THE POWER OF
EXTRAORDINARY PRAYER

THE POWER OF
Extraordinary
PRAYER

Robert O. Bakke

CROSSWAY BOOKS · WHEATON, ILLINOIS
A DIVISION OF GOOD NEWS PUBLISHERS

Cover design: Liita Forsyth

First printing 2000

Printed in the United States of America

Library of Congress Cataloging-in-Publication Data
Bakke, Robert O., 1950-
   The power of extraordinary prayer   / Robert O. Bakke.
      p.   cm.
   Includes bibliographical references and index.
   ISBN 1-58134-154-7 (pbk. : alk. paper)
   1. Prayer meetings. 2. Prayer groups—Christianity. 3. Prayer—
Christianity. I. Title.
BV285.B25 2000
269—dc21   00-025256
                                               CIP

15	14	13	12	11	10	09	08	07	06	05	04	03	02	01	00
15	14	13	12	11	10	9	8	7	6	5	4	3	2	1

To Sally

CONTENTS

INTRODUCTION

At 10 P.M. on May 6, 1999, I stood in front of an international television, radio, and Internet audience and waved good night. It was the close of the National Day of Prayer. Beginning at Moody Memorial Church in 1994 with a handful of stations, this annual prayer meeting was the sixth and largest ever. For three hours hundreds of television stations and hundreds of radio stations had joined in a partnership spanning three continents and two dozen other countries. Christians by the millions were given a means to pray simultaneously for the outpouring of God's grace upon our generation. Some of the nation's most prominent Evangelicals have helped with the broadcast—Lloyd Ogilvie, Jack Hayford, Tony Evans, Jim and Shirley Dobson, Twila Paris, Bill Bright, Joe Stowell, Joni Eareckson Tada, John Perkins, Ron Sider, Fernando Ortega, and Michael Card.

Since 1993 I have lived, preached, researched, and ministered full time for such moments. Domestically and internationally, I have logged over 700,000 miles on airplanes—preaching, teaching, writing, conferring, and leading prayer meetings in hundreds of venues, large and small. But my story begins in 1988 at a prayer meeting in New York City.

In September of 1988, I was senior pastor of Grace Church of Ridgewood, New Jersey. Ridgewood is a bedroom community for New York's financial district. My wife, Sally, and I heard from Neil Rendall, a staff member of Inter-Varsity Christian Fellowship and our church chairman, about a special prayer meeting to be held at the First Baptist Church of Flushing, Queens, New York. Neil said that the meeting represented a fledgling movement of men and women whose dream was to see God powerfully visit the New York metropolitan area. The prospect excited us, and on short notice we called a baby-sitter and then First Baptist for directions.

Upon arrival at the church, we found the atmosphere expectant and electric. The sanctuary was packed and cacophonous, with movement and noise from every quarter. A black Pentecostal choir was warming up in one corner, and Hispanic musicians were tuning up in another. Around us 800 other participants had gathered from the five boroughs of New York, Long Island, and New Jersey.

Once the meeting was under way, the organizers introduced the leader of the evening. Up to the pulpit stepped a baby boomer from Madison, Wisconsin, named David Bryant. Since I had produced Christian concerts and preaching events for years and was an experienced attendee of Christian "happenings," I had preconceived notions of what these "hired guns" were like. I also had my suspicions about speakers imported from elsewhere who liked to say they have preached in the "Big Apple" but who owned no intentions of staying. Most lacked real confidence that their ministry agendas could work in the capital city of the world.

Within moments after Bryant began to speak, however, he showed himself to be a man who passionately loved God and was powerfully used of God. He owned a powerful vision, and his dream was gripping.

Preaching compellingly from Paul's majestic letter to the Ephesians, Bryant told how he had experienced the call of God some twelve years before to leave the pastoral ministry and begin challenging the church worldwide to unite for fervent prayer, to earnestly seek God for revival and spiritual awakening. All this, he declared, to the glory of God who "is able to do exceeding abundantly above all that we ask or think, according to the power that worketh in us" (KJV). Bryant sought a new outpouring of God's Spirit upon the church and then, through the church, upon the whole earth.

Since his call, Bryant explained, God had used him to spearhead and encourage prayer movements across the United States and in different parts of the world. The previous year he had been in Korea and gathered with one million(!) Korean Christians on an airport landing strip to pray that the "knowledge of the glory of God might cover the earth as the waters cover the sea." The thought of one million Christians in a single prayer meeting calling out to God for spiritual awakening made my head swim. This didn't sound remotely like the prayer meetings I grew up with. God was drawing me in.

While Bryant spoke, I perused the room. A rainbow of races listened intently—red, yellow, black, brown, and white. It was among my first authentic glimpses of heaven: The righteous from every nation are summoned before the throne of God by the blood of Christ. Color wasn't the only diversity. Throughout the evening I heard several languages (110 languages are spoken within a ten-block radius of First Baptist alone).

We were asked to form "huddles" for prayer—four to eight people per huddle. In each group we introduced ourselves to each other. To my left were two white Presbyterian men, lawyers from Staten Island. Behind us were three black Pentecostal women from the Bronx, and on the other side was a newly married couple of Asian descent. As we exchanged names and backgrounds, we understood clearly that we were one in Christ, belonging to the same church. For three hours our huddle prayed and praised God together.

I was also introduced to black independent Baptists, Conservative Baptists, American Baptists, Episcopalians, Presbyterians, independent Charismatics (black, Hispanic, and Caucasian), Pentecostals, Lutherans, Methodists, those from the Christian and Missionary Alliance, the Assembly of God, the Evangelical Free Church of America, etc. I was struck by the fact that even though many of these Christians would not feel comfortable ministering together, they felt compelled to pray together.

Throughout the evening we prayed individually, we prayed in small huddle groups, we prayed congregationally. Hundreds groaned in repentance before God—confessing sins to one another and to God in prayer. I had never witnessed such depth of passion in prayer. We prayed for our churches, asking God to forgive them for sins of neglect, for prayerlessness, for carnality and materialism. We prayed that the church would once again find its first love. We prayed for the church regionally, nationally, and globally. We pleaded with God that he would anoint his church afresh and unleash it.

We prayed and we sang, and we prayed and we sang, and we prayed and we sang. For three hours thousands of prayers rose to God. I had been a Christian all my life, had pastored two churches, and had been in various ministries since my teens, but I had never prayed three hours for anything before. We prayed for the forgiveness of sin, the revival of the body of Christ, the transformation of our communities, the advancement of Christ's kingdom, and the salvation of the lost.

At the end of the meeting, we all joined hands and streamed out of the church. Out into the night we walked, across Sanford Avenue, through a gate in a chain-link fence into an asphalt-covered park. The sounds of the city surrounded us. On all sides apartment buildings rose straight into the air. The glow from lighted apartment windows and street lamps provided the only light. Once we filled the park, we were asked to pray in huddles again and cry out to God once more. We prayed that God would begin a miracle of spiritual awakening that night.

As our praying in small groups wound down for the last time, the entire throng spontaneously began to sing:

> *To God be the glory—great things He hath done!*
> *So loved He the world that He gave us His Son,*
> *Who yielded His life an atonement for sin*
> *And opened the Lifegate that all may go in.*
> *Praise the Lord, Praise the Lord,*
> *Let the earth hear His voice!*
> *Praise the Lord, praise the Lord,*
> *Let the people rejoice!*
> *Oh, come to the Father through Jesus the Son,*
> *And give Him the glory—great things He hath done!*[1]

As 800 voices reverberated off the asphalt and apartment buildings, curious people gathered at their windows and on their balconies to hear what was going on. We cemented the call of God upon our lives not simply to pray but to take our witness to the streets. We determined before God to be the answer to many of our own prayers. Into the darkness we took the light. What a wonderful night.

We were participating in a "Concert of Prayer." When I first heard the title from my church chairman, I thought to myself, *How clever, how fresh, how new!* It reminded me of the glory days of the Jesus Movement some twenty years before when all kinds of new ways of doing Christianity were invented.

But I was mistaken. Bryant informed us that what we were doing was rooted in history and similar to a movement of prayer initiated by Christians a long, long time ago. This intrigued me. A little fire was ignited in my soul, a curiosity that would not go away until I understood the Concert of Prayer more fully.

Within a few weeks I convinced the missionary committee of my church to make prayer the centerpiece of our missions conference scheduled for the following March. We agreed that "Reaching the World Through Prayer" would become our theme. I contacted David Bryant, and he accepted my invitation to speak on the final Sunday of our conference and to hold a Concert of Prayer on the Friday night preceding our conference.

In order to prepare the missions committee, we packed into a church van that January and went to a follow-up Concert of Prayer at the same Queens location. The same kind of crowd was present, with the same energy. The atmosphere was Spirit-filled and joyous. The missions committee members were amazed at the power and the wonderful sweetness of spending three hours in continual praise and prayer to God, united with all kinds of Evangelicals.

As the March conference drew near, it was my responsibility to send out invitations to the very modest number of pastors I knew and the few ministries I dealt with. Along with the several dozen invitations, I sent in an announcement to a local Christian radio station.

In trying to determine how many would attend our Concert of Prayer, I figured we'd get a couple hundred from my church and beyond that a handful in response to my invitations. After all, it was a prayer meeting. If what I knew about Wednesday night prayer-meeting attendance in our area was any indication of what might happen that night, I was not hopeful of a significant turnout. Who wants to go to church on a Friday night and pray for three hours? I consoled myself with the fact that great movements of God often start with humble beginnings.

On that Friday night, I escorted David Bryant from my study into the church sanctuary (which seats about 500). Having warned him not to be too hopeful, I was shocked at what I saw. The church was flooded with people—standing room only. I was thrilled. I couldn't believe that with so few invitations a crowd of this size could be generated to pray.[2] Moreover, I was flabbergasted to find out how many pastors were in attendance.

The night had enormous significance. At the end of the evening, visitors came up to me thanking me profusely for the service. Pastor after pastor stated with conviction that we had to do it again and soon. One veteran pastor of over thirty-five years in the New York metropolitan area, who ministered in prestigious churches, stood before me with tears in his eyes and said it was the most powerful night he had experienced in a generation. It gave him hope for the region, he said, where previously he had had little.

Over the following three years I organized four more Concerts of Prayer. Each was larger than the previous one. The fourth grew to three times the size of the first, with more than 1,500 attending. Thanks to the vision of my friend and radio station manager Joe Battaglia, the last three were broadcast live over radio to the entire New York metropolitan area. Listeners wrote to the station saying it was the best programming the station had ever offered.

To increase the impact, one weekend we coordinated our radio efforts with nine other Concerts of Prayer in New York City and Long Island so that we had as many as ten prayer concerts going on. Thousands of people—rich, poor, black, white, Hispanic, etc.—poured out their hearts to God for revival in the church and spiritual awakening.

During this same period, I began to gather with prayer leaders from across the country in what are known as Consultations on United Prayer. I heard testimonies and strategic plans for mobilizing God's people in prayer. I learned from leaders in the Pacific Northwest that prayer concerts were helping to lead the way to what many believed was a burgeoning revival. In Portland 15,000 Christians had gathered for a Concert of Prayer on the heels of 200 area pastors taking part in a four-day prayer retreat. In California's Los Angeles and Orange Counties thousands were gathering in Concerts of Prayer called "Love LA." In Cleveland, Ohio, between 6,000 and 7,000 people, including 1,000 teenagers, took part in a citywide Concert of Prayer. In Boston as many as 800 Christians from seventy-five different churches gathered at historic Park Street Church. In the Southeast and the Rocky Mountains, similar stories were being told, not to mention the international movements.[3]

These heady stories solidified my interest in the history of the Concert of Prayer. David Bryant informed me that the concerts were the brainchild of Jonathan Edwards while he pastored in Northhampton, Massachusetts. This surprised me. I was graduated from Gordon-Conwell Theological Seminary, a prominent New England seminary, and ministered in a white-clapboarded New England church for seven years thereafter. I had heard and read much about this great American theologian, pastor, and preacher. However, I had never heard of Edwards's passion for united prayer nor anything of his call for a carefully orchestrated prayer movement in the colonies.

I began to ask myself what had inspired Edwards to call for these prayer concerts. Why were they started, what impact did they have, and why are they perceived as a powerful model for today?[4] And, finally, does what is happening today bear resemblance to what Edwards originally envisioned? Since no one could satisfy my curiosity, I decided to find out. That decision changed the course of my life. Since 1993 I have devoted my ministry to this singular passion of Jonathan Edwards and his friends. What follows, then, represents my quest to understand the origins of this growing modern movement and learn the lessons of history for the church today.

One

First Things First

Before we embark on the wonderful story of the Concert of Prayer and introduce ourselves to men, women, churches, and revivals that have changed history, let's briefly root ourselves in the fundamentals of prayer so as to grasp the grace of God poured out in response to the prayers of people. Prayer, after all, is God's idea. He longs for it. He commands it. The unfolding of his will in history demands it.

WHAT IS PRAYER?

In *Knowing God*, J. I. Packer writes:

> Men [and women] who know their God are before anything else men who pray, and the first point where their zeal and energy for God's glory come to expression is in their prayers . . . the invariable fruit of true knowledge of God is energy to pray for God's cause—energy, indeed, which can only find an outlet and a relief of inner tension when channeled into such prayer—and the more knowledge, the more energy! By this we test ourselves. . . . If . . . there is in us little energy for such prayer, and little consequent practice of it, this is a sure sign that as yet we scarcely know our God.[1]

But what is the essence of this capacity? Often I ask Christians to define prayer. "By the raising of hands, how many believe that prayer is basically communication with God?" I ask. Most hands go up. The majority of hands that stay down belong to those who think it is a trick question. It is, of sorts.

If we think of communication in the normal sense—that is, the passing of information between two or more parties—then prayer is not fundamentally communication with God. In Psalm 139:1-4 we read:

O LORD, you have searched me and you know me.
You know when I sit and when I rise;
  you perceive my thoughts from afar.
You discern my going out and my lying down;
  you are familiar with all my ways.
Before a word is on my tongue you know it completely,
  O LORD.

Likewise, in Matthew 6:8 Jesus said that our Father in heaven knows what we need even before we ask. The reality is as clear as it is simple: There is nothing we can say to God that he doesn't already know.

Some years ago my son Joel was injured on a summer camp playground. He had watched older boys jump from the top of a nearby slide and grasp the bars of the jungle gym. Joel tried to do the same, but he didn't make it. He hit the ground with a frightful thud. The next thing his mother knew, an ambulance was taking Joel away to the hospital. When I heard of it, my first instinct was to cry to God, "Lord, my son Joel is hurt. Please be with him. Keep him safe and heal him."

Could you imagine God responding: "Joel did what? Where? Oh, of course I'll come. How do I get there? I'm so glad you called!"

In fact, God knows Joel fully. He's gone before him and comprehends his past. God knew him before the foundations of the earth were laid, knit Joel together in his mother's womb, and loves him more deeply than I possibly ever could (he sent *his* son to die for Joel). In sum, there wasn't a single thing that I could have told God that he didn't already know *completely* and was more passionate about than I. Yet God wanted me to pray and cry out to him. No, he commanded it.

If he knows all things completely, does it mean that our thoughts don't matter to God? To the contrary, for various reasons prayer is vital. The unfolding of God's purposes requires prayer. But apart from sheer efficacy, one of the reasons God wants us to pray is his deep affection for us.

My son Erik has a wonderful disposition and can disappear for hours to fiddle with crafts, a pencil and paper, or a set of watercolors. One day I was reading my *New York Times* on the living room couch when Erik, then six years old, plopped down prostrate on the floor nearby. With newsprint sprawled out in front of him and colored markers in his clutch, he drew and colored with passion, his whole being focused on the task while his feet were suspended in the air above him. Out of the corner of my eye I watched the creation of Erik's work of art—the entire process, start to finish. Forty-five minutes later he was done. He stared at the picture for over a minute, laid down his markers, folded the paper carefully into a little square, and rose to his feet. With a few pokes of his finger into the back of my newspaper, he asked proudly, "Dad, do you want to see what I drew for you?"

Now since I take newspaper reading seriously and since I had watched everything he had done, I could have announced that I had seen the whole thing. I knew what he had in his hand, so he needn't bother to bother me—especially while I was reading the editorial page. Only a silly or cruel father would say such a thing (and I have been either at other times). I gathered him up into my arms and said, "Yeah! Show me what you've done." Such moments are the delight of our hearts. They are important to our heavenly Father, too. He longs for the moments when we pour out ourselves to him, whether to display the works of our hands or to cry in our times of need. Moreover, because of the way God has designed his kingdom to work, these moments are filled with spiritual power.

So if prayer isn't fundamentally communication with God, perhaps, like with Erik in my lap, prayer is essentially *communion* with God. I use communion in a popular sense—warm, intimate fellowship.

I travel a lot. No matter where I find myself when I am away from home, my wife, Sally, wants to hear my voice. I could be in Chicago or China—she just wants to hear my voice, even for a few minutes. Each night when I am at home and after the kids are asleep, Sally and I sit outside on our front porch or back deck, or when the Minnesota winters settle in, in front of our fireplace. My wife needs about forty-five minutes to talk to me. I think the need for these times is knit into the DNA of wives. After years of this, however, I now look forward to it as much as she does.

Perhaps this is what prayer is essentially—getting in contact with our heavenly Lover, or better yet, cuddling up into his arms once or twice a day so as to make sense of our lives and find his reassurance. God and man need to hear each other's voices and reconnect.

In certain ways, this idea draws us closer to the essence of prayer, but there is something deeper still. Rather than communication or communion, prayer is essentially *union* with God. It is the dynamic, measurable act that helps define the Christian's spiritual state.

A husband and wife, for example, are declared to be one flesh. Sally and I are united as one whether I am at home beside her or in Johannesburg. But there is an activity—dynamic, measurable, and intimate—God-given to husbands and wives and celebrated by Solomon and other poets, whereby our union is fully expressed. And likewise prayer as an act of essential union with God jibes with the declaration of the Gospel concerning our faith. The apostle Paul says, for example:

For to me, to live is Christ. (Phil. 1:21)

Our encouragement is derived from knowing we are "united with Christ" (Phil. 2:1).

I have been crucified with Christ and I no longer live, but Christ lives in me. The life I live in the body, I live by faith in the Son of God, who loved me and gave himself for me. (Gal. 2:20)

Christ is in you. (Rom. 8:10)

And Peter adds that the goal of God's precious promises to us is "that through them [we] may participate in the divine nature" (2 Peter 1:4).

Through prayer we pour our lives, our thoughts, our longings into God and receive the life, power, character, mind, and authority of God in return.

Every morning when I sit down in my office, one of the first things I do is boot up my computer. As the screen fills up before me, I click on my Compuserve icon and launch the program. A second time I click the picture of an envelope, and a wonderful process is initiated. A box appears on my screen telling me that the modem is being "initiated," and then the computer starts dialing. At my instruction the modem is flying out into cyberspace to find Compuserve. I don't know where Compuserve is—perhaps behind Mars—but my modem can find it.

Once it does, an exchange takes place between Compuserve and my computer: What's your name? What's your account number? What's your password? And when Compuserve determines that I am part of its family, Compuserve connects and *downloads* all my E-mail and an almost inexhaustible supply of resources and tools for the accomplishment of my purposes that day. I launch up into Compuserve; it downloads into me. And because I have paid $24.95 a month, I can stay online *all day*. While doing other tasks with other software, occasionally Compuserve will break through and announce, "You have mail!" or, "You have messages waiting."

This is a great illustration of the essence of prayer: We thrust our lives and souls into the person of God; God downloads his person and grace into us, all through the modem of the Holy Spirit. And because of the price Jesus paid, I can stay logged on all day.

A generation ago E. Stanley Jones was a missionary to India. About this issue of union Jones wrote:

> The first thing [in prayer] is to get God. If you get him, everything else follows . . . allow God to get at you, to invade you, to take possession of you. He then pours his very prayers through you. They are his prayers—God-inspired, and hence, God answered. . . .
>
> Prayer is like the fastening of the cup to the wounded side of a pine tree to allow the rosin to pour into it. You are now nestling up into the side of God—the wounded side, if you will—and you allow his grace to fill your cup. You are taking in the very life of God.[2]

Jesus used a similar analogy when he spoke to his disciples the night before he died. The context in which these words were spoken mean that they are grave, weighty words, the words of a man about to die who is passing on the most important of truths. It is the nature of dying words to be poignant.

I remember the last words my father spoke to me. He was dying of a brain tumor at the age of sixty-four. As a young pastor, I refused to believe that my father, my hero, would die—that God would not hear my prayers and raise him up. Every weekend, after preaching Sunday morning, I traveled from my small Connecticut church to my parents' home in New Jersey. Sometimes when the house was quiet and my father asleep, I would kneel beside his bed, lay my hands on his feverish head, and pray for his healing. He was often too sick to be aroused by such a thing. When Monday night arrived, my wife and I drove home.

As I was leaving for what was to be the last time, suitcases in hand, I said good-bye to my dad—now a fading shadow of the man I had known and reverenced—and assured him that everything would be fine. I would see him again the next weekend. I talked fast and filled up all the parting moments with words so that no one could suggest anything different. While I was jabbering away, defending myself from the obvious, my father meekly raised himself from his bed and waved to me to draw near. I did so, still filling up the air with noise and false reassurances. I bent over as he reached up with the only arm he could use. Grabbing me behind the neck—I can still feel his arm trembling—he pulled me to his cheek. While I continued to talk, he wept. His tears fell down his face onto mine; his tears ran down my cheek. He whispered in my ear, "I love you. Good-bye."

In his humbled, weakened state, his arm holding me tightly, he poured into me the most important words he had left, his breathless last words. Moreover, with those few words he poured into me millions of words unspoken but attached by thirty-three years of affectionately raising his third son. His words haunt me to this day, because in my denial of his impending death, I refused to hear him. I wish I could have just held him and cried with him.

On the night that Jesus was to die, he gathered his dearest friends near him. It was a moment for the most important things to be spoken. If he could have held them close to his cheek, I think he would have. Perhaps he did. Unfortunately, the words he spoke were ones that would haunt his disciples because of their denial; they refused to believe that their master would die.

Jesus said:

> "I am the true vine, and my Father is the gardener. He cuts off every branch in me that bears no fruit, while every branch that does bear fruit he prunes so that it will be even more fruitful. You are already clean because of the word I have spoken to you. *Remain in me*, and I will *remain in you*. No branch can bear fruit by itself; it must *remain in the vine*. Neither can you bear fruit unless you *remain in me*.
>
> "I am the vine; you are the branches. If a man *remains in me and I in him*, he will bear much fruit; *apart from me you can do nothing*. If anyone does not *remain in me*, he is like a branch that is thrown away and withers; such branches are picked up, thrown into the fire and burned. *If you remain in me and my words remain in you, ask whatever you wish, and it will be given you.* This is to my Father's glory, that you bear much fruit, showing yourselves to be my disciples." (John 15:1-8)

To fully grasp the weight of these words we must remind ourselves one of the ways Semitic languages make a word significant: They repeat it. For example, when Jesus said something particularly important, he often prefaced it by saying *"Amen, amen,"* translated by certain English versions as "Truly, truly." This means "listen carefully!" Or again the angels in heaven who serve before the throne of God cry to God, "Holy!" But God is not just holy; he's "holy, holy." But even twice does not suffice; instead the cherubim identify God as "holy, holy, holy." In other words, "You, O God, are enormously, stupendously unlike any other, holy."

Well, Jesus on the night he was to die spoke to his dearest friends and said, "Remain *in me* . . . remain . . . remain . . . remain . . . remain . . . remain . . . remain . . . remain . . . remain . . . remain!" Remain in me; let my words remain in you so that you bear fruit—much fruit!—showing yourselves to be like me, all to the Father's glory. But if you don't remain in me, you'll wither and die. Apart from me you can do nothing.

The chief means given to us by which we remain *in Christ* and he *in us* is prayer. Union with God is demonstrable: We pray.

Later on the night before his death, Jesus' high-priestly prayer (John 17:20-26) strikes a similar note. Having prayed for the twelve disciples, Jesus prays for the rest of us:

> "My prayer is not for [the twelve apostles] alone. I pray also for those who will believe in me through their message, that all of them may be one, Father, *just as you are in me and I am in you.* May they also be *in us* so that the world may believe that you have sent me. I have given them the glory that you gave me, that they may be one as we are one: *I in them and you in me.* May they be brought to complete unity to let the world know that you sent me and have loved them even as you have loved me.
>
> "Father, I want those you have given me to be with me where I am, and to see my glory, the glory you have given me because you loved me before the creation of the world.
>
> "Righteous Father, though the world does not know you, I know you, and they know that you have sent me. I have made you known to them, and will continue to make you known in order that the love you have for me may be *in them and that I myself may be in them.*"

As Christ poured himself into his Father, he received from his Father, too. Jesus declared forthrightly, "I and the Father are one." But his prayers made the union manifest. Jesus, in these moments before the cross, was involved in a measurable act called prayer that put on display the unity of Father and Son—a form of consummation. It was also the instrument whereby God manifestly poured out himself into his Son.

So the chief question regarding prayer is not about mouthing words (although words *are* important) or subscribing to an obligatory religious discipline that promises benefits over the long haul (akin to jogging or lifting weights), but about giving your life away to God and receiving the life of God in return. As E. M. Bounds noted: "Prayer is the contact of a living soul with God. In prayer God stoops to kiss man, to bless man and to aid man in everything that God can devise or man can need." The very act of prayer, then, is our confession to him that *in him* we have all things (the world, life, death, the present, the future—all are ours because we are of Christ and Christ is of God, 1 Cor. 3:22), and apart from him we can do nothing.

It is the Holy Spirit who unites us with God and makes us participants in the divine nature. In part, that explains why the apostle Paul commands Christians to "pray in the Spirit." And just so we don't confuse this kind of prayer with any charismatic gift, praying in the Spirit, Paul writes, is for "*all* kinds of prayers and requests" (Eph. 6:18). In other words, no matter how you pray, do it in the Spirit. In this manner, when we pray, the Spirit of God is praying in us and through us.

JESUS AND PRAYER

In every area of a Christian's life, Jesus is our model. In Luke 11, Jesus commanded that we should pray and never give up; we should log on and stay online. Well, as with everything else he taught, Jesus was the chief example of his own words. He was first of all a man of prayer. Prayer was present in every facet of his ministry. The Bible records that Jesus' greatest triumphs were coupled with great praying. It was after praying that Jesus raised Lazarus from the dead. I love John 11, which records this resurrection. The passage speaks volumes about the character of God.

Upon entering the village of Bethany and speaking with the sisters of Lazarus, Martha and then Mary, Jesus was "deeply moved in spirit and troubled." This description joins multiple thoughts. First, the aorist middle of the verb *embrimasthai* describes an articulate expression of anger. In the Greek translation of the Old Testament, this verb is used to describe intense indignation. For example, the word is used in Daniel 11 to tell us that in the end times God will "vent his fury" on his enemies. In the New Testament, Mark 14:5 tells of an unnamed woman who anoints Jesus with expensive oil. Those watching, we are told, "rebuked her harshly" for wasting the oil. Same word.

In Bethany our Lord stood in a state of fervent anger, his soul raging at the sights and sounds of mourning and unbelief. But the description goes further. John tells us that Jesus was furious *to pneumati*, "in spirit." In other words, angry to the very core of his being. But there's more.

Jesus "was deeply moved in spirit and *troubled*." Literally, he "trembled" or "shuddered." Deep down in his soul, his emotions were so turbulent that they were physically manifested. He was shaking.

The Greek adds a qualifier that tells us that Jesus stirred himself up to this point. The trouble in his soul was Jesus' own doing. These words do not depict a spontaneous, uncontrolled human reaction. This fury of Christ is intentional.

I have stood at the scene of fatal car accidents and witnessed spontaneous, uncontrolled human grief. Likewise, I have stood at deathbeds, and I have buried children. I've seen survivors come unglued. Jesus in Bethany is not like these. His emotion is willed.

What was happening? Well, from elementary school through college I played football. I learned early that on game day you put on a "game face." That is, you prepared yourself for a battle. Some players stared at the floor quietly; others foamed at the mouth and butted their helmets into the lockers and smashed into teammates. Once dressed, we made our way to the field, and the crowd cheered as we ran past the cheerleaders to the fifty-yard line. Once around the coach, we began a rhythmic cheer—starting off low and ending in a frenzied roar as we ran out onto the field, psychologically prepared to fight. This was Jesus before the tomb of Lazarus—a conscious gathering up of divine potency and holy indignation.

Os Guinness comments on this passage, arguing that there are two things Christians need—the compassion of Christ and the outrage of Christ:

John uses [the expression *embrimaomai*] twice in his account of Jesus at the tomb of Lazarus. This deep emotion is usually interpreted in relation to the verse "Jesus wept." Certainly as he stands at his friend's grave with Lazarus's two mourning sisters, Mary and Martha, this is not unnatural. But the Greek word has a twist which the English unfortunately fails to convey. Weeping, or sorrow, does not exhaust what is meant by Jesus' being "deeply moved," for Jesus

knew that Lazarus would be alive and standing beside him in a matter of moments. Where is the sorrow in that? . . . The Greek gives
us a clue to what is really involved here, for the root meaning of
embrimaomai is to "snort in the spirit." It was used by Aeschylus to
describe Greek stallions before battle, rearing up on their hind legs,
pawing the air and snorting before they charged. Similarly, Jesus
"snorted in the spirit": He was moved deeply in the sense of a furious inner anger. Entering his Father's world as the Son of God, he
found not order, beauty, harmony and fulfillment, but fractured dis-
order, raw ugliness, complete disarray—everywhere the abortion of
God's original plan. Standing at the graveside, he came face to face
with a death that symbolized and summarized the accumulation of
evil, pain, sorrow, suffering, injustice, cruelty and despair. Thus,
while he was moved to tears for his friends in sorrow, he was also
deeply moved by the outrageous abnormality of death.[3]

Christ, in coming to Lazarus' tomb, faced all the misery of sin and
all the ramifications of fallenness—faithlessness, hatred toward himself,
hardness toward God, sickness, sadness, and death itself. As he gazed
upon the mourners and heard their cacophony of grief and despair, he
saw everything he never intended for humankind when he formed us
from the dust of the ground and blew his life into our nostrils.

Moreover, Jesus stared into the face of Satan himself, in whose
demonic grip mankind was held. Christ, the Word made flesh, was both
grieved and outraged. Like a great, fierce stallion—his eyes wide and
glinting with fury, adrenaline coursing through his veins, anticipating
the charge—our Lord stood before the opened grave with the smell of
death in his nostrils. He was, as John Calvin said, "as a champion who
prepares for a conflict." The tyrant of death, whom he had come to overthrow, stood before Jesus like Goliath—taunting the chosen one of
Israel.

At this point we would expect Jesus to burst out with a cry. Instead,
the Christ stopped, lifted his head toward heaven, *and prayed.* Before
his battle with death and hell, he worshiped the Father. The heart of
Jesus booted up into God, and God downloaded his power and authority into his Son. Jesus clothed himself with his Father, dressed himself
in the strength and mighty power of the Lord, and pointed to where all
the glory is due. Then our champion drew his weapon—a sharp two-
edged sword, aflame with the Holy Spirit's power—and leveled a deci-
sive blow against the gates of death.

John tells us that having prayed, Jesus cried *phone megale*—"in a loud voice"—a cross between an anguished wail and a furious command, crying out as if calling through time and space beyond this reality into the next, through the door of this world into another. The Lion of Judah roared, "LAZARUS! COME OUT!" It was a command as powerful as "Let there be light." The Lord's voice resounded across eternity like the voice of a shepherd crying out in the wilderness for his sheep, and his sheep heard his voice and obediently stumbled to the entrance to the tomb. Someone once noted that if Jesus had not identified Lazarus by name, all the dead would have been raised. All of this happened after Jesus prayed.

Jesus continues in prayer to this day. The role of the resurrected and ascended Lord in heaven is prayer. Romans 8:34 tells us plainly that one of the principal reasons we should not fear the threat of charges against us, or condemnations, or that someone will snatch us away from God is because Jesus "is at the right hand of God and is also interceding for us." Likewise, Hebrews 7:25 states that Jesus can "save completely those who come to God through him, because" the glorified, heavenly high priest "always lives to intercede for them."

The implications are breathtaking. For one, I can trust more in the prayers of Jesus for me—prayers that can never be thwarted—than I can trust my own prayers. And second, before the foundations of the earth were laid, we were predestined to be conformed to his image. That is, we were predestined to become pray-ers. If I put an acorn in the proper soil, it will grow to be an oak. It cannot produce a beech, an apple tree, or any other kind of tree. So, too, Jesus has planted his seed within us. We will grow to be like him. We will grow up to be men and women who pray. Prayer is the first means by which God works in us and through us. It is among his principal means by which his purposes are accomplished in history.

While Jesus is interceding for us and conforming us to his image, it is the Holy Spirit who makes prayer efficacious. That is, apart from the Holy Spirit prayer is empty, without grace or power, like peddling a bicycle without a chain. Christians are not the only people who pray. Billions of people pray. Hindus, Buddhists, Muslims, animists, and witches pray. But only the ministry of the Holy Spirit enables prayer to be an encounter with God, let alone move his hand.

In 1990 I sat on the platform of the Long Island Billy Graham Crusade as a member of the Invitation Committee for the next crusade

Dr. Graham would hold. Dr. Graham had recently been diagnosed with Parkinson's disease, and questions about his future persisted. That evening his voice was weak, and his sermon simple and without drama. Because it was New York, I feared for the response. Would hardened New Yorkers react well to such a sermon? The previous 1979 visit to New York had not gone well for the Graham organization. I worried. My palms were sweaty.

Then came the invitation for people to believe in Jesus as their Savior. I can still see Dr. Graham silhouetted against the lights as he prayed. What happened next stunned us all. The people flooded out of their seats, filled the floor of the Nassau Coliseum, filled the entrances to the floor and the hallways beyond the entrances. The response was enormous. It was as if the Holy Spirit swept through this crowd like a scythe through wheat ripe for harvest. As my friend Ron Hutchcraft and I stood on the platform watching, we wept at the sight. It dawned on us what was happening. Simultaneously, God answered the prayers of millions of people—prayers kept in heaven for this very moment—and his Holy Spirit swiftly and graciously accomplished his glorious ends.

UNITED PRAYER

The union of Christians with God and with each other isn't just nice, that is, as opposed to conflict, but it constitutes the wisdom and the power of the church. Unity is a matter of the theology of the church and how God accomplishes his purposes in history. United prayer is something too few Christians understand, so they rarely practice it. The era in which we live is demanding rediscovery of united prayer.

I often tell people that if they ever visit New York City, the best thing in New York on a Tuesday night is the prayer meeting at the Brooklyn Tabernacle. Over the past twenty-five years this church has grown from a handful who were about to close its doors to 10,000 members. Because Pastor Jim Cymbala takes Jesus seriously when he said that God intends his church to be a house of prayer,[4] every Sunday morning for a generation Pastor Cymbala has told his congregation that the Tuesday night prayer meeting is the most important meeting of the week. Cymbala leads it, models it, and his people come.

The meeting starts at 7:00 P.M., but the doors open at 5:00 P.M. with the sanctuary dimly lit and soft instrumental music playing. By 5:30 hundreds of people are already on their knees or standing at the altar in prayer. By 6:30 fifteen hundred are in prayer. At 7:00 three hundred chairs have been set up in the lobby to accommodate the overflow crowd of 2,200. Then for the next three hours praise, intercession, and earnest pleading fill the auditorium. The prayers pack enormous spiritual power, and there is a strong sense of the presence of God. This prayer affects everything the church does. The whole life of Brooklyn Tabernacle's ministries flow out of that prayer meeting. Their union in prayer isn't just nice; it's the power of the church.

In Matthew 18:15ff., Jesus taught about how to rectify an offense between two people. There is much in this passage about the nature of the church. But in so teaching, Jesus appeals to truths that transcend the specific context of the Matthew 18:15ff. lesson: "I tell you the truth, whatever you bind on earth will be bound in heaven, and whatever you loose on earth will be loosed in heaven. Again, I tell you that if two of you on earth agree about anything you ask for, it will be done for you by my Father in heaven. For where two or three come together in my name, there am I with them."

Jesus grants to a united church enormous spiritual authority centered on requests on which Christians "agree." The old King James Version translates the verse "agree as touching"—that is, what is held in unison among believers, as if many hands held a common thing.

A couple of years ago I was preaching at a conference in Mexico City. My hotel was on the ancient central square and across from the "White House," or old parliament building. The church I was preaching in was on the outskirts of town. One night I preached on Matthew 18, and I asked each in my Mexican audience to turn and face one other person. Then I asked them to hold up their hands, palms up, and touch the end of their fingers to the other person's fingers as if the two of them were holding a soccer ball between them. They all did it. Then I said, "This is what Jesus is asking you to do in prayer—hold the prayer between you in agreement and then give it to God."

The following night was my final service, but at 7:00 P.M., the starting time of the service, no one had picked up my wife and me. We sat in the lobby and waited. At 7:15 the desk clerk came to us saying I had a phone call. I went to the desk and our host apologetically explained that no one had been given the responsibility of picking us up. I offered to take a cab but, given the fact that I don't speak Spanish, would he explain to the cab driver where I needed to go. "No problem," he said.

A cab driver was found. He listened carefully to the phone directions and seemed gleefully confident. Off we went.

Within two minutes I knew we were in trouble. For the next forty-five minutes we went on a wild goose chase into seedy parts of Mexico City I had never seen before. After nearly an hour, we wound up in front of the Mormon Tabernacle. The cabbie stopped the car and signaled with a relieved smile that we had arrived. "No, no, no," I cried and tried to direct him out toward the airport where I knew the church was. An hour and many sidewalk conversations with locals later, we pulled up at the church with a dozen or so missionaries and locals out front waiting anxiously.

It seems there had been a recent spate of deadly and brazen car-jackings against American tourists, and my hosts had become fearful that we had been victimized. I was escorted quickly into the packed-out service. The worship center was full of people praying. Hundreds of Mexicans were standing, two by two, palms up, touching the ends of each other's fingers as I had instructed them the night before. They were holding my wife and me in their hands and vigorously offering us to God in agreement that we should be delivered safely to their service. They erupted into praise when we walked onto the platform. The presence of the Lord was sweet and unmistakable, and they had learned a powerful lesson on agreement in prayer.

The verb for agree in Matthew 18 is *symphoneo*, from which we get the modern word *symphony*. But this needs explanation. The root of *symphony* does not speak of fine music but of the agreement that produces fine music. For a beautiful orchestral piece to be played well, those playing it must make certain fundamental agreements among themselves. Though they may be entirely different kinds of people who play different kinds of instruments, they must agree on at least two things to the exclusion of all else—the score and the conductor. With these two agreements, beautiful music can result. Likewise, Christians are asked by Jesus to come to "one mind" with each other regarding that for which they will seek God. In response God offers two enormous promises: 1) I'll give you anything you ask, and 2) Jesus will be manifestly present.

Whereas the Word of God has been preeminent in twentieth-century Evangelicalism, especially in light of the Fundamentalist controversies early this century, prayer is only now reemerging as the other of the two pillars of local church ministry, evangelism, or revival ministries. The

Bible studied, rightly handled, and prophetically preached is the mark of the modern Evangelical. Our conviction regarding this Word must not be compromised at any cost. Skilled exposition of the text of Scripture is paramount. But the practice of united prayer has been neglected. The ministry of the Word of God must be coupled with united prayer.

Prayer means spiritual power flowing from our union with God. It is the life and power of Jesus (the vine) flowing through his people (the branches), and we should rejoice for men and women within the body of Christ who today are reordering their lives and ministries so that prayer is always coupled with the ministry of the Word and with all other ministry.

THE SEGUE: EXTRAORDINARY PRAYER

Lastly, there are times in our lives and moments in history that call out for extraordinary prayer—prayer that is above and beyond normal requirements. Pentecost was such a time, as was Acts 4 when Peter and John were arrested, the arrest and miraculous release of Peter in Acts 12, and the commissioning of Paul and Barnabas in Acts 13, but there are many other such occasions in the Bible. For example, extraordinary prayer was necessary when Haman conspired to kill the Jews. Mordecai persuaded Queen Esther to approach King Xerxes to plead with him to stop this plot. Such forwardness could be deadly for anyone, even a queen. Esther agreed to go to Xerxes under one condition: "Go," she told Mordecai, "gather together all the Jews who are in Susa, and fast for me. Do not eat or drink for three days, night or day. I and my maids will fast as you do. When this is done, I will go to the king. So Mordecai went away and carried out all of Esther's instructions" (Est. 4:15-17). What happened? The Jews were saved, and Haman was executed.

When, upon the threat of death, Daniel was asked by the king of Babylon to interpret the king's dream—a dream the king would not reveal and that pagan wise men and astrologers could not discern— Daniel called his friends together to unite with him in prayer: "He urged them to plead for mercy from the God of heaven concerning this mystery. During the night the mystery was revealed to Daniel in a vision" (Dan. 2:18-19). God revealed the dream, Daniel was saved, and God's name was exalted. Ordinary prayer would not have sufficed.

During their wilderness travels Israel was attacked by Amalek at Rephidim. Israel seemed easy prey. Moses, Aaron, and Hur went then to the top of a hill. While the hands of Moses and his staff were held high in prayer to the Lord (Aaron and Hur helped prop up his hands), the Israelites prevailed. Israel fought in faith. Upon the victory "Moses built an altar and called it The LORD is my Banner. He said, 'For hands were lifted up to the throne of the LORD'" (Ex. 17:15-16).

In 1 Samuel 7, in the wake of the Ark of the Covenant's capture, its habitation at Kiriath Jearim, and the great oppression of the Philistines against Israel, Samuel ordered that "all Israel" gather at Mizpah where he would intercede with the Lord. As they fasted, prayed, and sacrificed, rulers and armies of Philistia attacked them. Frightened, the Israelites cried to Samuel, "Do not stop crying out to the Lord our God for us." And as they prayed and sacrificed, "the LORD thundered with loud thunder against the Philistines and threw them into such a panic that they were routed before the Israelites" (1 Samuel 7:10).

In Isaiah 62:1-2 the prophet cries out the hope of God for a people in captivity and a city in ruins:

> For Zion's sake I will not keep silent,
> For Jerusalem's sake I will not remain quiet,
> Till her righteousness shines out like the dawn,
> Her salvation like a blazing torch.
> The nations will see your righteousness,
> And all kings your glory.

For the glory of his name and the splendor of his purposes for his people, God summons people of prayer, intercessors who will unitedly, urgently, and relentlessly seek God.

> I have posted watchmen on your walls, O Jerusalem;
> They will never be silent day or night.
> You who call on the Lord,
> Give yourselves no rest,
> And give him no rest till he establishes Jerusalem
> And makes her the praise of the earth. . . .
> The LORD has made proclamation
> To the ends of the earth:
> "Say to the Daughter of Zion,
> 'See, your Savior comes!
> See, his reward is with him,
> And his recompense accompanies him.'"

> *They will be called the Holy People,*
> *The Redeemed of the LORD;*
> *And you will be called Sought After,*
> *The City No Longer Deserted. (vv. 6-7, 11-12)*

On and on the stories go. From the reports of the Scriptures to those of pastors, missionaries, and historical figures down through the centuries, we are told of those times when ordinary praying is not enough. Crises, periods of danger, or times of great sin compel God's people to seek God for the glory of his name. Sometimes the prayers are answered swiftly. Sometimes the answers come after years of praying.

There are many Christians today who believe we live in times that demand extraordinary praying. Millions of Christians are pursuing God, fasting, and uniting with each other in order to unite with God for a new work of the Holy Spirit in this generation. The stories that follow in this book should encourage and teach us because our generation is not unique. We shall read of great praying men and women of God upon whom the presence of God rested with much grace and effect, the powerful union of Christians before God's throne, remarkable movements of the Spirit, and the fundamental altering of history as the hand of God moved. It is the hope of many that future generations will remember us in the same manner.

My friend David Bryant is known for defining revivals as "approximations of the consummation." It's the best definition I know. Keep this definition in mind as you read, because all of the stories from the Bible and church history point to a day soon coming when a great confluence in heaven will change history forever. The prayers of those now beneath the throne in heaven asking, "How long, Sovereign Lord, holy and true, until you judge the inhabitants of the earth?" will merge with the intercession of the glorified Christ at the right hand of God, the intercession of the Holy Spirit who groans in prayer, and the incense of heaven, which is the prayer of all the saints, and with a shout of the archangel, their prayers will be answered. The eastern sky will crack, and the glorious ending (and new beginning!) of all things will follow. In the midst of a new heaven and on a new earth, God will then reign forever in the presence of his people.

All this in answer to extraordinary prayer.

Two

Edwards, Prayer Societies, Cambuslang, and the Concert of Prayer

Jonathan Edwards (1703-1758) was arguably America's greatest theologian and philosopher. His genius and remarkable religious faith helped shape America's theological landscape. His writings were broad and voluminous, his preaching articulate, his vision for the kingdom of God profound, and his energies for the advancement of Christ's reign inexhaustible.

Edwards was born in East Windsor, Connecticut, the only son in a family of ten daughters. His father, Timothy Edwards, was a pastor, and his mother, an extraordinarily godly woman, was the daughter of the renowned and venerable Samuel Stoddard of Northampton, Massachusetts.

To prepare for the ministry, Edwards entered the Collegiate School of Connecticut (afterwards Yale College) at the age of thirteen. He was graduated four years later at the head of his class. After a stint in New York and again at Yale as a tutor, he was called to Northampton, Massachusetts, to serve as an assistant pastor to his maternal grandfather, eventually succeeding him as senior pastor two years later upon Stoddard's death. Stoddard's first-hand familiarity with revivals surely influenced Edwards.[1]

In 1735, during America's Great Awakening, Northampton and the Connecticut River Valley were shaken by religious fervor. Edwards was seen as a principal catalyst and apologist for the stirring, a member of that nuclear core of individuals whose fusion with the Holy Spirit produced the spiritual explosion. While many viewed the awakening with skepticism, fear, and even anger, Edwards's lucid preaching and writing convinced many that the awakening was an authentic work of God, abuses and unusual manifestations notwithstanding.

In the mid-1730s, this phenomenon swept through Edwards's church, the town of Northampton, Massachusetts, and the entire Connecticut River Valley. In the early 1740s the move of God revisited this area during the public ministry of George Whitefield.

In line with the vision in Ezekiel 37, Edwards was aware that spiritual awakening is the result of both preaching (prophesying to the bones) and praying (prophesying to the wind). His famous sermon, "Sinners in the Hands of an Angry God," provides an example. This message, though chilling and graphic, was dispassionately delivered, as were all his sermons. That Lord's Day, July 8, 1741,[2] however, his words were attended by an extraordinary anointing of the Holy Spirit. The sermon drew from Deuteronomy 32:35 (KJV): "Their foot shall slide in due time." Edwards's preaching produced such profound alarm in his congregation that parishioners groaned under the weight of their sin, and some held fast to supporting posts in the church, so fearful were they of literally sliding into hell.

It was later revealed that a group of Christians in nearby Enfield had met the night before. They were worried that because of God's anger the outpouring of God's grace so manifest in other places would pass them by. So they spent the whole night crying out to God in prayer. In less than twenty-four hours God answered and brought the Northampton parish to its knees.

Leaving Northampton after being expelled from his pulpit in 1750, Edwards served for seven years as a missionary to American Indians in Stockbridge, Massachusetts. In 1757, upon the death of his son-in-law, Aaron Burr, Sr.,[3] Edwards was invited to be president of the College of New Jersey (now Princeton University). However, he died from a smallpox inoculation before he could serve.

In 1747, some twelve years after the 1735 revival and five years after the second wave of the Holy Spirit's grace, Jonathan Edwards wrote a treatise that was to profoundly impact many evangelical Christians on both sides of the Atlantic. The work was a compilation of material he had developed over a lifetime of study, a series of sermons he preached in the 1740s, combined with a new and exciting plan of action proposed to him by good friends in Scotland. His treatise was entitled *An Humble Attempt to Promote Explicit Agreement and Visible Union Among God's People, in Extraordinary Prayer for the Revival of Religion, and the Advancement of Christ's Kingdom on Earth, Pursuant to Scripture Promises and Prophecies Concerning the Last Time.*[4]

Even though *Humble Attempt* has escaped the scrutiny given to many of Edwards's other works and has attracted only modest scholarly attention in recent years,[5] it can be argued that it had as much practical effect on the spread of the Gospel in England and America as anything Edwards ever produced.[6] Ironically, Edwards wrote the treatise on the eve of his expulsion from his Northampton pulpit and would see only limited fruit borne from the treatise during his lifetime.

As the title suggests, *Humble Attempt* was Edwards's call to Christians and churches everywhere to visibly unite in a workable strategy of synchronized prayer. The prayer union foreseen was identified as the "Concert of Prayer" (COP).

In the introduction to *Humble Attempt*, Edwards indicated that the scheme was not original to himself. He co-sponsored the call with a group of pastors from northern Scotland with whom he had corresponded for some years. The scriptural justification for the scheme, however, to which the larger part of *Humble Attempt* is dedicated, is distinctively Edwards's own. The COP, he argued, fitted into the prophetic unfolding of God's plan for the nations of the earth.

Concerning the mission of the COP, Edwards delineated two goals: (1) prayer for the revival of the Christian church (as the primary agency through which Christ manifests his glory on earth), and (2) prayer for the church, once revived, to be active with God's Spirit in the advancement of God's kingdom throughout the world.

The simplicity and clarity of these prayer targets was part of the COP's genius. Since few Christians would have difficulty with either prayer request, and since earnestly seeking God's face on behalf of the glory of Jesus' name was a goal on which evangelical Christians could agree, Edwards expected the Concert of Prayer to spread quickly across denominational lines. Moreover, he imagined that the plan would go beyond the mere cooperation of Christians to the creation of a marvelously harmonious "catholic"[7] church. Disparate Christians earnestly engaged in such harmonious prayer with one another would create "one family, one holy and happy society."[8] If the union of praying Christians in "different towns and cities" and in "different countries" could be realized, "who knows what it may come to at last?" he asked. Perhaps united prayers would even "open the doors and windows of heaven, that have so long been shut up, and been as brass over the heads of the inhabitants of the earth as to spiritual showers."[9] So taken was Edwards with the vision of a unified church literally covering the earth with harmonized praying that he dedicated much of his energy throughout the last ten years of his life to promoting it: "I shall not cease . . . to do what in me lies to promote and propagate it, according as favorable junctures and opportunities do present," he wrote.[10]

Before we examine Edwards's *Humble Attempt* more closely, however, we need to see something of the context within which the call was issued, as well as the constituency to which it was addressed. If the COP can be considered a jewel, we must picture its setting. Certain particulars of the 1735-1750 context will be addressed later when we examine the effect of the Great Awakening on the population and church leadership of northern Scotland and Northampton, Massachusetts, and we will also look at the particular theological justification for the COP. Each of these aspects is important for us to understand. But first we will look at the constituency to which *Humble Attempt* was addressed, one that transcended any provincial concern or geographical delineation. Edwards wrote with the "prayer societies" popularized in Europe, England, and the American colonies in mind.

THE PRAYER SOCIETIES

Prayer societies first emerged as a result of the spread of European Pietism.[11] By the 1740s, Yale historian Stephen Stein notes, prayer societies were everywhere, going wherever evangelical Christianity spread. They were prominent on both sides of the Atlantic. Not only were they prominent, but they were powerful. Tens of thousands of Christians, including some of the most important leaders in the history of Protestantism, were members. Given the magnitude of their influence, one wonders why the prayer societies are nearly overlooked by history scholars today.[12] For our purposes, to overlook them would make Edwards's vision of the COP appear as a utopian pipe dream.

Though prayer societies were widespread at the time *Humble Attempt* was written, their roots extend back more than a century before Edwards.

PRAYER SOCIETIES IN EUROPE AND ENGLAND

In Frankfort, Germany, some sixty years before *Humble Attempt*, a Lutheran pastor named Philipp Jacob Spener (1635-1705) codified what it meant to be an evangelical Christian and laid out a plan for the renewal of Christian living. His famous and hugely influential work *Pia*

Desideria was a reaction to barren Christian intellectualism.[13] Distressed over the condition of the Lutheran church in Germany, Spener stressed a personal experience with God and the duty of all Christians to grow in their love and devotion to the Savior.

As a forerunner to John Wesley, with his Methodist small-group strategy in the eighteenth century, and Paul (David) Cho, with his cell-group emphasis of today, Spener called upon pastors and laypeople to form small "societies," or pastoral care groups, within their churches for Bible reading and prayer. He saw these as vital to his goal of revival in the church.[14] Simply put, "the goal of all these [societies] for Spener was to have the contemporary church reflect the early Christian community."[15] Though prayer societies existed prior to Spener, his work put them in a whole new light and established them as the preferred *modus operandi* of Evangelicals and their churches.

Spener was a Pietist, a group concerned principally with the devotion of the Christian heart over and against the dominance of rigid and often dead orthodoxy. The theological center of the movement was at the University of Halle (1694). The champion was Spener's soul-mate, August Hermann Franke (1663-1727). Similar to Pentecostalism's long-term effect on modern Fundamentalism, Pietism prompted a remarkable surge of ministry. Just a few examples of its outreach—ragged schools were formed for the poor (models for later schools such as those introduced a century later by Lord Shaftesbury in England); orphanages were organized (which influenced George Muller of Bristol, who was educated at Halle and converted to Christ in a prayer society); an embryonic form of the modern missionary movement took shape as the king of Denmark sent men to Halle to be trained as missionaries for Tranquebar, India. All of these activities were bathed in systematic, united small-group prayer.

By 1727, a generation later, Count Nicholas Von Zinzendorf organized the *Unitas Fratrum*, and the enormously influential Moravian movement was born. Zinzendorf was Spener's godson and a student under Franke. The count had actively mobilized prayer societies since his youth (he organized seven while he studied at Halle). The Moravian emphasis on prayer societies for the spread of Christ's kingdom was plucked right out of Pietism's vision for the Christian life. Moravian prayer societies and missions deeply affected William Carey fifty years later. It was the Moravian prayer societies at Aldersgate Street and Fetters Lane in England that brought John and Charles Wesley to salvation through Christ and cemented other Oxford Methodists like Whitefield to the Savior.[16]

On his estate at Saxony Zinzendorf gave sanctuary to oppressed Moravians. Saddened by the divisions and critical spirit evident among them, he drew up a covenant, *Unitas Fratrum,* calling the divided group "to seek out and emphasize the points in which they agreed." Once in agreement on paper, he set the whole of them to united, sustained, and extraordinary prayer. Their hearts were knit together by prayer.

In July of 1727, tears came in their praying. Days later they covenanted together on their own for more prayer and hymns. On August 5, many Moravians spent the whole night in prayer with Zinzendorf. On Sunday, August 10, the worship service was overwhelmed by the power of God. Then on Wednesday, the 13th, the Holy Spirit was poured out upon the whole community, transforming it by an enormous work of grace. From that point forward, a united prayer meeting was established that continued twenty-four hours a day without interruption for 100 years!

Prayer societies flourished with Pietism's rise and affected every sector of the Protestant church. One of the principal leaders behind the migration of these prayer societies to London, and thus to the Church of England, was Dr. Anthony Horneck (1641-1697).[17] He was appointed preacher at Savoy shortly after his arrival in England from Heidelberg in 1661. During the persecution under King James II, Horneck helped foster a movement of covert prayer societies. The movement grew like a weed.

Concerning one such secret prayer society, Horneck records: "they adjourned to some Publicke-House where they could have a Room to themselves; under the Pretext of spending a Shilling or two, they conferr'd seriously together."[18] Since the London societies determined to be evangelistic, the members agreed to bring one friend each to their various meetings. Forty distinct groups existed in London by 1701.[19]

In Europe Pietism spread among the Germanic Lutherans. For our concern, the most important of these peoples was the Dutch. Holland was a major center for the transport of Pietism to England and beyond. Throughout the seventeenth century Holland was an important asylum for English religious refugees. Among them were the Separatists who sailed to America as the Pilgrims of Plymouth Rock.

But there were also many others who, having fled to Holland, returned to England once the heat of religious persecution dissipated.

Among them were many who had been deeply affected by Pietism's passion for God. While in Holland, English expatriates emulated their Pietistic hosts, meeting regularly in prayer societies. Having grown to appreciate the impact of Bible reading, fervent and regular prayer, and mutual accountability, these English Christians embraced the prayer societies as their own.

Upon their return to England, the newly fashioned English Pietists brought their societies home with them.[20] In 1724 Robert Wodrow noted that there were "multitudes of these meetings, both young men and elder persons in London."[21] Concerning the nature and regularity of their meeting, Wodrow speaks of a certain Mr. Kemp who lived in London and who "joyned in a private fellowship-meeting, who conveened every Monday, about six of the clock, and spent some hours in prayer and conference, where he was much afreshed."[22]

Societies were found elsewhere. Among the numerous prayer societies at Oxford was the Methodist society, better known as the "Holy Club." Still more were found in Cambridge. To the north, after a rough first fifty years, private prayer societies spread through Scotland like yeast through dough.[23] For years the popularity of the prayer societies in Scotland grew almost unimpeded. By the end of the seventeenth century, every social class was involved in them.[24]

As I intimated before, one can easily appreciate that there were times when the popularity of the prayer societies was perceived as a threat. Early on, the Scottish kirk was alarmed by them. As principally a lay movement,[25] the influence of these societies became significant, and some churchmen and the state (church and state were joined at the hip) feared that that power was excessive and pernicious. As early as 1639 the revered Samuel Rutherford intervened to thwart potentially severe actions against the societies by the Scottish kirk. After a lengthy point-by-point defense of the societies, Rutherford likened them to the Jews of Jeremiah 50:4-5, who bound themselves in a covenant to "seek the Lord their God." A sympathetic Rutherford wrote:

> Now a word of the manner of their seeking to Zion. They go weeping to seek the Lord. They weep because they had angered the Lord, and weep for the desolation of the holy city, and truly a work of reformation, it requires weeping. And it should not have so much rejoicing and so much security joined therewith. And it looks the liker a judgment, that so few are drawn to repentance by this work of reformation, for the former breach of our covenant and our turn-

ing away from the Lord. The work of reformation should draw us
to this, as the harlot wife who has been put out from her husband
for her harlotry, when she is brought home again to her provoked
husband, and he delivers to her again the keys of the house. If she
be honest, it grieves her and makes her heart to melt, that she
should have provoked such a loving husband. Even so; when the
Lord has dealt so graciously with us after our falling away from
Him, should there be so many dry cheeks among us as there are?
"They asked the way to Zion." All the tears in the world without
this, they are but like to Esau's tears, for he resolved in the days of
mourning to kill his brother; and like Judas's tears of desperation.
But these are better tears that are spoken of in Acts 20:19, when the
apostle was there leaving the Ephesians to serve the Lord, with
many tears and temptations. It is nothing to weep for sin for a time,
but to have their faces towards Zion, and asking the way to it, and
to weep, that is more![26]

Within a hundred years the societies were fully integrated into
Scottish church life and were carefully regulated and organized by
the local Sessions.[27]

PRAYER SOCIETIES AND THE AMERICAN COLONIES

During the years of Pietism's ascendancy, America came under its influence through many people.[28] Though he was of the Dutch Reformed
rather than the Lutheran tradition, Theodorus Frelinghuysen[29]
imported his passion for pietistic "experiential religion" to the Dutch
immigrants in New Jersey's Raritan Valley. Frelinghuysen was schooled
by Pietists in Utrecht and Hernorn, and over the course of his life he
argued passionately regarding the issues of the heart as opposed to simply knowing doctrine.

His preaching, that placed greater importance on the heart than the
head, influenced the founding of the famous, yet derisively named "Log
College" by William Tennent.[30] Tennent established this one-room
school in rugged eastern Pennsylvania to train pastors zealous after
God. It was an alternative to formal academic institutions that turned
out educated clergymen whose heads were full of learning but whose
hearts were cold toward heaven. If they couldn't import godly men from
Europe or Boston, they determined to grow them locally. The powerful
fires of revival lit by Frelinghuysen's ministry in the 1720s were among
the earliest signs of America's Great Awakening, a monumental move

of God that affected millions of lives, galvanized a montage of colonial immigrants, and forged a semblance of common life among them.

Another person in the colonies whose zealous pursuit of God closely mirrored Spener's was Cotton Mather (1663-1728). Mather's family was renowned within American religious circles. His father, "the Reverend and famous Increase Mather,"[31] was president of Harvard College and possessed a prayerful longing for spiritual revival. He passed on this longing to his son.[32] Like the German Pietists who were burdened for the Lutheran church in Europe, Cotton Mather was deeply and continually concerned for the spiritual state of affairs in the American colonies. As we will see later, he was also motivated by an urgent, unshakable conviction that Jesus was soon to return. Mather did not simply bemoan the condition of the church; he proposed a plan to heal it.

At the end of the seventeenth century, Mather began a long correspondence with Hermann Franke. In 1706 Mather's pressing concern for New England and the influence of Franke merged into an essay titled *Private Meetings Animated and Regulated.*[33] Though Mather called it "a short essay to preserve and revive the ancient practice of lesser societies formed among religious people to promote the great interest of religion," it was clearly intended for a wide audience. It was reprinted under the title *Proposals Concerning Religious Societies, Humbly Offered unto GOOD MEN, in several Towns of the County: For the Revival of DYING RELIGION.*[34]

In the essay Mather observed that the times had become perilous, and the church showed little spiritual power. Like the Europeans, he saw the pressing need for lay Christians to mobilize themselves in order that the smoldering coals of spiritual life might be fanned into flames. As to the shape this mobilization should take, Mather insisted that prayer societies were "the most Effectual Engines" to accomplish revival[35] and reverse the spiritual fortunes of the colonies. He encouraged his readers to form a variety of such groups. He proposed that "a Dozen families or less, of a Vicinity, Agree to meet (Husbands and their Wives) at each other's Houses, Once in a Fortnight of a Month, and spend a Convenient Quantity of Time together." Besides neighborhood groups, he also advocated age- and sex-targeted groups such as "young men's meetings" and "women's societies."[36]

In the following excerpts from Mather's essay, we can glean the dynamics of the proposed societies. He writes:

One special *Design* of the *Meeting* should be, with *United Prayers,* to ask the Blessings of Heaven on the *Family* where they are Assembled, as well as of the rest. . . . Wonderful, wonderful is the Force of *United Prayers*, when the Faithful, *Two or Three shall agree on Earth, to ask such Things, as are to be done for them of our Father which is in Heaven.* . . .

Supplication of such Affected Families; and the *interests of Religion* may be mightily preserved and prompted in the *whole flock*, by their Fervent Supplications; and the *Spirit of Grace*, mightily Poured out upon the Rising Generation, Yea, *all the Land*, may fare the better for them. . . . Especially, when a *Society* shall set apart *whole Days* for *Prayer* with *Fasting* before the Lord, as it may be proper for them to do now and then upon some Occasions. The *Success* of such *Days* has been sometimes very marvellous. . . .

[O]nce in Two Months, let the *whole Evening* be Devoted, unto Supplications for . . . the Success of the Gospel.[37]

As American prayer societies grew in popularity throughout the colonies, they became a constituency to which churches and political leaders could turn in times of extraordinary need.

In 1745, for example, the American colonists faced the threat of French troops to the north. There was general alarm throughout New England as colonists mobilized to defend themselves. The Americans took their stand at Cape Breton on the Canadian frontier.

In the wake of a stunning American victory came unrestrained joy throughout the colonies and a general conviction that God had been mightily at work. In July of 1745, Thomas Prince, pastor of South Church, Boston, praised the Lord for "the *happy Accomplishment*" of God's providential protection of New England. It was encouraging, said Prince, "to think how many *pious* and *prayerful* Persons were embarqu'd in the Cause, which we accounted a Cause of GOD and his People; it gave further Ground of Hope, to see such a *Spirit of Supplication* given to many in this Town and Land on this Occasion."

In particular, Prince applauded "the solemn Days of *publick* and *general Prayer* appointed" and the "*particular Days* observed in several Congregations." But then he turned his praise toward a distinct group of people—those who belonged to the "Societies."

. . . some of Women as well as others of Men, which met *every Week*, more privately to pray for the Preservation and Success of their dear

Countrymen: And I have been well informed of their extraordinary Fervency, Faith and Wrestlings, as so many *Jacobs*, in this important Season. . . . [That our victory came] in such a Manner as the *Work* and *Glory* might appear to be *his alone*. . . .

It was in the wake of the fervent, united "wrestlings" in these praying societies, Prince said, that God "began in a remarkable Manner to hear our Prayers."[38]

So the societies became a powerful resource in times of great need in towns and cities or in the colonies as a whole. And apart from the popularization of prayer societies, the call for united praying generally was not unfamiliar to the colonial period. Solemn Assemblies of prayer were commonly decreed. The annual Fast Day is a case in point.

Fast Days were observed regularly throughout New England. They were days designed to focus the colonists' attention on their great need for God. Many Fast Day sermons still exist, providing a wealth of evidence that evangelical pastors were acutely aware of the relationship between united and fervent prayer and God's action on their behalf with power.

Like Mather, Prince, and Edwards, the Reverend John Webb of the New North Church, Boston, was a man of deep personal piety. He, too, was deeply concerned with united prayer and its relationship to revival.[39] In 1734 he preached the annual Fast Day sermon at the New North Church. He spoke of the "declining Years" for Christianity and exhorted his audience with the necessity to fervently seek the face of God for the revival of the church:

[W]e are indispensably bound to pray that God would pour down his Holy Spirit upon all Orders and Ages amongst us. . . . And if we do not presently see the success of these Prayers, we must not be discouraged and give over the Duty; but we must humbly resolve with Holy Jacob in his wrestling with the Angel of the Lord (Gen. 31:24, 26) *that we will not let him alone till he bless us*. That is, we must persevere in the Duty, and Cry to God with all possible Importunity, till we find the Holy Spirit reviving his own Work both in Ourselves and Others. And if God does but once open and enlarge our Hearts to pray to Him with this persevering Importunity, we need not doubt the success of our Prayers. For God can as soon deny Himself as deny an answer to the fervent Prayers of his People. . . . We must, with our Prayers to God, for this Mercy *unite our best Endeavors* to obtain what we pray for.[40]

This sermon was preached only months before the general out-break of spiritual awakening under Edwards.

Transcending the particular emphasis on prayer societies, Pietism's emphasis on the importance of united prayer, then, was profound. The significance is more fully realized when we are aware that one of Pietism's central messages, especially in the Lutheran and Moravian strains, was the unity of all true Christians. This point in principle affected Evangelicals as deeply as the societies did in practice. Edwards illustrated the effect on his thinking when he explained his vision for "one family, one holy and happy society" through the COP. Unity was seen as uniquely manifested in the corporate prayer life of all true Christians. This unity was the context in which God designed to man-ifest his greatest glory (e.g., Pentecost).

All this is to say that when Jonathan Edwards sat down to compile *Humble Attempt*, he did so knowing that his call for the COP would be addressed to ears generally familiar with the themes of united and fer-vent praying. More specifically, he addressed a significant constituency of evangelical Christians already committed to the unity of true Christians and knowledgeable of or already participating in a design that could quickly and efficiently embrace his scheme: prayer societies. None of the above would have been perceived as a particularly exotic or novel idea. The only new thing in Edwards's vision was the plan to coordinate the prayer agendas of all prayer societies, harness their inherent spiritual energies, and combine them with large-group, Fast-Day dynamics into a single worldwide movement. But as we are about to see, even the idea of fashioning a single prayer movement out of many existing prayer soci-eties had a proven track record to which Edwards could point.

The model to which Edwards looked was to him the perfect illus-tration of how all these elements could merge into a smoothly orches-trated movement. It was found in the city of Cambuslang, Scotland. There a successful COP had been established six or seven years before *Humble Attempt* was published.

CAMBUSLANG

Cambuslang is in the north of Scotland about five miles southeast of Glasgow. Throughout the seventeenth and eighteenth centuries, the city was engaged in weaving, agriculture, and mining. The town was situ-ated in a district of beautiful rolling hills and valleys, fertile land, and extensive woods.[41] By the early eighteenth century the city's population stood at about 1,000 people, or about 200 families.[42] As in much of England at this time, prayer societies were to be found everywhere in northern Scotland, including Cambuslang. By the 1730s, however, the prayer societies, like the general state of the Christianity, were experiencing decline.

In 1731 the Reverend William M'Culloch[43] (1691-1771), a 1712 graduate of Glasgow University, was ordained pastor of the Cambuslang parish. His religious heritage was glorious. His father had been a parish schoolmaster in Anworth under the ministry of Samuel Rutherford, a man noted for his emphasis on prayer and his sympathies toward the prayer societies. Rutherford had come to the aid of the societies when they were deemed a threat to the Scottish kirk.

M'Culloch was a bright and studious man, noted for his unusual skills in the sciences and biblical languages. He taught for a time at the University of Glasgow and was described by its dean as "a learned, unostentatious scholar, a slow, cautious and prudent parish minister."[44] M'Culloch, however, was not a gifted preacher. His parishioners gave him the name "Ale-minister," for when he rose to speak on the Lord's Day, many of his congregation suddenly got thirsty and slipped out of church to the local public house.[45]

When M'Culloch arrived in Cambuslang, he could never have imagined how God was about to use him to affect his city, Scotland, and the world.

In the mid to late 1730s, M'Culloch came into the possession of a report from the American colonies describing an ongoing and marvelous work of God along the Connecticut River Valley. Sometime after 1735, *A Faithful Narrative of the Surprising Work of God in the Conversion of Many Hundreds of Souls in Northampton*, written by Jonathan Edwards, hit Scotland. It received a wide reading and moved many hearts. After a long period of spiritual declension, the surprising news of God's awakening activity spread like wildfire among drought-ridden fields of the evangelical world.

Reading of lives being transformed by the Gospel and churches exploding with new life, M'Culloch was deeply moved. He dreamed of seeing his own Cambuslang experience a similar work of God. This vision became M'Culloch's passion and prayer. To help instill a similar hunger in the hearts of his congregation, M'Culloch began reading excerpts from Edwards's *Faithful Narrative* and the latest reports of spiritual awakening from the colonies during worship services. The accounts stirred a sense of holy jealousy among some of his people.[46] Sometime between this time and the publishing of his first edition of *The Weekly History*,[47] M'Culloch began an ongoing correspondence with Jonathan Edwards. Their letter writing lasted to the time of Edwards's death.[48]

With splendid glory, M'Culloch saw the answer to his prayers for Cambuslang in the early 1740s. Revival and spiritual awakening shook his city and beyond. This work of God came on the heels of a long and serious trouble throughout Scotland and England.

In January 1741, a furious hurricane roared across the British Isles. The storm did extensive damage to shipping and property throughout the British realm and Europe. What seemed to be two terrible omens also appeared that month. Glasgow's most important cathedral was heavily damaged and its steeple demolished. And on January 13, immediately following the storm, a total eclipse of the sun occurred.

To compound the misery of the storm's carnage, the winter weather was bitter and hard. The general devastation was so widespread that it never allowed people to recover during the warmer months of 1741 and prepare for the following winter.

By the winter of 1742, conditions in Scotland were dreadful. Harsh weather revisited the country, and the people suffered from famine and disease. As in scenes out of modern Somalia, hungry mobs attacked food wagons. "Bands of haggard and emaciated women and pale, skeleton-like children" were seen "creeping slowly among the trees, stripping the branches of the beech of their tender leaves, returning to pick them day by day."[49] "Little children searched among the miller's huscks, hoping for some stray grains of corn, gnawing the stems of vegetables from the dunghill."[50] *Scots Magazine* recorded that rioting broke out at Leith, Edinburgh, Musselburgh, Prestonpans, and other places and that troops had fired on the mobs. Beggars filled the streets of Edinburgh.[51] An estimated 2,000 people perished of hunger and cold.[52]

Added to the natural disasters were problems with Cambuslang's church life. In 1741 the parish was so fraught with trouble and spiritual decline that the Glasgow presbytery refused to ordain any elders from Cambuslang. In the whole of the parish not a single man could be found worthy of ordination.

Throughout these difficulties M'Culloch faithfully preached, reminding the people that God often used the calamities of nature and troubles of other kinds to cause his people to return to him. Because of the hardships, M'Culloch preached to an attentive audience.

Then in 1741 a phenomenon visited the town. One of the most gifted preachers in the history of the church, a common denominator of the Great Awakening, arrived in Cambuslang to preach. Though conditions had not yet reached their worst in Scotland, the passionate and powerful evangelist George Whitefield came to minister.[53] Onto the soil of Scotland, made fallow by decline and disaster and harrowed by the plow of despair, God sent a sower to scatter the seeds of spiritual awakening. Preaching ten times in five days to eager listeners and large audiences, Whitefield made a surprising impression upon the city and countryside.

In the months after Whitefield's first visit, the lives of people in Cambuslang began to change. M'Culloch witnessed a remarkable hunger for God within his parish.[54] By the end of January 1742, two converts of Whitefield's preaching, Ingram More, a shoemaker, and Robert Bowman, a weaver, went door to door with a petition requesting that M'Culloch begin a weekly midweek teaching time. Almost half the total households in the Cambuslang parish, ninety families, signed the petition.

Excited beyond words, M'Culloch not only started the midweek service but organized the ninety families into prayer societies by February. Conscious of the ongoing despair and spiritual ruin in his parish, M'Culloch decided to coordinate the prayer efforts of the societies so they could all focus on certain agreed-upon prayer targets. This prayer agreement he called "a Concert." Writing in the third person, he said:

> On *Monday the 15th of February* there was a general Meeting at the Minister's House, of the particular Societies for Prayer which had been subsisted in the Parish for several Years before . . . and *Tuesday* there was another Meeting for Prayer there, the Occasion of which was a Concert with several serious Christians elsewhere about solemn Prayer, relating to the public interests of the Gospel; in which Concert only a small Number of People in *Cambuslang* were engaged at first, but others getting Notice of it determined to join, and were admitted: The People who met for Prayer those two Days apprehended that they had been so well employed and found so much Leisure for it that they had a third Meeting on *Wednesday*: But on all these three Days they returned tim[e]ly in the Evening to

their own Houses, so far is it from [source unreadable] that they rushed from some of these Meetings to the Church, and continued *immersed* there for some Days and Nights, as was reported.

. . . [On Friday] a considerable Number of People, reckoned by some present about fifty, came together to the Minister's House, under Conviction and alarming Apprehensions about the State of their Souls, and deciding [sic] to speak with him. . . .

After this, Numbers daily resorted to that Place. . . . He found himself obliged, without any previous Intimation, to provide them a daily Sermon, a few days excepted . . . the number of persons awaken'd to Deep Concern about salvation, and against whom there are no known Exceptions as yet, has amounted to above 300.[55]

Once the Concert was under way, the church was soon packed. The third service "proved to be the spark which ignited the ensuing blaze."[56] The morning after this particular service, M'Culloch assembled the leaders of prayer societies in his house. He "read over . . . [the agreement for prayer] to a General Meeting of the Societies [sic] for Prayer in the Parish that met at his House that day; they were greatly affected in hearing it."[57] Three straight nights of meetings followed, and soon the surrounding towns heard about a remarkable "wark" of God burgeoning in Cambuslang. Condemnation from those who criticized what was happening only served to fuel the fire.

By the end of May it was obvious that God was stirring up deep conviction within many, many people. In the span of two months 300 had been "awakened," and the compounding of conversion upon conversion created a remarkable, almost delirious joy throughout the parish. The midweek lectures and the prayer societies were packed, and many meetings lasted throughout the night.

Soon M'Culloch needed help with the crowds. He was overwhelmed. He appealed to the other ministers of the region, and they came. Shortly after that the revival spread all over the Scottish lowlands.[58]

Because of these awakened lives and because of the critics who would scoff at such sensational spectacles, M'Culloch emulated Edwards[59] in systematically recording the events at Cambuslang. Through detailed reporting and interviews, M'Culloch wrote the *Narrative of the Extraordinary Work at Cambuslang in a Letter to a Friend with Proper Attestations by Ministers, Preachers, and Others.*[60]

By July the awakening had assumed enormous proportions. As the startling events in Cambuslang were duplicated in other towns and villages, Whitefield was summoned to return. He accepted the invitation to help further the Cambuslang work and arrived the week of July 11-17, 1742.

By this time the prayer societies, which had been barely alive the previous year, were thriving.[61] The change in corporate prayer life immediately impressed Whitefield. Everywhere he turned the people were pleading with God to multiply the work begun among them. Reflecting years later on this second visit, Whitefield wrote:

Much prayer had previously been put up to the Lord. All night in different companies, you might have heard persons praying to, and praising God. The children of God came from all quarters. It was like the Passover in Josiah's time.[62]

And again, listing the reasons for the remarkable work of God:

1. The Revival was not something humanly planned, but was manifestly the sovereign work of the Holy Spirit of God.

2. It began under the ministry of a man who did not possess outstanding pulpit gifts—William M'C[ulloch]—and who was simply doing his regular task, but with grave earnestness.

3. The Revival was born in and produced much prayer. M'C[ulloch] and Robe were men of prayer and under their influence the Societies for Prayer in their areas came into a strong new life and Christians prayed with new intensity and power.[63]

Cambuslang, however, was not alone in its extraordinary praying. Prior to the awakening James Robe of Glasgow wrote: "Our Societies for Prayer came gradually to nothing. . . . All the Societies for PRAYER were then given up." Nothing could be done, Robe continued, to stem the spiritual slide, the poor attendance at church services, and the general state of immorality among his people. Even after the reports began to flood back to Glasgow about the Cambuslang awakening, he could see no immediate effect upon his city. But then came what Robe described as "*this uncommon Dispensation of his Grace.*" Robe saw "[w]hat appeared *the most hopeful*" sign: "[T]here appeared a *concern more than ordinary* among the Hearers of the Gospel, and . . . there were Proposals for *setting up Societies for Prayer*, which had been long intermitted." Soon, little by little, the effects of the awakening became more noticeable. He heard that prayer societies were being formed: "Near this Time . . . there were some *Societies for Prayer* erected in the Parish; I was also informed that *several young girls* in the town of *Kilsyth*, from *ten* to *sixteen* Years of Age, had been observed *meeting together for Prayer.*" Shortly afterward, Robe reported, the awakening erupted, and the good minister of Glasgow was inundated with counseling.[64]

The Reverend Mr. Willison, shepherd of the Dundee parish near Cambuslang, wrote to Robe on June 14, 1742:

> O that we could praise him and call Heaven & Earth to praise him, for the Comforter's Continuance at *Cambuslang*, and for his coming so many Miles on this Side of *Glasgow*. . . . We have a great number of young People in *this Place* who have changed their Ways, are in love with Sermons and join Societies for Prayer. . . . If a Spirit of *Faith* and *Prayer* were poured out, we might hope the blessed Work would spread, and go through the breadth of the Land.[65]

Further on, Willison noted that the most compelling "*Fruits* of the Dispensation" were the "many societies for Prayer erected in the Parish."

On September 13, 1742, John Hamilton of Glasgow wrote Robe telling a similar tale. Hamilton rejoiced about "erecting *new Societies* for Prayer and spiritual Conference." To Hamilton, the forming of the prayer societies was ample reason by themselves to give him hope of "the joyful Prospect of a considerable Enlargement of the Messiah's Kingdom."[66]

From the nearby town of Muthil came yet another dramatic testimony. A letter from a William Haley was received by Robe. Haley recounted the activity of that time both in his parish and that of Madery:

> Sept. 28, 1742
> Our praying Societies are in a most flourishing Condition, and still more Members [are] flocking to them: their Meetings are frequent, and the Lord is observably present with them—The *Meetings for Prayer* among the *young Boys* and *Girls*, give me great Satisfaction, one whereof began [with] the Number of *twenty*. Till of late they met in the *Town:* But several of them falling under deep Concern, that I was sent for to speak with them, where I found some of them all in Tears; Since that Time (that I may have them near me) I give them a Room in the *manse*, where they meet *every Night*. And O how pleasant is it to hear the poor *young Lambs* addressing themselves to God in Prayer. O with what Fervour, with what proper

Expressions, so I hear them pouring out their Souls to a Prayer-hearing God; so that standing at the back Door, I am often melted into Tears to hear them. We have another *praying society* of the *young Ones,* lately, desired his Allowance to meet in the *School-House* for *Prayer;* which he very readily went in to (for his Pleasure, to promote and encourage Religion both in Young and Old), and there about *twenty* of them meet *twice every Week,* tho' they have a good Way (many of them) to travel in the Night-Time. I may say in general, that such a *praying Disposition* as appears among this People, both *young* and *old,* was never seen nor heard of before. . . . As to the Parish of MADERY, which you desire to be inform'd about; soon after the Sacrament at *Fowels,* a neighboring Parish, some few *Boys* met in the *Fields* for *Prayer;* and when observed were brought to an *House;* to whom, many others, both *young* and *old* resorted since, and are now according to my information, in a very flourishing Condition. This *Presbytery* is resolved to divide themselves into *Societies for Prayer,* for the *Progress of this blessed Work.*

Wm. Haley[67]

So as Whitefield returned, the region was buzzing with fervent, expectant prayer. The people of God were earnestly and hopefully praying "in concert" for the revival of the church and general spiritual awakening. On July 11, Whitefield preached on the Braes at Cambuslang. Considering that Cambuslang's population stood at about 2,000, the size of the crowd was breathtaking—an estimated 20,000! M'Culloch reported that "Mr. Whitefield's sermons were attended with much power . . . very great but decent weeping and mourning was observable throughout the auditory . . . a much greater increase of the power and special presence of God." Robe added, "Some who attended, declared they would not for a world have been absent from this solemnity. Others cried, 'Now let thy servants depart in peace,' if it were the will of God, to die where they were attending God in his ordinances, without ever returning to the world." As Whitefield preached, multitudes came under deep conviction. They wept over their sins, and some fell to the ground. Over 1,700 people received Communion in the open air.

A month later, on August 15, Whitefield returned for a third visit. This time he estimated the attendance to be 30,000 people[68] with 3,000 taking Communion.[69]

The hand-in-glove relationship between spiritual awakening and united prayer did not go unnoticed by the religious leaders of northern

Scotland. This lesson made a deep and lasting impact upon them. If such an awakening could happen as a result of a single season of united praying, these leaders could only imagine what a sustained movement of prayer might mean for the whole of Scotland and the ministry of the Gospel throughout the earth.[70]

Flush with the wonder of God's awakening grace, in 1744 twelve pastors from the revived regions of central Scotland decided to coordinate all their efforts for the glory of God and the global advancement of Christ's kingdom. The Cambuslang revival caused many to consider global possibilities. Many of those who attested to the authenticity of the 1742 awakening called Cambuslang the "little cloud." What they had witnessed reminded them of the account in 1 Kings 18:44 when the prophet Elijah, fresh from vanquishing the prophets of Baal, pleaded with God to end his judgment against rebellious, drought-ridden Israel. After Elijah had prayed a seventh time, his servant looked and saw a little cloud. The cloud was the sign, said Elijah to his servant, that a mighty outpouring of God was imminent. The Scottish pastors believed such an outpouring was foretold for the latter days of the earth and across the face of the globe.[71]

On October 28, 1742, John Erskines wrote that it was his conviction that Cambuslang's awakening was a presage of much greater things to come. While asserting that he had no knowledge of the exact times and seasons for the fulfillment of scriptural prophecies, he argued that the fulfillment of certain signs about the end of history were being seen at every hand. He concluded his thoughts with a fervent prayer: "It is hoped that this Work will not only go through our Land in the Length of it and the Breadth of it, but spread from Kingdom to Kingdom, till all the Kingdoms of the Earth shall become the Kingdom of God and His Christ."[72]

M'Culloch himself suggests similar thoughts in a letter to Jonathan Edwards. Even though he and Edwards constituted a "brotherhood at such great distances," M'Culloch wrote that they could still see manifested together:

> the mighty hand of the Lord; Great controversies and obstacles overcome by the power of the Lord, [and can] anticipat[e] more formidable enemies; and his prophetic promises unfolding before their eyes; Christ conquering more and more "till the whole Earth be filled with his Glory."[73]

So in their excitement, these Scottish pastors dreamed up a glorious experiment. Since their people were wonderfully alive to Christ, and prayer societies were blossoming in every locale, they took a page from William M'Culloch's parish strategy and decided to coordinate all the praying societies of all their parishes into a single movement of concerted prayer. Through this, they believed, the whole world would be impacted.

The prayer societies were asked to meet once a week to pray by themselves, and then once a quarter they were to unite in larger multiple-parish gatherings for a solemn day of prayer. The prayer concerns were kept simple:

1. for the revival of the church of Christ
2. for the advancement of Christ's kingdom throughout the earth.[74]

Initially they agreed to pursue this concert for two years, after which the leaders would reevaluate the arrangement to see if its continuation had further merit.

As for the logistics of such a plan, the sheer numbers involved meant it was no small feat. In Edinburgh alone there were some thirty societies with as many as thirty members apiece. Glasgow boasted forty-five prayer societies, not to mention the scores of others in the major population centers of Aberdeen, Cambuslang, Kilsyth, and Dundee.[75] But organize them they did.

At first the pastors agreed not to advertise their prayer concert but to spread the COP by word of mouth and letter writing.[76] Given the religious networks the Scottish pastors had access to, this meant that some very important people were soon to hear of the experiment. In 1745, for example, John Wesley (1703-1791) heard of the plan from John Erskines. Wesley readily agreed to join in with it, and suggested that Erskines also inform Jonathan Edwards and Gilbert Tennent in America.[77] When the proposal arrived in Northampton, Massachusetts, Edwards was instantly delighted, regarding the prayer union as "exceedingly beautiful, and becoming Christians." "[I]t is apparent," Edwards added, "that we can't help ourselves, and have nowhere else to go, but to God."[78]

Sereno Dwight's account gives us greater detail of Edwards's reception of the proposal:

> In Oct. 1744, a number of ministers in Scotland, among them whom I believe, were all the correspondents of Mr. Edwards in that

country, thinking that the state of the church and the world called loudly for United Extraordinary Prayer to God, that he would deliver the nations from their miseries, and fill the earth with his glory; proposed that Christians universally should, for the two years then next ensuing set apart a portion of time, on Saturday evening and Sabbath morning, every week, to be spent in prayer for this purpose; and that they should still more solemnly devote the first Tuesday in the last month of each quarter of the year, to be spent either in private, social, or public prayer to God, for the bestowment of those blessings on the world. Mr. Edwards not only welcomed the proposal as soon as he received it, but did all in his power to promote its general acceptance by the American churches.[79]

After the two years of praying together (1744-1746), the Scottish pastors agreed that the plan merited another commitment by all. Greatly encouraged by their success and the rising interest on every front, the leaders of the COP decided to publicize the plan by the distribution of a printed "memorial." Five hundred memorials were sent to New England alone.[80] Others were sent to the remaining colonies and were said to be "wonderfully spreading in . . . England, Wales, [and] Ireland." Evidence suggests, too, that they went to Holland. In sum, the Scots intended to invite all Christians everywhere to join them in united prayer.

The fact that the COP plan so delighted Edwards raises questions as to why it fitted as perfectly as it did into his scheme of things. To answer this question, we have to examine two important areas: Edwards's Northampton ministry context and his understanding of the coming millennial reign of Christ.

NORTHAMPTON

Like many other places in New England during the 1730s, prayer societies were active in Edwards's parish.[81] The last half of the decade was marked by the extraordinary spiritual activity surrounding the Great Awakening, and, needless to say, this period was characterized by flourishing prayer societies. Even though the evangelical community already prized occasions for united prayer, throughout this time Edwards grew in his convictions about and his passion for such prayer.

For example, during the 1730s and 1740s (especially in the waning years of the Great Awakening), Edwards developed a system whereby "prayer bids" could be submitted by individuals within his congregation.[82] These were scraps of paper on which members of his Northampton congregation could submit requests for general prayer. Many of these prayer bids exist among Edwards's papers. Once the requests were collected, they would be distributed among the prayer societies. The requests gave rise to "prayer conventions"—large-group prayer times of extended, fervent, united intercession. Through these activities Edwards hoped to keep the fires of revival alive and help foster the idea of the priesthood of all believers.

But Edwards did much more than simply work hard to keep united prayer alive in his church's congregational life. He was driven by deeper eschatological convictions and expectations, and he became convinced that prayer, especially united prayer, was foundational to the inexorable unfolding of God's designs in history. He was intensely curious about those Bible books and passages—at once full of glory, wonder, and mystery—dealing with the end of the world and the ultimate glorification of Christ and his church. Edwards began writing *Notes on the Apocalypse* (that is, notes on the book of Revelation) when he was in his twenties[83] and regularly worked on it until near the end of his life. Dozens of sermons on Revelation remain among his collection of sermons, and many others exist on related subjects.

Without trying to simplify this remarkable man, I think it is safe to say that Jonathan Edwards was driven and animated by three things— a vibrant, personal devotion to Christ, Reformation theology, and his convictions and expectations concerning God's plan for the culmination of history. Regarding the latter, historian Perry Miller called him "the greatest artist of the apocalypse" in colonial America.[84] This part of Edwards greatly impacted his Scottish friends and cemented their admiration for him.

Edwards had very clear sentiments regarding the millennial reign and the personal return of Jesus Christ. Like many evangelicals of his day, he was a postmillennialist. In a nutshell Edwards believed that both the church of Jesus Christ and the reign of God were predestined to expand with ever-increasing glory until all the nations of the earth and the relationships of people and nations were captured for the sake of the Gospel. As the nations turned to Christ, the Redeemer would establish a glorious penultimate state through a reign of righteousness, justice, prosperity, and joy among the nations of the earth. At this time the prophecies of Isaiah and Habakkuk would be fulfilled: "The earth shall be full of the knowledge of the Lord, as the waters cover the sea." After this quasi-utopian period (interrupted by occasional rebellions, upheavals, and the various sad fruits of sinful behavior), Jesus Christ would personally return to earth, judge it and every person, and transform all creation by creating a new heaven and a new earth. In this final state, the Lord would reign personally and his glory would fill the universe.

To these ends, Edwards was persuaded that the awakenings he was involved in and the numerous other extraordinary works of God reported to him from elsewhere were indications that history was thawing and showing signs of the budding of the millennium.[85] Moreover, he saw prayer, especially united universal prayer, as chief among the evidences of the glorious, inexorable unfolding of God's historical design for the earth. For this reason, the Concert of Prayer must be seen in its theological-eschatological context.

EDWARDS'S MILLENNIALISM

Edwards's zeal for examining eschatological themes in the Scriptures was unquenchable. Throughout his adult life, he was preoccupied with apocalyptic material.[86] A personal notation by Edwards in 1739 reflects the general disposition he maintained on the matter: "My heart has been much on the advancement of Christ's kingdom in the world. . . . And my mind has been much entertained and delighted with the Scripture promises and prophecies of the future glorious advancement of Christ's kingdom on earth."[87]

The millennium factored into everything Edwards did. As Gerald McDermott points out, for Edwards, "history and the millennium were inseparable. The first was preparation for the second; the second the *telos*[88] of the first. . . . Since the millennium was the last earthly stage of . . . history, no part of . . . history could be properly evaluated without consideration of its earthly *telos*. Only the future could give proper meaning to both past and present."[89] In other words, Edwards was continually pondering what the culmination of history would look like so as to know where present history ought to go. Clear visions of the future are always compelling with regard to the present.

For example, in Martin Luther King's famous "I Have A Dream" address on the mall in Washington, D.C., he drew from the Bible story of Moses atop Pisgah, viewing the *telos*, if you will, of Israel's exodus—

the promised land. Rev. King said he had been to the mountaintop and had seen the promised land of freedom and equality for all peoples. Since then he could not rest until racism was expunged from American culture. Many saw the same thing through King's eyes, and history was changed.

Well, Edwards was continually climbing Pisgah[90] in his studies of eschatology to view the splendid graces of the kingdom of the Lord. What he saw, he yearned for, and he pointed the way toward what will be. For generations afterward, many who looked through his eyes were convinced, too, and yearned and prayed with him.

Edwards's *Notes on the Apocalypse* were to him a living document, even while he worked on other matters—theological, exegetical, and philosophical. For over thirty years he regularly worked on the *Notes*— amending and expanding it—even during his days among the Native Americans in Stockbridge, Massachusetts. *Humble Attempt*, which greatly widened the call for the Concert of Prayer, was his biblical/eschatological justification for it. *Humble Attempt* is predominantly an exposition of apocalyptic passages from the books of Zechariah, Ezekiel, and Revelation, for the most part. The book was a compilation of sermon material he preached in Northampton during the last half of the 1740s on the culmination of history and the role the Concert played in it.

But Edwards's interest in the Apocalypse did not lie simply in private biblical studies and theological musings, nor was it confined to his preaching duties. The Apocalypse was also among his chief interests in conversations with close friends. When he wrote his *Personal Narrative* at the age of thirty-six, he recalled with delight conversations he had had while visiting his friend John Smith in New York: "Sometimes Mr. Smith and I walked together, to converse on the things of God; and our conversations used to turn much on the advancement of Christ's kingdom in the world, and the glorious things that God would accomplish for his church in the latter days."[91] In the final days of David Brainerd's life, during that time when Edwards had taken the sick young missionary into his home in order to care for him, the two dear friends sat for long hours and warmly conversed about the "future prosperity of Zion which is so often foretold and promised in the Scriptures."[92]

To all of his numerous correspondents, Edwards reported on and sought "intelligence" concerning the kingdom's advance. Many of his pen pals eagerly compiled such accounts.

John Erskines, a lasting admirer of Edwards, was a prolific Scottish author. His correspondence networked him with the most prominent evangelicals in England, on the European continent, and in America. Throughout the 1740s and 1750s Edwards and Erskines wrote frequently.[93] The two men exchanged not only letters but publications and critiques of each other's work. Erskines vigorously promoted Edwards's material abroad.[94] In 1742 Erskines, heavily dependent upon Edwards's New England experience and views concerning the coming of Christ's kingdom, wrote *Signs of the Times Considered, or the high PROBABILITY that the present APPEARANCES in New England, and the West of Scotland, are a PRELUDE of the Glorious Things promised to the CHURCH in the latter Ages*.[95] In the treatise, Erskines established himself firmly in Edwards's camp regarding the "hopeful signs" they saw in their day as "a Prelude of greater Things yet to come." After Edwards's death, Erskines had several volumes by Edwards published abroad.

In addition to gathering information from his friends, Edwards consumed newspapers and publications of all kinds to gather clues as to how his generation fitted into God's unfolding plan. His *Notes on the Apocalypse* show careful, detailed scrutiny of all kinds of world events— political, military, and ecclesiastical.[96] Edwards wrote:

> If I hear the least hint of anything that happened in any part of the world, that appear'd to me, in some respect or other, to have a favorable aspect on the interest of Christ's kingdom, my soul eagerly catch'd at it; and it would much animate and refresh me. I used to be earnest to read public news-letters, mainly for that end; to see if I could not find some news favorable to the interest of religion in the world.[97]

Most of Edwards's views on the millennium were a result of his evangelical heritage. He was reared on a post-Reformation school of thought that "spawned a host of Protestant commentators who planted the love of the Apocalypse deep in the soul of English [and thus American] Protestantism."[98] John Bale (1495-1563), an ex-Carmelite monk, was one such scholar and writer who greatly influenced Puritan thinking on the Apocalypse. Others who influenced Edwards directly were Moses Lowman (1680-1752)[99] and Petrus Van Mastricht (1630-1706).

Part of the modern-day discomfort with Edwards's millennialism stems from his intense anti-Roman Catholic fervor. Edwards, like the other evangelical ministers of his generation, was weaned on an anti-Catholic perspective.[100] He was convinced that the spirit of the Antichrist found its gravitational center in Rome. Edwards may have expressed uncertainty about many aspects of history's unfolding, but he was absolutely convinced that the papacy was the incarnation of satanic evil.[101]

This prevailing view of Rome must be seen in its historical context. During this and the previous epoch Rome was at times a vicious enemy of Protestant Britain and Europe, vying for thrones and nations, employing aggressive designs for global colonial expansion. Rome had teeth. She commanded armies and her emissary, the French army, was poised on the American border especially to the North—within shouting distance of New England. In the eyes of many Protestants, Rome looked like an apocalyptic monster indeed.

Where Edwards parted with many of his American contemporaries was his rejection of imminentism and his espousal of globalism. In 1706 Samuel Danforth proclaimed that the millennium was at hand. The Mathers, Increase and his son Cotton, were vehement in their certainty that the millennium was near. Increase expected it within the eighteenth century. Cotton, outdoing his father, expected Christ's return by 1716. When the Second Coming failed to materialize, Cotton Mather predicted that it would happen at any time thereafter.[102] Thomas Prince's *The Christian History*, which included weekly reports of revival activities on both sides of the Atlantic, frequently cited the enthusiastic suspicions of numerous evangelical leaders that the Day of the Lord was at hand.

But Edwards did not expect to see the millennium. In *Humble Attempt*, he agreed with other scholars of the Apocalypse, such as Moses Lowman, and did not foresee the final destruction of "Satan's kingdom till after the year 2000."[103] Rather than something imminent, the millennium would be preceded by the gradual progress of the ever-surging tide of Providence. Amidst "violent and mighty opposition,"[104] likened to the birth pangs of an expectant mother, God's ultimate goal would advance by the heavenly Father's initiating successive outpourings of the Spirit, fomenting many a "glorious work of God."[105] And then the kingdom would be born in its fullness:

> [I]t is meet that the *last kingdom* which shall take place on *earth* should be the kingdom of God's own *son* and *heir*, whose right is to

rule and reign; and that whatever revolutions and confusions there may be in the world, for a long time, the cause of truth, the righteous cause, shall finally prevail, and God's holy people should at last *inherit the earth*, and *reign on earth*; and that the world should continue in tumults and great revolutions, following one another, from age to age, the world being as it were in *travail*, till truth and holiness are brought forth. It is meet, that all things should be shaken, till that comes which is true and right, and agreeable to the mind of God, which *cannot be shaken*; and that the wisdom of the ruler of the world should be manifested in bringing all things ultimately to so good an issue. The world is made for the Son of God; his kingdom is the *end* of all changes that come to pass in the state of the world. All are only to prepare the way for this.[106]

Unlike most of his contemporaries, Edwards was a globalist. He dismissed all ideas of a millennial scheme based on tribal or parochial interpretations, considering such a scheme "ill-suited to a deity who superintends the entire cosmos."[107] Departing from a popular notion that America was to be central to the geography of the millennium,[108] Edwards declared that the triumphant reign of Christ "shall *universally* prevail, and . . . extend over the whole habitable earth."[109] "All nations from one end of the earth to the other are subdued by the spiritual David," he wrote, "and firmly and quietly established in subjection to his crown."[110] Additionally, the millennium would eradicate "hypocrisy, strife, charismatic enthusiasm, and racism,"[111] ushering in an age of extraordinary agreement and sweet union "embracing all peoples of all nations . . . a paradise restored."[112] Edwards foresaw:

. . . a time wherein the whole earth shall be united as one holy city, one heavenly family; men of all nations shall as it were dwell together, and sweetly correspond one with another as brethren and children of the same father. . . . A time wherein this whole great society shall appear in glorious beauty, in genuine amiable Christianity, and excellent order. . . . And then shall all the world be united in peace and love in one amiable society.[113]

All of this is to say that Edwards's vision of the future was custom-made for the Concert of Prayer proposal. Edwards was at home with it immediately. The millennium was the chief end of history, and prayer for the millennium was among the chief goals of each Christian moving through history: "The Scripture does not only abundantly manifest to be the duty of God's people to be much in prayer for this great mercy, but it also abounds with manifold considerations to encourage them in it."[114] Praying for the millennium was simple Christian obedience to how Jesus instructed us to pray: "Thy kingdom come, Thy will be done on earth as it is in heaven." In *Humble Attempt* Edwards appeals to Isaiah 26:16-17 as instructive for every Christian: "'Lord, in trouble have they visited thee; they poured out a prayer when thy chastening was upon them. Like as a woman with child, that draweth near the time of her delivery, is in pain, and crieth out in her pangs, so have we been in thy sight, O Lord.'" He adds, "And certainly it is fit that the *church* of God should be in travail for that for which the whole *creation* travails in pain."[115]

At the same time he started his investigation of the Apocalypse, Edwards also began praying for the glorious reign of Christ. In a diary entry when he was only twenty, he criticized himself over the insufficiency of his prayers for the millennium.[116] In 1741 Edwards wrote to a newly converted "dear young friend" replying to a request for instructions on how to "maintain a religious life." He urged his friend to pray regularly that God "would carry on his glorious work which he had now begun, till the world shall be full of his glory."[117] Edwards insisted it is God's will

> through his wonderful grace, that the prayer of his saints should be one great and principal means of carrying on the designs of Christ's kingdom in the world. When God has something very great to accomplish for his church, it is his will that there should precede it the extraordinary prayers of his people; as is manifest by Ezek. 36:37: "I will yet for this be inquired of by the house of Israel, to do it for them." And it is revealed that when God is about to accomplish great things for his church, he will begin by remarkably pouring out the spirit of grace and supplications, Zech. 12:10.[118]

The idea of united prayer, then, combined Edwards's passion for prayer with his vision of the millennium as a period of wonderful union among believers.[119] He saw the former as a means to the latter. The Concert of Prayer proposal was a fulfillment of prophecy. Citing Zechariah 8:20-23,[120] Edwards foresaw that the future and glorious enlargement of the church would actually be inaugurated by a movement of international cooperation and union in prayer:

In [Zechariah 8] we have an account of *how* [the] future glorious advancement of the church of God should be brought on, or introduced; viz., by great multitudes in different towns and countries taking up a *joint resolution*, and coming into an express and visible *agreement*, that they will, by united and extraordinary *prayer*, seek to God that he would come and manifest himself, and grant the tokens and fruits of his gracious presence.[121]

For these reasons Edwards wrote:

And I hope that such as are convinced it is their duty to comply with and encourage this design [for concerted prayer], will remember we ought not only to go speedily to pray before the Lord, and seek his mercy, but also to go constantly. We should unite in our practice those two things, which our Savior unites in his precept, praying and not fainting. If we should continue some years and nothing remarkable in providence should appear as though God heard and answered, we should act very unbecoming believers, if we should therefore begin to be disheartened, and grow dull and slack in seeking of God so great a mercy. It is very apparent from the word of God, that he is wont often to try the faith and patience of his people, when crying to him for some great and important mercy, by withholding the mercy sought, for a season; and not only so, but at last succeeds those who continue instant in prayer, with all perseverance, and "will not let him go except he blesses. . . ." Whatever our hopes may be, we must be content to be ignorant of the times and season, which the Father hath put in his power: and must be willing that God should answer prayer, and fulfil his own glorious promises, in His own time.[122]

Three

Harvests, Missions, America's Pentecost and the Concert of Prayer

From victory, unto victory
His army shall He lead,
Till every foe is vanquished,
And Christ is Lord indeed.[1]

The progress, evolution, and ultimate effect of the Concert of Prayer is among the most wonderful of stories and best-kept secrets. I must admit that the tale is greater than my ability to track it, but what I have found clearly indicates that Edwards (and M'Culloch et al.) could not have devised a more potent game plan to alter the course of history.

Looking back from his perch fifty years after Edwards's death, Sereno Dwight reported that the *Humble Attempt* package[2] had "exerted an influence, singularly powerful" because it had created a "concentrated movement of the whole Church of God, to hasten forward the Reign of the Messiah."[3] While *Humble Attempt* was new and controversial, according to Dwight, the plan gained momentum. Both the Concert of Prayer and Edwards's interpretations of prophecy became broadly accepted.[4] Dwight, caught up in his appreciation of his mentor, concluded that *Humble Attempt* presented the unfolding will of God in history so clearly and convincingly that "the necessity of any subsequent treatise on the subject" was wholly unnecessary.[5]

1747-1760

As we noted earlier, shortly after Jonathan Edwards received his invitation from Scotland to join his friends in the Concert of Prayer, he began with great energy, excitement, and hopefulness to promote the prayer plan among his own parishioners, friends, and colleagues.[6] At the outset Edwards's success at mobilizing people was minimal at best, but he made progress. In 1747, before he had published *Humble Attempt*, he wrote to William M'Culloch: "[P]ropagation of [the Concert of Prayer] is slow, but yet so many do fall in with it, and there is that prospect of its being further spread, that it is a great encouragement to me." With regard to those already active in the plan, Edwards reflected with concern: "I earnestly hope that they that have begun extraordinary prayer for the outpouring of the Spirit of God and the coming of Christ's kingdom will not fail or grow dull and lifeless in such an affair, but rather that they will increase more and more in their fervency."

He assured M'Culloch that he had "taken a great deal of pains to promote this Concert . . . in America." "[I] shall not cease to do so," Edwards wrote, "if God spares my life." It was in this letter that Edwards first informed M'Culloch that he had written material for the purpose of promoting the Concert of Prayer (i.e., *Humble Attempt*). The treatise, wrote Edwards, was targeted toward "insisting on persuasion, and answering objections." To show his desire to distribute the work quickly, the printer had promised Edwards it would be "speedily printed."[7]

Two years later (1749), with *Humble Attempt* having been in circulation for over a year, Edwards sounded decidedly more upbeat. In his response to a M'Culloch letter, he writes:

[The news of the Concert's success in Scotland has] been of great benefit, particularly to excite and encourage God's people, in the great duty of praying for the coming of Christ's kingdom, and to promote extraordinary, united prayer in the method proposed in the Memorial from Scotland. I read these articles of good news to my own congregation, and also to the association of ministers to which I belong, when met on one of the quarterly seasons for prayer; and read them occasionally to many others; and sent a copy of one of the aforementioned abstracts to Connecticut, which was carried into various parts of that government, and shown to several ministers there. I sent on to Mr. Hall of Sutton,[8] a pious minister about the middle of this province; who, according to my desire, communicated it to other ministers. . . . I sent a copy to Mr. [John] Rogers of Kittery,[9] I suppose seventy miles eastward of Boston; who in reply, wrote to me, and in his letter says as follows: "I was well pleased [with your plan]. . . . And Dear Sir, I am full on the belief, that so many of the Lord's people agreeing upon a time to unite in prayer for the pouring out of the Holy Spirit, and the coming of the Redeemer's kingdom is from the Lord . . . that all his ministers and people, who are engaged in so delightful a work, for so noble an end, will give him no rest, till he shall make Jerusalem a quiet habitation, a name and a praise in the earth."

I sent another copy to John Brainerd.[10] . . . The next Tuesday after . . . was the quarterly day appointed for Extraordinary Prayer: which I called my people together.[11]

In addition, wrote Edwards, a memorial was sent to Governor John Belcher of New Jersey.[12] In May 1748, Belcher was chiefly concerned about the charter to found the "New-Jersey College," but he thanked Edwards for sending him *Humble Attempt*: "I am led to thank you for your book, wrote in consequence of the Memorial from Scotland, for promoting a concert in prayer. I am much pleased with this proposal and invitation to all good Christians, and with your arguments to encourage and corroborate the design."[13]

Edwards told M'Culloch, too, that he had sent a memorial to Philadelphia for Gilbert Tennent[14] "as a means to excite a spirit of Prayer and Praise." Likewise, Edwards had notified "Mr. Davenport of Elizabethtown in New Jersey," who read it to a group of ministers who met at his house for prayer.[15] Edwards had sent still another "to Long Island [where] Mr. Rivel took a copy of it and read it in his congregation on the Island," and to "Mr. [Samuel] Buell of East Hampton[16] . . . [and] . . . Mr. Brown of Bridgehampton, and Huntington," Long Island. Closer to home, Edwards read the proposal "to the ministers who met at my house for prayer."[17]

Less than a year later, Edwards's heart was cheered by news from Buell of a revival at East Hampton.[18] We will examine a second East Hampton revival below.

By 1748 the Concert of Prayer was regularly complied with in Edwards's part of New England. To John Erskines, minister of Old Greyfriars, Edinburgh, Scotland, Edwards wrote:

I have taken a great deal of pains in communicating to others, in various parts, the pleasing accounts [from Scotland] . . . which have been very affecting to pious ministers and people in New England, and also in the provinces of New-York and New-Jersey . . . animating many in the duty of extraordinary, united prayer for a general Revival of religion, and promoting the Concert for prayer proposed from Scotland; which prevails more and more in these parts of the world.[19]

Of these "pleasing accounts," Edwards rejoiced to M'Culloch that news he had received about breakthroughs in England had "greatly encouraged" his local fellow ministers, who had "lately united by explicit agreement in extraordinary Prayer for general Revival of Religion and the coming of Christ's Kingdom."[20] He told M'Culloch that his colleagues were faithful in observing the Quarterly Day for Prayer, spending "the former part of the day in prayer among [the neighboring ministers], and the latter part in public services in one of our congregations."[21] By April of the same year, Edwards found himself busy distributing the newly printed *Humble Attempt*, asking friends to report back to him as to how the plan was faring.[22]

But for all the activity Edwards generated over those first few years, the comments of his close friend Joseph Bellamy[23] speak volumes about the real progress of the Concert of Prayer. In a letter to Thomas Foxcroft (one of the signatories of *Humble Attempt*),[24] Bellamy confided that "to this day I believe not half the Country have ever So much as heard of Edwards's piece upon the Scotland Concert."[25] This sober reality seems to be reflected in Edwards's 1749 letter to James Robe.[26] In it Edwards speaks of the "very dark and melancholy" state of Christianity in New England and says that he is only comforted by the reports of the Concert of Prayer's progress and revivals elsewhere.

It is a sad and pregnant irony that at precisely the time Edwards was organizing the Concert of Prayer, drafting and later dispersing *Humble Attempt*, and preaching to his congregation on the glorious reign of Christ, he faced the most disheartening period of his life. The seeds of this difficulty had been planted during the wonderful 1741-42 awakening in his church.[27] Within three years of publishing *Humble Attempt*, Edwards was forced out of his pulpit.[28] Leaving Northampton, he settled in the mission outpost of Stockbridge to minister among Native Americans, hoping at least for a lifestyle that would allow him to write and think. Even there, however, he was harassed from a distance.[29]

The overseas mobilization was a different story. For example, in 1754, when the first seven-year agreement came to an end, the Scottish participants readily recommitted themselves to another seven years of prayer.[30] Not only did the Concert of Prayer thrive in parts of England

and Scotland, but it made its way into Holland with powerful consequences.

In 1751 Edwards wrote John Erskines and encouraged him to correspond with his associates in the Netherlands.[31] Edwards reminded Erskines that they were living in "a remarkable time in the Christian world," but adds with unmistakable urgency: "things are going downhill so fast." Edwards expressed his worry to Erskines that "a crisis is not far off, and what will then appear, I will not pretend to determine." The letter, too, reveals the ongoing pressure Edwards felt to maintain the Concert of Prayer's momentum and his acute disappointment whenever a prayer concert petered out.

After relaying some news about revivals in America, especially among the American Dutch (which, Edwards thought, would be of great encouragement to those in Holland), Edwards adds:

> [The news of these revivals should be of] such great encouragement to those who have engaged in the Concert for United Prayer, begun in Scotland, to go forward, but binds it strongly upon them so to do; and shows that it will be an aggravated fault, if, after God does such glorious things, so soon after we have begun in a extraordinary manner to ask them, we should grow cold and slack, and begin to faint. And I think what God has now done, may well cause those, who seemed at first, with some zeal, to engage in the affair, but have grown careless about it, and have left off, to reflect on themselves with blushing confusion. What if you, dear Sir, and other ministers in Scotland, who have been engaged in this affair, should now take occasion to inform ministers in the Netherlands of [the Concert of Prayer], and move them to come into it, and join with us, in our united and extraordinary prayers, for a universal revival of religion?

Writing to Erskines again in 1752, Edwards asked his friend about how his contacts in the Netherlands were going.[32] This suggests strongly that Erskines did indeed invite his Dutch colleagues to join the Concert of Prayer. Of the Scotland Concert, Fawcett reports that during this time "those who were banded in the Concert for Prayer made mention of [a] revival in Holland in their intercessions."[33] Considering the magnitude of the spiritual awakening shaking the Netherlands between 1748 and 1754, we have no doubt that the Concert of Prayer played a central role. Fawcett relates how the power of the Cambuslang prayer society model was copied in the Netherlands. In the wake of the Cambuslang revival, Hugh Kennedy, who was

> "one of the best pulpit men" in Scotland and who in 1742 declined an invitation to leave Holland and succeed Ralph Erskine at Dunfermline, learned of the surprising news of Cambuslang quickly. The *Narrative of the Work at Cambuslang* was translated into Dutch the same year [it was published in Scotland]. . . . By 1750 Kennedy was sending encouraging news to Scotland and London. Writing from Rotterdam on October 2, Kennedy tells of an awakening at Nieuwkirk which began under the ministry of Gerardus Kuypers in 1748 and tells of "Fellowship Meetings" similar to the private meetings of Christians held in Scotland for prayer. Hundreds frequented these meetings after their daily labour was over and by Monday, November 17, 1748, a general awakening gripped Kuypers's congregation and "the work increased and spread beyond all description. . . . [It is] in substance the very same Work which was some years ago carried on so remarkably in your happy Corner of the Lord's Vineyard."[34] On January 5, 1751, Kennedy rejoiced that the work was spreading to Aalten, Rheed and Groningen and notes "that the great Works of God in Scotland . . . are blessed to Multitudes in these Provinces and through Germany."[35]

Back in America Joseph Bellamy reported that the Concert of Prayer produced fruit in 1757, when a revival broke out after the student body of the College of New Jersey (at Princeton) prayed for the outpouring of the Spirit and then for the coming of the millennium. This revival "was not begun by the ordinary means of preaching" but by prayer.[36] The previous year, Aaron Burr, Sr. (1715-1757), president of the college and Jonathan Edwards's son-in-law, addressed the Presbyterian Synod of New York on the subject of the millennium, preaching for nearly four hours![37] In the address he not only employs Edwards's *Humble Attempt* imagery of the apocalypse but also points to the Concert of Prayer. With regard to how God will manifest his wondrous plan, Burr suggested one means: "I hint at these Things, as possible *Means* whereby the glorious Designs of God's grace will be carried on, in the latter *Day*, that with our fervent *Prayer*, we may unite our earnest Endeavors for their Accomplishment."[38]

The timing of the Princeton revival is important because it illustrates how another of Edwards's friends joined him in his preoccupation with the earth's final epoch. It was in 1757 that Bellamy wrote *The Millennium* (basically an extension and modification of Edwards's expectations). This book deeply affected ministerial students and the evangelical community for years to come.[39] Two years later, in 1759, Robert Smith (1723-1793)[40] noted that so many praying for the millennium gave him "hope that the Dawn of the aforesaid glorious Day is not far off."[41] United prayer for the millennium and expectations that "periodic pulsations of the Spirit"[42] would one day break loose and establish Zion commanded the attention of many.

1760-1800

In the early 1760s the incense of the Concert of Prayer seemed to manifestly delight the throne of God. Numerous outpourings of the Spirit spread through the colonies.[43] While renting a cabin on the coast of Ipswich, Massachusetts, for the summer 1992, I came upon a remarkable story in the official town history's eighteenth-century sermon collection. Ipswich,[44] Massachusetts, may be an illustration of how certain churches and towns participated in the Concert of Prayer.

IPSWICH, MASSACHUSETTS

The town of Ipswich was settled in 1633[45] by barrister John Winthrop, Jr., son of the famous governor of the Massachusetts Bay Colony. Situated on the beautiful Atlantic coast of Cape Anne northeast of Boston, Ipswich became a way station on the major east-west route between Boston, Massachusetts; Portsmouth, New Hampshire; and Portland, Maine. The village grew to be a bustling town.

The town's landscape is pastoral. Covering the municipality are rolling hills as high as 200 feet, from which a panoramic view opens of the ocean. The sea was always a part of the town's livelihood. From the elevated hilltops many wives and lovers watched for their seamen to return. Heartbreak Hill is one such summit, getting its name from an ancient legend about a hunter's daughter who watched in vain for her lover to return from the ocean. As the story goes, she died of a broken heart.

Along the coast where necks jutted out into the ocean lay "vales, open meadows and marshes, woodland and fields, winding rivers and tidal rivers, ponds stocked with perch and black bass and dotted with lilies, and streams of pickerel and trout, and the banks of the major rivers lined with grist-mills and saw-mills and tanneries,"[46] in the words of a nineteenth-century chronicler. The everyday scenery was painted with "wild-flowers, huckleberry bushes, and cattle upon the hillsides, waving grass, fruit trees (apple, plum) large fields of corn and grain . . . roads lined with farms and tables, long stretches of white sandy beaches, [and] open harbors for commerce to Portsmouth, Portland or Boston."[47]

The First Church of Ipswich was founded in 1634. Since its founding, the congregation was known for the remarkably high caliber of its people, with ministers to match. Cotton Mather called it a "renouned [sic] church, consisting mostly of illuminated Christians, that their pastors in the exercise of the ministry might, in the language of Jerome, perceive that they had not disciples so much as judges."[48]

In 1820 David Kimball, then pastor of the First Church, looked back upon the church's rich history of outstanding pastors and scholars:

[M]y friends, there is not a town in New England under stronger obligations to serve the Lord, than this. You are children of the covenant [Puritan settlers]. . . . You tread on ground consecrated by prayers and tears of pious progenitors, through successive generations. For you, their unborn posterity, they wrestled in their supplications. You inhabit a place, on which showers of divine grace have copiously descended. Here the word of God has been preached *with the Holy Ghost sent down from Heaven.* Here at different periods have been powerful revivals. Here many precious immortals have been trained up for glory. Cherish an affectionate remembrance, as of your pious ancestors in general, so in particular of those who with demonstrations of religious joy, early erected temples for God's worship here, and laid the foundation for the promotion of religion in future time.[49]

One of those "outstanding pastors and scholars" was Nathaniel Rogers (Harvard, 1721). Rogers became pastor of the First Church in 1726. He was a brilliant, godly evangelical pastor. As for other ministers in New England during 1740-1743, the Great Awakening proved to be watershed years for Rogers. During this time, he witnessed "a happy and remarkable revival of religion in many parts of this land, through uncommon divine influence, after a long time of great decay and deadness."[50] He had invited William Tennent and George Whitefield, twin pillars of Great Awakening preaching, to declare the

Gospel at his meetinghouse. Their ministry "engaged, heart and soul . . . with . . . gratifying results."[51]

Whitefield preached to throngs from the hill on which First Church still stands, right in the center of the business district. It was "the most prominent hill in the town."[52] In an outcropping of bedrock near the sanctuary, there is a sizable indentation resembling a great footprint. The townspeople call it the "Devil's Footprint." The story is told that the devil once haunted the belfry of First Church. When Whitefield preached on the hill there, the devil became so angry and terrified that he fled from the sound of the Gospel, jumping from the belfry (which rose 118 feet in the air) and crashed into the hilltop, leaving his footprint in stone.[53]

The Great Awakening years, however, would be important to the future of Ipswich in more ways than an immediate increase in church attendance.

While the winds of awakening blew lustily across New England, there were sharp divisions in the Protestant—predominantly Congregational—churches. Although men and women by the thousands were transformed in the wake of powerful itinerant evangelical preachers, ecclesiastical foundations also shook, and power structures were threatened.[54] Some pastors, such as Webb, Foxcroft, Edwards, Dickinson, Appleton, Prince, and others, warmly embraced the "new measures" of Whitefield and Tennent. They praised God for the effect wrought upon New England. These supportive pastors were called "New Lights." Others, however, such as Charles Chauncy, angrily dismissed and denounced everything about the Awakening, especially the itinerancy of the preachers and the emotional responses (i.e., "religious enthusiasm") their preaching caused. The detractors became known as "Old Lights." It was a classic struggle between new wine and old wineskins.

Yale College was deeply embroiled in the controversy. For a time the college trustees expelled students associated with the New Lights, and the school forbade attendance at any New Light meeting. David Brainerd, future missionary to the Native Americans along the Delaware River, was the most famous casualty of this policy.[55] Eventually these stringent tactics resulted in a split at the school, and for a time half the student body left in support of the new work of God and with the intention of establishing another school.

While all of this messiness was breaking loose in New Haven, a young student by the name of John Cleaveland was studying there for the ministry. His brother Ebenezer was in attendance, too.[56] In John Cleaveland's freshman year (1740-41), New Lights flooded Yale with preaching. That October George Whitefield preached on campus.[57] In the first three months of 1742, Cleaveland heard fifty-two sermons and lectures from New Light proponents. During February Cleaveland spent a memorable day with David Brainerd. In March Gilbert Tennent preached seventeen sermons in a single week. To top the year off, the commencement address was delivered by Jonathan Edwards, who, in Cleaveland's own words, presented "an eloquent and sophisticated defense of the revival and the new methods."[58] Edwards's sermon was later published entitled *The Distinguishing Marks of a Work of the Spirit of God.*[59]

Any romantic notion that revivals or awakenings are solutions "solving all our problems, clearing up all the difficulties that have arisen in the church, and leaving us in a state of idyllic peace and contentment, with no troubles to perplex us anymore," are silly notions.[60] If Cleaveland ever entertained such ideas, they were quickly smashed. In the same year (1742), his junior year, while at home on vacation, the young ministerial candidate attended a New Light revival meeting featuring a lay evangelist. Cleaveland's family was in attendance, as was most of his church. As he began his senior year, Cleaveland's rebellion was found out by the trustees of Yale, and he was expelled from the college.[61]

After leaving Yale, Cleaveland moved to Boston where he ministered to a separatist society for two years.[62] During this period, the Second Church of Ipswich[63] was weathering a church split over the New Light controversy. When Rev. Theophilus Pickering, the pastor of Second Church, heard George Whitefield preach in 1740, Pickering found the service offensive and refused to support the revival or its leaders. From the moment he expressed his disgust, discontent with Pickering grew among his parishioners.[64] After a bitter fight over the matter (which Pickering lost), he literally died. Pickering lived long enough, however, to witness the New Light contingent of his parish invite John Cleaveland to pastor their separate church and to watch Nathaniel Rogers (a New Light) officiate at Cleaveland's ordination. So bitter was this ordination to Pickering that he wrote *A Bad Omen to the Churches in the Instance of Mr. John Cleaveland's Ordination over a Separation in Chebacco[65] Parish.*[66]

The stature that Nathaniel Rogers lent to his ordination gave Cleaveland immediate credibility. Cleaveland would pastor the Second Church until his death in 1799.

In contrast to the erudite Pickering, Cleaveland was a brusque, straight-shooting, rough, and boisterous fellow. "In the pulpit he was more forcible than eloquent."[67] It was once reported he preached so loudly that "persons sitting at an open widow on the opposite side of the street, when the windows and the doors of the church were open . . . distinctly heard the greater part of his sermon."[68] Though Cleaveland was frank, outspoken, and plain-dealing, he was known for the courage of his convictions and was "magnetic in his oratory." Whenever he preached, there was "a constant and devout attendance."[69]

Cleaveland volunteered himself for a chaplaincy in the French and Indian Wars, serving the Essex County Regiment.[70] In Cleaveland's mind the conflict was ripe with eschatological overtones. America was facing down the armies of the Antichrist. He "preached every man in his parish into the American army," including three of his own sons.[71] Rejoicing over what seemed to be a miraculous victory over the French, Cleaveland returned home a hero.

The year of most importance for the Concert of Prayer is 1760. In that year this Yale alumnus—New Light, Calvinist chaplain, warrior battling the forces of the Antichrist and admirer of Whitefield, Tennent, and Edwards—called upon his church to comply with the Concert of Prayer.[72] Sensing that vital religion was waning, Cleaveland established an agreement among his people to seek the face of God. His parish not only agreed to unite in the Scotland scheme but faithfully kept the Concert. Once every two weeks his people promised to pray, privately or in societies, for the revival of true religion and the advancement of Christ's kingdom. Then once a quarter, a large corporate meeting was held for the same purpose.

Within three years (1763), a "very remarkable revival of religion commenced . . . which resulted in the hopeful conversion of very many" in Cleaveland's church. Within a short time, the revival spread throughout the whole of Cape Anne.[73] To record this outpouring of the Spirit, Cleaveland wrote *A SHORT and PLAIN NARRATIVE of the late WORK of GOD's SPIRIT at CHEBACCO*[74] *in IPSWICH, in the YEARS 1763 and 1764: Together with Some Accounts of the Conduct of the Fourth*[75] *Church of Christ in IPSWICH, in admitting MEMBERS—and their Defense of said Conduct.*[76] Much like the Northampton awakenings in 1735 and 1741, Cleaveland reported that the Ipswich/Cape Anne revival started among his church's young people before fanning out into the rest of the parish. Soon he had nightly meetings at his house. These meetings overflowed with "persons wounded in spirit, and some in the greatest agony of distress in every room."[77] He took the gatherings to the meetinghouse, but within a short time even that overflowed with men and women serious about the things of Christ: "There was a solemn silence through the whole assembly, during the time of service, and a sacred awe on every countenance."[78]

Like M'Culloch in Cambuslang, Cleaveland was quickly overwhelmed by the needs of the people and had to call outside assistance. When the dust settled, the list of those from whom he received help was substantial, including Nathaniel Rogers and John Rogers, and many other New Light leaders.[79] Surges in church membership were reported to Cleaveland.[80]

In the introduction to Cleaveland's *Narrative*, he explained how the fallow spiritual ground of Ipswich was made fertile for the wonderful work of heaven. The credit for the revival is placed on the Concert of Prayer:

> A LITTLE better than three Years before the late Effusion of the divine Influences among us, This Church agreed to spend one Day of every Quarter of the Year, in a congregational Fasting and Praying for the Out-pouring of God's Spirit upon us and upon all Nations, agreeable to the Concert for Prayer, first entered into in *Scotland* some Years since; and also to spend a Part of a Day once a Fortnight in a private religious Conference, which for near half a Year before this Effusion was held once a Week for the most part, and divers, at these Meetings were favor'd with a remarkable Spirit of Prayer for the rising Generation.[81]

There was no doubt in Cleaveland's mind that when his church members agreed with each other to seek God earnestly for the outpouring of God's Spirit, the foundation for revival was laid. The harvest was certain; it was only a matter of time.

For twenty years Cleaveland's parish members kept the Concert of Prayer among themselves. Then in 1780 Cleaveland reached out to three other Congregational churches—the First Church of Ipswich, the South Church (which had broken off from Cleaveland's fellowship years before), and the Church "at the Hamlet"[82]—and invited them to participate. These four churches agreed to "visible union" in "extraordinary prayer" and made arrangements for the quarterly day of prayer to be rotated among them.[83]

Over the years that followed, a series of revivals came to the area. In his 1834 Centennial Discourse honoring 200 years of history at the First Church, Rev. David Kimball, then pastor of First Church, remembered the Ipswich revivals of the past and bade his listeners to look back with pride at the history of orthodox Congregationalism in their town and New England. He rejoiced "in the heritage of Edwards, Bellamy, and Dwight—free schools to every child, moral instruction and influences upon the nation."

However, Kimball worried about the future and hungered for revival. With great agitation, he lamented "the degradation of Unitarianism" spreading like a plague throughout their land. Exhorting his people to counter this abomination, Kimball sounded like the New Testament writer to the Hebrews recalling the "great cloud of witnesses" from the Old Dispensation. He pointed his people back to their evangelical heritage for the purpose of recapturing what seemed to be slipping away. The importance of the Concert of Prayer was central to his thinking:

> [The orthodox Congregationalists in Ipswich] highly valued and zealously promoted *revivals of religion*. In their day there was a happy concurrence in sentiment between magistrates, and ministers, and private Christians,[84] with respect to the duty of praying for the influences of the Holy Spirit. And in answer to united prayer for this purpose, showers of divine grace came down on most of the settlements of New England. It becomes us to cherish a high veneration for the character of our ancestors and a deep respect for their principles, and carefully to follow their example.[85]

This was no fleeting notion of Kimball's. In a sermon nine years earlier, he bemoaned the spiritual declension of the town. Considering the outstanding pastors and scholars who had served Ipswich since 1634, he concluded that "there is not a town in New England under stronger obligations to serve the Lord than" Ipswich.[86] Soberly he prompted his people to remember that they "tread on ground, consecrated by prayers and tears of pious progenitors, through successive generations." It was for them, Kimball said sternly, that their forefathers "wrestled in their supplications." "You inhabit a place," he cried, "on which showers of divine grace have copiously descended."

Longing for another glorious visitation of the Lord, an outpouring of the Spirit like those in the 1700s, Kimball mourned:

How small the number now presented for baptism! There has been a decrease in the proportion of four to one, since the time of the last Mr. Rogers. How many families now call not on the name of the Lord! How many pews are entirely empty! and, more lamentable still, how many *seats of professing Christians* are empty, on days of preparatory lecture! Where is the man at the present day . . . who frequently, I do not say, *walks* to *Boston*, to attend Thursday lecture, but who *rides* to *Essex* or *Hamilton*,[87] to unite in the quarterly concert of prayer for the prosperity of Zion, throughout the limits of ancient Ipswich, and for the influences of the Spirit upon all nations?[88]

For years the Concert of Prayer played a vital role in the life of Ipswich. But Cleaveland could never have imagined the Concert's staying power. On December 31, 1859, the four Ipswich churches that had entered into the prayer covenant in 1780 celebrated the *centennial* of the Quarterly Fast/Concert of Prayer.[89] For 100 years the Concert of Prayer was kept. Throughout those 100 years the four churches remained orthodox and evangelical in the face of a tide of Unitarianism, universalism, and liberalism that swept away many Congregational churches in New England.[90]

The status of the four churches was to change, however. After the Civil War, the Concert of Prayer disappears from town records. The existing published sermons from the four churches show a decidedly nonevangelical bent by the 1880s. Several of the sermons reflect upon the town's Puritan past as one might chuckle over the memories of one's grandmother who refused to wear makeup, wore her hair in a bun, and trusted in cod liver oil for every ailment.[91] Mary Connelly, archivist for the Ipswich Historical Society, confirms that until the 1980s it had been over a century since any evangelical had pastored these churches.[92]

While the churches of Ipswich agreed in concerted prayer, revivals visited their towns, and the congregations remained orthodox and evangelical. When churches ceased to pray, their evangelical vision and convictions dissolved. There hasn't been a significant work of revival throughout Cape Anne in nearly 150 years.

Ipswich wasn't alone in recording revivals in the wake of the Concert of Prayer.[93] For example, Edwards's young friend Samuel Buell of East Hampton, Long Island, witnessed a revival shortly after beginning the Concert of Prayer in his congregation.[94] Then he reported another extraordinary work of God in 1764. Buell, who was a central figure in the 1741 awakening at Edwards's church, witnessed four awakenings in his tenure at East Hampton: 1748, 1764, 1785, and 1791. Buell testified that the 1764 episode was the greatest. To chronicle the 1764 awakening, he wrote (again, in a very Edwardsean manner) "A FAITHFUL NARRATIVE of the *Remarkable Revival of Religion* in the CONGREGATION of EASTHAMPTON on Long Island, *In the year of our Lord,* 1764."

Alluding to the ongoing Concert of Prayer rhythm of once a week in societies and once a month in large corporate gatherings, Buell noted that the prayer warriors of East Hampton had larger goals than simply the revival of their own parish:

> . . . we are praying for divine influence in more copious measures. We have several praying societies meeting every week for prayers. In the afterpart of the day upon the first Wednesday of every month, our people meet for prayer: When many prayers are offered up to God, that He would continue to pour out his *spirit* upon us, and dwell with us . . . and also according to his promise, "He would pour out his Spirit upon all flesh."[95]

Buell reported, too, that East Hampton was not unique in either its praying or the stirring of the Spirit. Similar things were under way in "The Jerseys," "the city of New-York," "Maryland and Virginia," "New England," "several places in Holland,"[96] "Morristown, [New Jersey]," and "Huntington, [Long Island]."[97] Some historians, in fact, refer to this as the Revival of 1764.

Buell echoed Edwards's statement that God answers the fervent, travailing prayers of his people by enlarging Christ's household. Quoting Isaiah 66:8, Buell writes: "'as soon as Zion travailed she brought forth her children.'"[98] While Buell reflected on why the revival at East Hampton occurred in the first place, Edwards's justification for the Concert reverberated in Buell's declaration of the lesson of the East Hampton revival: "God] made [His people] with a design to fulfill [His promises], resolving their exact accomplishment, and that the prayers of His people should be a means by which He would execute his eternal purposes . . . *till* He make *Jerusalem* a praise in all the earth."[99]

1760-1805

On the other side of the Atlantic, the spread of the Concert of Prayer accelerated the preaching of the Gospel throughout the world. In April 1784, Andrew Fuller, a pastor and member minister in the

Northamptonshire Association of Baptist Churches, was sent a "parcel of books" from Jonathan Edwards's old friend, "Dr. John Erskines of Edinburgh, [and] a copy of Jonathan Edwards's [*Humble Attempt*]—a stirring call to prayer."[100] Fuller was especially captivated by Jonathan Edwards's apocalyptic interpretations. So taken was Fuller by Edwards's vision and the godly design of united prayer that he appealed to the Northamptonshire Association of Churches for an opportunity to speak before them at their meeting in Nottingham.

On April 11, two months before he preached at Nottingham, Fuller's diary records that he was already complying with the Concert of Prayer in his own circle of friends: "Devoted this day to fasting and prayer, in conjunction with several other ministers, who have agreed thus to spend the second Tuesday in every other month, to seek the revival of real religion, and the extension of Christ's kingdom in the world. . . ."[101]

In the meantime, Fuller made arrangements for *Humble Attempt* to be reprinted and circulated. This was followed by a small work of his own titled *The Nature and Importance of Walking by Faith: PERSUASIVES to a GENERAL UNION in Extraordinary PRAYER for the Revival of Real Religion*. Its opening lines read: "Addressed to the churches in the Leicestershire and Northamptonshire Association, and to any others who love and long for the coming of Christ's blessed kingdom, and whose hearts may be inclined to unite in seeking its welfare."[102]

Then on June 2, Fuller preached in Nottingham. In a stirring message of hope and encouragement, he challenged the association to comply *en masse* with Edwards's design for the Concert of Prayer.[103] His sermon was titled "Walking by Faith." So bad were the conditions of evangelical religion in England and so terrible were the conditions of culture in general that many Christians had lost heart. Fuller exhorted his listeners, assuring them that God was on the verge of doing the greatest thing he had ever done and that the whole of his church should face the present darkness with confidence, walking by faith that God's great blessing was forthcoming. As he preached, Fuller acknowledged the struggles faced by the churches of his day:

> Those that had been used to sound the high praises of God in Zion now hang their harps upon the willows, as having no use for them! Nor is this the worst; they must be taunted, and their God derided, by their insulting words: "Come," said they, "sing us one of those songs of Zion:" as if they had said, Now see what your religion has

availed you! This was your favorite employ, and these were the songs wherewith you addressed your Deity, in whom you confided to deliver you out of our hands: what think you now? Poor Zion! "She spreadeth forth her hands, but there is no one to comfort her. The Lord hath commanded that her adversaries should be round about her: her captive sons can only remember Jerusalem and weep! Alas, how can they sing the Lord's song in a strange land!"

But is there no help from above? Is there no physician there? Yes, the God whom Babel derides, but Judah adores, looks down and sees their affliction. . . . For a season you must walk by faith, and not by sight; but trust me, that season shall soon be over. Seventy years, and Babylon shall fall, and Judah return! . . . This may encourage and direct us in larger concerns; concerns which respect the *whole interest of Christ* in the world. . . . By these prophecies the Christian church is encouraged to look for great things. . . . She is taught to look for a time when "the earth shall be full of the knowledge of the Lord, as the waters cover the sea" . . . when "the kingdoms of this world shall become the kingdoms of our Lord and of his Christ; and he shall reign from sea to sea, and from the river unto the ends of the earth." . . . Let us take encouragement, in the present day of small things, by looking forward, and hoping for better days. Let this be attended with *earnest* and *united prayer* to him by whom Jacob must arise. A life of faith will ever be a life of prayer. O brethren, let us pray much for an outpouring of God's Spirit upon our ministries and churches, and not upon those only of our own connection and denomination, but upon "all that in every place call upon the name of Jesus Christ our Lord," both theirs and ours![104]

Within two weeks, Fuller was in Olney. His diary shows clearly what was on his mind during these crucial weeks and the depth to which Edwards had affected him. On July 9, Fuller recorded the following:

Read to our friends this evening, a part of Mr. Edwards's *Attempt to promote Prayer for Revival of Religion*, to excite them to the like practice. Felt my heart profited and much solemnized by what I read.[105]

On July 11 he wrote:

A good forenoon in preaching on *fellowship with Christ*. Felt some tenderness of heart several times in the day, longing for the coming of Christ's kingdom and the salvation of my hearers.[106]

On July 12:

> Lord Jesus, set up Thy glorious and peaceful kingdom all over the world. Found earnest desires . . . in prayer that God would hear the right as to them, and hear our prayers, in which the churches agree to unite *for the spread of Christ's kingdom.*[107]

And on July 13, he recorded:

> Spent this day in fasting and prayer, in conjunction with several of my brethren in the ministry, for the revival of our churches and the spread of the gospel. Found some tenderness and earnestness in prayer, several times in the day. Wrote a few thoughts on the desirableness of the coming of Christ's kingdom.[108]

When Fuller's Nottingham sermon was published, his *Persuasives* was attached to it. In *Persuasives* he listed some of the great biblical examples of God answering the united prayers of his people. Of the first days of the church, Fuller wrote:

> Just before that great outpouring of the Spirit on the day of Pentecost, the church was in a low and disconsolate condition, having lost Christ's personal presence: however, they united with one another in one accord in ardent prayer, in an upper room, to the number of about an hundred and twenty. Presently, and their light brake forth as the morning—a little one become a thousand, and a small one a strong nation, thousands are converted by a single sermon, and Satan falls before the gospel of Christ like lightning from heaven—Might we not make the same use of the glorious works of God? . . . Oh, let us pray to the Lord Jesus that the work may be carried on—that the kingdom of our Lord and of his Christ may come, and that he may reign for ever and ever.[109] . . . [Our praying] *will not be in vain* whatever be the immediate and apparent issue of it. Could we but heartily unite to make a real earnest effort, there is great reason to hope great good might follow. Whenever those glorious outpourings of God's Spirit shall come, all over the world, no doubt it will be in answer to the prayers of his people . . . our petitions may prove like seed in the earth, that shall not perish though it may not spring up in our days.[110]

Edwards's vision of history had instilled such confidence in Fuller, confidence in "those glorious outpourings of God's Spirit" to come, that

Fuller declared the blessing sought would surely come in answer to their prayers even if they never lived to see it. Their prayers were like a farmer planting seed in the ground. It may take time and patience, and maybe another generation would be the beneficiaries, but there was no doubt the harvest would come.

After Fuller preached at the Nottingham meeting, his good friend and prayer partner, John Sutcliff[111] of Olney,[112] made the motion to begin the Concert of Prayer. The association adopted it. Agreeing with Fuller, it was decided that the quarterly meeting was too infrequent, so the first Monday evening of every month was settled on.

> Upon a motion being made to the ministers and messengers of the associate Baptist churches assembled at Nottingham, respecting meetings for prayer, to bewail the low estate of religion, and earnestly implore a revival of our churches, and of the general cause of our Redeemer, and for that end to wrestle with God for the effusion of his Holy Spirit, which alone can produce the blessed effect, it was unanimously RESOLVED, to recommend to all our churches and congregations, the spending of one hour in this important exercise, on the first Monday in every calendar month.
>
> We solemnly exhort all the churches in our connection, to engage heartily and perseveringly in the prosecution of this plan. And thus it may be well to endeavour to keep the same hour, as a token of our unity therein. . . .
>
> We hope also that as many of our brethren who live at a distance from our places of worship may not be able to attend there, that as many as are conveniently situated in a village or neighbourhood, will unite in small societies at the same time. And if any single individual should be so situated as not to be able to attend to this duty in society with others, let him retire at the appointed hour, to unite the breath of prayer in private with those who are thus engaged in a more public manner.—The grand object in prayer is to be, that the Holy Spirit may be poured down on our ministers and churches, that sinners may be converted, the saints edified, the interest of religion revived, and the name of God glorified. And at the same time remember, we trust you will not confine your requests to your own societies, or to your own immediate connection; let the whole interest of the Redeemer be affectionately remembered, and the spread of the gospel to the most distant parts of the habitable globe be the object of your most fervent requests.—We shall rejoice if any other Christian societies of our own and other denominations will unite

with us, and do now invite them most cordially to join heart and hand in the attempt.

Who can tell what the consequence of such an united effort in prayer may be! Let us plead with God the many gracious promises of his word, which relate to the future success of his gospel. He has said, I will yet for this be enquired of by the house of Israel, to do it for them, I will increase them with men like a flock, Ezek. 36:37. Surely we have love enough to Zion to set apart one hour at a time, twelve times in a year, to seek her welfare.[113]

They determined as well to invite Christians from all other denominations to join them. Such a work could not be the exclusive domain of Baptists.[114]

The impact of this particular Concert of Prayer has been immeasurable. It continued in a thriving condition well into the twentieth century.[115] All through its existence, information was printed and distributed for the express purpose of helping participants pray intelligently for the advancement of Christ's kingdom worldwide.[116]

Following the 1784 adoption of the Concert, eight years of praying for the revival of religion and the advancement of Christ's kingdom passed before the Northamptonshire Association was to hear its most well-known proposal. During these eight years, a young cobbler participated in the Concert and was deeply affected by it. His name was William Carey (1761-1834). He was baptized the year before Fuller's call to prayer. Fuller's preaching and call impressed themselves on Carey's soul, forming within his heart a missionary vision to the nations.[117] Carey bore testimony to the "quickened spiritual life which showed itself" in his own life "as a result of special monthly prayer meetings." Then in 1792 Carey challenged the Northampton Association to form a missionary society, and the Baptist Missionary Society was born. The ones who prayed for the advancement of the kingdom—to fill the earth with the knowledge of the glory of the Lord—were now becoming an agency through which God would answer their prayers. The society's first goal was to send Carey to India.[118]

In his famous *ENQUIRY Into the OBLIGATIONS OF CHRISTIANS, to use Means for the CONVERSION of the HEATHENS,*[119] a booklet still widely read and influential after 250 years, Carey laid out before his Northamptonshire brethren his convictions about the responsibilities inherent in Christ's call to every believer. The final section of the

ENQUIRY is essentially Edwards's *Humble Attempt* distilled.[120] Carey states plainly that Christians must pray together "as our blessed Lord has required us to pray, that his kingdom may come."

> After the resurrection the disciples continued in Jerusalem till Pentecost. Being daily engaged in prayer and supplication . . . when they were all assembled together, a most remarkable effusion of the Holy Spirit took place. . . . [Even after the Apostles were opposed and arrested, they persisted to] assert their divine warrant, and as soon as they were set at liberty addressed God, and prayed that a divine power might attend their labors, which petition was heard, and their future ministry was very successful.[121]

Referring to opinions popularized by Edwards and by then widely held, Carey writes:

> If the prophecies concerning the increase of Christ's kingdom be true, and if what has been advanced, concerning the commission given by him to his disciples being obligatory on us, be just, it must be inferred that all Christians ought heartily to concur with God in promoting his glorious designs, for *he that is joined to the Lord is one Spirit.*[122]

But the Carey story is richer still. For years Carey was impeded from going to India, principally by the East India Company, which had no intentions of letting the Gospel interfere with its capitalistic and monopolistic enterprises. When in 1801 Carey's persistence prevailed and he finally arrived in India (via Serampore) as professor of Bengali for Fort William College, it was due to Claudius Buchanan (1766-1815), who had secured his appointment.

Buchanan, an Anglican, was a protégé of the great Charles Simeon and a friend of John Newton. Newton was pastor at Olney,[123] John Sutcliff's church, one of the Northamptonshire Association of Churches. Buchanan, too, was raised in Cambuslang, Scotland, born in the parish of William M'Culloch! His father, a teacher in Cambuslang, had come to faith in Christ during the 1742 revival and Whitefield's preaching. Later Buchanan's father became an elder and a treasurer in M'Culloch's church.[124]

So in 1801 one born out of the parish where the Concert of Prayer was conceived and later flourished, whose father's life was forever changed by the great move of God in central Scotland, invited one "born" out of the Concert of Prayer in Northamptonshire, England, to join him in a divine enterprise that inaugurated a new age in the spread of the Gospel—the modern missionary movement. This age was given impetus by a genius-saint from Northampton, Massachusetts.

Simultaneous with the Northamptonshire story is another missionary endeavor in New York City where the first mission society of the new United States formed in 1797. Like the Concert of Prayer in Northamptonshire, England, where those who met for prayer united to become the agency whereby God would answer their prayers, so it was with the New York Missionary Society.

In their initial plan to form the society, the leaders distributed *Thoughts on the PLAN FOR SOCIAL PRAYER proposed by the DIREC-TORS of the NEW-YORK MISSIONARY SOCIETY.*[125] Following the British design for the Concert, they proposed a monthly meeting:

> That the second Wednesday evening of every month, beginning at candle-light, be observed, from _____ next, by the Members of this Society, and all who are willing to join with them, for the purpose of offering up their prayers and supplications to the God of grace, that he would be pleased to pour out his Spirit on his Church, and send his gospel to all nations. . . .[126]

The plan included a scheme for the rotating of their monthly praying from church to church "beginning with the Old Presbyterian Church, and proceeding next to the Scots Presbyterian Church, and proceeding next to the New Dutch Church, next to the First Baptist Church, next to the Brick Presbyterian Church, and then the service to revert to the place it began."[127]

Anticipating the anxieties of some who feared that praying with other Christians and congregations would "break down the outward distinctions of" each church, the leaders reminded members that for over twenty years, since before the Revolutionary War, "a concert of prayer held by the Ministers of the Churches mentioned" clearly proved that the breakdown of doctrinal convictions never need occur.[128] Furthermore, they added, "Our brethren in Great Britain, of different denominations, have united in prayers, on a more catholic plan than what is proposed here, notwithstanding their many obstacles; ought we to imbibe their spirit, and imitate their example?"[129] And more importantly, the proposal argued, the anxieties expressed about praying together were themselves evidences of spiritual deterioration. That

Christians would want to unite in a modest scheme of prayer was seen as a divine drizzle before the deluge, a small sign of a much larger and deeper work God desired to pour out upon his people. Division and opposition within our churches, the proposal declared,

> arises from the declension of the times, and is an additional argument for our prayers. Behold a reviving prospect! Let us bless God for the day of small things. The cloud which is now only as large as a man's hand, may soon cover the heavens. God is giving to some of his people the spirit of grace and supplication, a more than common engagedness in his service. This is a presage of more plentiful blessings. If we regard our own progress and comfort in the divine life; if we with the success of the gospel among ourselves unite; and if we long for the day when our blessed Lord shall be, in the most extensive sense, "a light to lighten the Gentiles, and the glory of his people Israel," let our mingled flames of love and devotion arise like pure incense before his throne.[130]

Years later the monthly Concert was everywhere and was still being adapted by missionary societies and the missionary-minded. In 1824, for example, the upstart Sabbath Schools in England decided to emulate what their Christian friends were doing for world missions. A Concert of Prayer for revival and the kingdom's advancement was begun on behalf of Sunday school children. The idea made sense because Sunday school was originally a mission outreach to illiterate and unchurched children, rather than a ministry of edification to Christian families, as it is today. They saw Sunday school as a tributary to the widening stream of the advancing kingdom.

During the Industrial Revolution, an extraordinarily heavy price was extracted from children. Child labor laws were a generation away. Beginning at the age of four, boys and girls were set to work at hard labor. In England they worked ten- to twelve-hour days, six days a week, performing the most miserable work and subject to untold abuse in factories, mines, and various smaller enterprises. Life expectancy was short. Charles Dickens was among the many who portrayed the terrible conditions.

Those who wanted to reach children knew that the only day available was Sunday, and the best means was a school to teach remedial academic, social, and religious skills and to present the Gospel.

Early in the nineteenth century the Sabbath School movement took its cue from mission societies. When the leaders of the Sunday school, or Sabbath School movement, established their Concert of Prayer, they chose the *second* Monday night of the month to pray for the evangelization and rescue of children. They did not want to conflict with the *first* Monday night of the month devoted to prayer for foreign missions.[131]

In 1845 the Sabbath-School Association printed a hymnal, titled *Union Hymns*, containing some 300 hymns.[132] This collection was a sequel to earlier Sabbath School hymnals, containing "the best part of the Sunday-School hymn books" then in use for many years. Only the texts of the hymns were printed, along with an indication meter so that many of the hymns could be sung to various tunes.

The largest section of the hymnal is devoted to the "Monthly Concert," the occasion when God is implored to come and shower grace upon their efforts, glorifying his name while rescuing the children. This section is filled with hymns that are still well known, but there are many others written specifically to implore God to pour out his favor on the children. The themes of dependence on God, the great power of united prayer, the sweet love of lost children, and a grand vision of his purposes are pronounced.

> *Blessed Saviour—thou hast told us,*
>   *In the midst of two or three,*
> *Thou art present to behold us,*
>   *If we humbly call on thee;*
> *Blessed promise—blessed promise—*
>   *May we thy salvation see!*
>
> *O instruct us, gracious Master,*
>   *While thy tender lambs we guide;*
> *May we lead them to green pasture,*
>   *By the living water's side,*
> *Where the fountain of salvation,*
>   *Pours its soul-refreshing tide.*
>
> *Lord, we bring our charge before thee,*
>   *Little ones of thine own fold;*
> *Teach them, Saviour, to adore thee,*
>   *As those children did of old,*
> *Who sang praises, high hosannas,*
>   *When the hearts of men were cold!*

> *Haste the time when all the islands*
>   *In the bosom of the sea;*
> *And the lowlands, plains and highlands,*
>   *Shall resound with praise to thee;*
> *And the children of all nations*
>   *Shall their God and Saviour see.*[133]

And again:

> *Saviour, visit thy plantation;*
>   *Grant us, Lord, a gracious rain!*
> *All will come to desolation,*
>   *Unless thou return again:*
> *Keep no longer at a distance;*
>   *Shine upon us from on high;*
> *Lest, for want of thy assistance,*
>   *Every plant should droop and die.*
>
> *Surely once thy garden flourished,*
>   *Every part looked gay and green;*
> *Then thy word our spirit nourished,*
>   *Happy seasons we have seen!*
> *But a drought has since succeeded,*
>   *And a sad decline we see;*
> *Lord, thy help is greatly needed—*
>   *Help can only come from thee.*
>
> *Let our mutual love be fervent,*
>   *Make us prevalent in prayer;*
> *Let each one esteem thy servant,*
>   *Shun the world's enticing snare.*
> *Break the tempter's fatal power;*
>   *Turn the stony heart to flesh;*
> *And begin from this good hour*
>   *To revive thy work afresh.*[134]

In America the Concert of Prayer spread among significant groups. In 1787 the new United States were summoned to pray for their troubled nation. From New Hampshire came *A Concert of Prayer propounded to the citizens of the United States of America. By an association of Christian ministers.*[135] The authors of this proposal are unknown, but both Daniel Rogers, who prayed passionately at the funeral of George

Whitefield, and Josiah Stearn were prominent evangelicals in Exeter where the proposal was authored. The Exeter call corresponded with other similar calls during this period—and for good reasons. This leads us to consider one of the most remarkable periods in American history.

THE REVIVAL OF 1800, OR THE SECOND GREAT AWAKENING

David Austin (1759-1831) pastored Presbyterian churches in Elizabethtown (modern Elizabeth), New Jersey, and Bozrah, Connecticut. Deeply affected by the Great Awakening, the Presbyterian church in Elizabethtown was instrumental in the founding of Princeton College to train pastors who walked with God. Princeton's revivalist founders, particularly Edwards, had heavily influenced this church. Rev. Austin was a Yale graduate (1779) who had studied under Bellamy, a disciple of Edwards.

In 1794 Austin republished a work of Bellamy's titled *The Millennium*.[136] As one might guess from its title, the work heralded the postmillennial expectations of the day, principally from Edwards's viewpoint. Austin bound Bellamy's work with two others: Halifax's essay on the present evidences of the immanent beginning of the millennium and Jonathan Edwards's *Humble Attempt*.[137]

In his preface Austin bemoans the sad state of the church. But he writes with confidence that God was soon to break in upon history, and the millennium was "soon to be revealed." He summoned Christians to apply themselves earnestly to the Concert of Prayer:

> "The Lord hath spoken, and the decree shall be fulfilled."—If, in ancient time, the people of God believed what the Lord had spoken respecting the redemption of his people; if, from the sacred calendar, they discovered the time of the promise of redemption—prayed for, and actually saw the fulfillment of the object of their hopes, in temporal and in spiritual deliverances; what forbids that, in this day of general captivity, the prophets of the Lord should look with the same faith and prayer for the fulfillment of those promises which expect the spiritual deliverance of the Christian Church.[138] . . . The object [then] in publishing Dr. Bellamy's discourse is to establish the doctrine of the Millennium as to matter of fact: and by Publishing President Edwards's "Humble Attempt to Promote explicit Agreement and visible Union in Prayer;" it is hoped attention will be excited to the use of those means which God hath

ordained to be used in view of a gracious fulfillment of every promise made to his Church and to his People. . . . [139] The arguments which [Edwards's] invaluable tract suggests for explicit Agreement and visible Union of God's People in extraordinary Prayer, for the Revival of Religion, and the Advancement of Christ's Kingdom on Earth, pursuant to Scripture-Promises and Prophecies, concerning the LAST TIME, are as applicable to the state of the Church, and of the world, now, as they were [when President Edwards was alive], and the encouragement, from present circumstances, much more animating.

If any individual Christian, any society of Christian People, or any Minister, or association of Ministers, should be so far impressed with the propriety of a present compliance with what President Edwards laboured to bring about in his day, as to desire that measures should be taken for the accomplishment of the objective of his work, and express a willingness to aid in laying a foundation for a general and united exertion in prayer throughout all the Christian Churches in our land; the Editor pledges his whole heart in aid to any such proposal. . . .

That the Great Head of the Church would graciously take this humble attempt to the honor of his name, and for the interests of his Zion, under his holy protection, and prosper, and do his own blessed will in all things which it strives to accomplish, is the fervent prayer of one, who knows no higher object of present or future ambition, than to approve himself, and to be approved of his Lord and Master, as an industrious hewer of wood, and a drawer of water for the church of God.[140]

> DAVID AUSTIN
> Elizabeth Town
> May 1, 1794

In the same year that he republished *The Millennium*, Austin and a fellow pastor, Walter King (1758-1815), sent out a circular letter inviting ministers everywhere to join the Concert of Prayer. Addressed to "ministers and churches of every Christian denomination throughout the United States," the letter invited each to "unite in an attempt to carry into execution the 'Humble Attempt' of President Edwards to promote explicit agreement, and visible union of God's people in extraordinary prayer, for the revival of religion and the advancement of Christ's kingdom on earth."

The large meetings were to meet "every Tuesday of the four quarters of the year, beginning with the first Tuesday of January, 1795." From that point on, the concert would continue "from quarter to quarter, and from year to year, until *the good Providence of God prospering our endeavors* we shall obtain the blessings for which we pray:—or until by the delegation or council from the Ministers and Churches in concert . . . it shall be signified that good and sufficient reasons are found for discontinuing the concert."[141]

Austin could not have been disappointed by the initial response. The signatories on the invitation alone must have encouraged him: Timothy Stone (Goshen, Connecticut), Zebulon Ely (Lebanon), Levi Hart (Preston), Samuel Nott (Franklin), Walter King (Chelsea), John Gut[ ] (Exeter), David Austin (E[lizabeth]-Town, New Jersey), Joseph Strong (Norwich, Connecticut), James Cogswell (Windham, Connecticut), Joseph Whatney (Brooklyne), Andrew Lee (Lisbon), Nathaniel Emmons (Franklin), Stephen Gane (Providence), Mase Shepard (Little-Compton), Peter Ph. Roots (same), David Avery (Wrentham), Thomas Andros (same), Calvin Chaddock (same), Herman Daggett (Southampton, Long Island), Solomon Morgan (Canterbury, Connecticut), Isaac Backus (Middleborough, Massachusetts), Jonathan Wilder (Attleborough), and Joseph Snow (Providence).[142]

The communications network group, the "Committee of Correspondence," charged with receiving "advice" from respondents and disseminating "the same to the subscribing agents" was a substantial group, too: Rev. Samuel Spring (Newburyport), Rev. Doct. Stillman (Boston), or Rev. Jedidiah Morse (Little-Compton), Rev. Stephen Gano (Providence), Rev. Doct. Hoplins (New-Port), Rev. Masse Shepherd (Little-Compton), Rev. Samuel Austin (Worcester), Rev. Walter King (Norwich), Rev. Timothy Stone (Goshen), Rev. Nathan Strong (Hartford), Doct. West (Stockbridge), Doct. Edwards (New-Haven), Doct. Lewis (Greenwich), Doct. Rogers, Doct. Levingston, Rev. Fuller or Rev. Mr. Pilmore (New York), Rev. Mr. Austin (E[lizabetown]), Doct. Green (Philadelphia), Doct. Davidson (Carlisle), Rev. William Graham (Lexington), Doct. Keith (Charleston), Rev. Thomas Reese (Salem), Rev. Silas Gildersleve (M[iddlesex?]).

Soon afterward Austin and Walters began hearing back from their mailing. From all quarters of the country they heard of enthusiastic initiatives underway to promote and "carry into execution 'the humble attempt' of President Edwards."[143] From Princeton, New Jersey;

Bethlehem, Pennsylvania; New York City; Hartford, Connecticut; and many towns throughout New England, associations, denominations, and presbyteries complied with the design.

The Concert persisted and pleased Austin for years to come. Six years after his circular letter, Austin published *THE DAWN OF DAY, Introductory to the RISING SUN, whose Rays Shall Gild the Clouds.*[144] At the end of the work, he writes to the "Fifteen Divines," who were editors of a new publication beginning in Hartford, Connecticut (*The Connecticut Evangelical Magazine*). The two things that gave Austin the greatest confidence that the reign of Christ was near, he wrote, were the "continuation of the attempt at general union of the Household of Faith" manifest in "the concert for prayer" and in their magazine.[145]

Simultaneous to the Austin-King effort, Isaac Backus, the esteemed patriarch of American Baptists and signatory of Austin's letter, mobilized his Baptist Association forces at their annual convention for the Concert of Prayer. It was a time universally recognized as one of national and spiritual declension. While churches were empty across America because of "careless neglect of religious worship," and a spirit of "fraud, oppression, and sensuality . . . prevailed to an amazing degree,"[146] Backus hungered for God to revisit the land.

To understand these urgent calls to prayer, we must know the depth of the problems in the United States. These were dark days for the nation and American Evangelicalism, perhaps the darkest in our history. The national economy was nearly wrecked, and there was talk of defaulting on debts (until Alexander Hamilton managed, barely, to engineer a rescue). Society generally seemed in complete disarray. Citizens wondered whether the nation would survive. There was famine in the land. The price of staples doubled and quadrupled. A plague of worms destroyed both corn and grass. Canker worms infested orchards and destroyed fruit. It was the worst that Backus had seen "in any year." Furthermore, human disease was widespread—"smallpox came into Boston . . . [and] many died." "Distemper" harassed "many other places," and thousands more succumbed.

In our own time, early 1990s, the mayor of Washington, D.C., asked President Clinton to send federal troops into the nation's capital to stem the tide of lawlessness and violence. Well, that request had a precedent. So nasty and explosive was the national mood two centuries earlier that Congress passed and President John Adams signed the Sedition Act of 1798, "a proclamation to prevent a rebellion."[147] Federal troops and prosecutors were sent into major cities to quell the fever of anarchy and open rebellion against the government. Free speech was curbed. Verbal or published material deemed to be "scandalous and malicious" criticism of the Congress or President was outlawed. America seemed on the verge of coming apart. On a day of fasting and prayer proclaimed by President Adams that May, there were widespread fears that certain camps would seize the opportunity for violence. Many openly worried that insurrection and rioting would break out across Philadelphia.

Externally, America faced powerful foes. Two belligerent superpowers, England and France, were poised to make trouble. They both wreaked havoc on American shipping, and a quasi state of war existed with the French. The British were more easily placated. Similar to our own recent anxieties about Chinese infiltrators in America, there were fears that foreign agents, particularly French, were at work in the government. The Alien Enemies Act followed the Sedition Act. Backus feared that all-out war with either England or France was imminent.

The threat of armed conflict wasn't the only thing blowing in from England and France. On the religious landscape, a series of European-born plagues swept America—the "creeping decay of Universalism and Deism."[148] Clergy, churches, and religious associations were being changed in every quarter, abandoning historic orthodoxy.

Among the intelligentsia—the press, the politicians, and the educational institutions—the French Enlightenment was the rule of the day. Jefferson, the Enlightenment's torchbearer in America, was seen by numerous Evangelicals to be either the Antichrist or the prophet of the Antichrist. Historic Christianity seemed to be dissolving. So bad was the state of the church that Voltaire confidently predicted that Christianity would not survive his lifetime.

Into this time of uncertainty and empty pews, Backus, a signatory of the Austin-King circular letter, rose before his Baptist Association in a 1799 meeting in Rhode Island and declared:

> While political earthquakes shake the kingdoms of the world; while the pillars of popery tremble on the verge of oblivion, and Pestilence, that aweful bosom of death, is sweeping by thousands our fellow mortals into eternity; we have thought proper to invite our Brethren of corresponding Associations to unite with us in fervent and solemn prayer to Almighty God, that the glorious work of grace begun in different parts of our land may continue and spread,

till the earth shall become a mountain of holiness and a habitation of righteousness.[149]

The association heartily complied. It busied itself in mobilizing its churches to pray in union with all those of like mind.

The frame of mind of these Christians is remarkable. In today's environment, dominated by a pessimistic premillennialism, the cry might be to circle the wagons; buy canned food, guns, and generators; protect the young; film a new video about how much worse everything will get; and wait for the end of the world or the Rapture. How very different were the thinking and convictions of our predecessors such as Edwards, Dwight, Fuller, Austin, and Backus. Their confidence of victory and the vindication of the church in the unfolding of history was firm. In the midst of grim days they could proclaim that, in answer to the earnest prayers of the saints, Christ was about to do the greatest thing ever, a thing so great it would gloriously change history, exalt the church, extend his rule, and capture the nations of the earth to boot.

In less than a year after calling Baptists to the Concert of Prayer, Backus's diary changed decidedly. By 1800 revivals were being reported to him from all throughout New England. His diary entries in 1800 were replete with the following: "The revivals of religion in different parts of our land have been wonderful!" In 1801: "Although stupidity has greatly prevailed in our land, yet religion has been revived in many places," and in 1803: "We hear joyful news from several places. . . ."[150] The Concert of Prayer had preceded the holy deluge of 1800. Historians have named it The Second Great Awakening. Historian Paul Conkin called what happened "America's Pentecost,"[151] suggesting that the episode was a spiritual explosion of almost cosmic proportions.

In the South, the story was remarkably similar and yet many times more dramatic. Here again we find Edwards's influence pronounced and the Concert of Prayer a central player.

The Southern story of the 1800 revival had its beginnings at Hampden-Sydney College in 1787, under the presidency of John Blair Smith (1756-1799). Because of sympathies that eventually led to "The Plan of Union" between Congregationalist and Presbyterians,[152] Edwards-influenced Congregationalists such as Smith found themselves in Presbyterian enclaves. This penetration had untold effects. One of these was that Congregationalist John Smith presided over the little Virginia school named Hampden-Sydney College.[153]

In 1786 Smith saw no religious vitality among his students. The spiritual desolation on campus reflected a generally depressing scene all over the South.[154] Influenced by his father's experience in the Great Awakening, Smith "pleaded with his elders"[155] to begin a Concert of Prayer "for a special outpouring of the Spirit of God."[156] By the fall of 1787, a student named Cary Allen was converted while on vacation. He was "the first student who made any public pretensions to religion in College."[157] Soon afterward two other students professed Christ and with President Smith formed a prayer society. Within a week the awakening widened. Shortly, a revival broke out and spread through the region. The effect reached as far north as Virginia.

With the scent of something new in the air, a fresh breeze named James McCready began to blow in nearby North Carolina. McCready, in appearance a profoundly ugly man, was born in western Pennsylvania. He returned there in 1784 to be tutored for the ministry at an embryonic institution under the care of John McMillan, a graduate from the College of New Jersey (Princeton). McCready surrendered his life to Christ in 1786.

During McCready's schooling, the writings of Jonathan Edwards made an impression on this young, newly converted minister. For example, like Edwards (yet surpassing him in vehemence), McCready demanded a clear, unequivocal testimony of salvation from every communicant: "An unworthy communicant . . . is more offensive to Almighty God than a loathsome carcass crawling with vermin set before a prince."[158] Like Edwards, too, he would promote the Concert of Prayer.

In 1797, after a stint of itinerant preaching and short ministry stays, McCready settled in Logan County, Kentucky. The county was the armpit of the nation, meagerly populated, poor, and full of scoundrels.

McCready was given a union parish made up of three "sparse congregations"[159]—one at Gasper River, another at Muddy River, and a third at Red River. Soon after taking charge, McCready bound his people in a solemn covenant, written and signed. They agreed to observe: (1) a monthly fast, (2) a Saturday Concert of Prayer at about twilight, and (3) a concert of prayer each Sunday morning when the sun rose to meet the day.[160] McCready wrote:

When we consider the word and promises of a compassionate God, to the poor lost family of Adam, we find the strongest encouragement for Christians to pray in faith—to ask in the name of Jesus for the conversion of their fellow-men. None ever went to Christ, when on earth, with the case of their friends that were denied, and although the days of his humiliation are ended, yet for the encouragement of his people, he has left it on record, that when two or three agree upon earth, to ask in prayer, *believing*, it shall be done. Again, *whatsoever ye shall ask the Father in my name that will I do, that the Father may be glorified in the Son.* With these promises before us we felt encouraged to unite our supplications to a prayer-hearing God, for the out-pouring of his spirit, that his people may be quickened and comforted, and that our children, and sinners in general, may be converted. Therefore, we bind ourselves to observe the third Saturday of each month, for one year, as a day of fasting and prayer, for the conversion of sinners in Logan County, and throughout the world. We also engage to spend one-half hour every Saturday evening, beginning at the setting of the sun, and one-half hour every Sabbath morning, at the rising of the sun, in pleading with God to revive his work.[161]

McCready copied the Cambuslang, Scotland, practice of holding the Lord's Table outdoors. During the visits of George Whitefield thousands participated in this phenomena. McCready held once-a-year gatherings of his three churches for the Sacrament at an open space on a mountainside. The dynamics he put into place—individual prayers, church-wide praying, and large-group gatherings—created a holy rhythm in his churches that was instrumental in creating a divine critical mass.

Boles argues that these kinds of prayer meetings made the South "like a room filled with oil-soaked cloths . . . primed to blaze."[162] "A universal deadness and stupidity," however, "prevailed in these congregations [Red River, Muddy River, and Gasper River] till the May following, when the Lord visited the Gasper River congregation with an outpouring of his Spirit," wrote McCready.[163]

One year after the Concert was begun, July 1798, hopeful signs were powerfully witnessed also at the Muddy River Sacrament.[164] For another year the churches prayed. At the Red River Sacrament in July 1799, a much larger work of God broke out among the people: "About this time," wrote McCready, "a remarkable spirit of prayer and supplication was given to Christians. And a sensible, heart-felt burden of the dreadful state of sinners out of Christ, so that it might be said that 'Zion travailed in birth to bring forth her spiritual children.'"[165] The revival caused tremendous excitement, and for the first time bodily agitations were witnessed. These agitations, like those witnessed during the Great Awakening sixty years earlier, would characterize the experience of many people over the next few years.[166] As God's Spirit came upon the people, McCready was deeply impressed by what he saw:

> All the blessed displays of Almighty power and grace, all the sweet gales of divine Spirit, and soul-reviving showers of the blessings of heaven which we enjoyed before, and which we considered wonderful beyond conception, were but like a few scattering drops before a mighty rain, when compared with the overflowing floods of salvation, which the Eternal, Gracious Jehovah has poured out like a mighty river, upon this our guilty, unworthy country. The Lord has indeed shewed himself a prayer-hearing God: He has given his people a praying spirit and a lively faith, and then he has answered their prayers far beyond their highest expectations.[167]

However moved McCready was, he had no idea how great the work of God was to become. The excitement of Red River couldn't be contained. Meanwhile McCready continued to encourage "prayer societies, fasts, intense and urgent sermons."

In the third year of the Concert of Prayer, June 1800, McCready called his three churches to meet together at the Red River meeting-house (by this time two colleagues had joined him in his ministry—William Hodge and John Rankin). As anticipation of a new work of God gripped Logan County, McCready summoned his churches to begin "actively praying and preparing for revival."[168]

The move of God spread from McCready's congregations to other parts. Soon delegations were sent to Logan County to bear witness to the "very extraordinary religious excitement." Convinced that a mighty work of God was afoot, the Sacrament at Cane Ridge was scheduled in August 1801. As Paul Conkin cautions, what took place at the Cane Ridge Communion was "a culmination rather than an event that surfaced out of thin air."[169] At Cane Ridge a work of God broke loose that hadn't been seen since the height of the Great Awakening. Enormous crowds of 20,000 to 30,000 gathered. People came on foot, by horse, wagons, and carriages from most of the states of the Union and from every denominational background. The roads and fields teemed with "Presbyterians, Methodists, Baptists, &c.,

&c. . . . as one mighty spiritual host, assembled together to fight the battles of the Lord. They had come up to the help of Zion. They preached and prayed and praised together. . . . Their objects and aims were the same; there was no schism."

> Nay, more. Together, in sweetest, holiest, symbolic communion, they sat down at the one table of the one Lord, and together commemorated his sufferings and death, affording to a gazing and admiring world, a monumental exhibition of an answer to the memorable prayer of the incarnate Jesus, to his and their Heavenly Father for the union of His people. Such were the glories of the times that many good people thought assuredly the Millennium had begun to dawn upon the world.[170]

Sabbath scenes of solemn, agonizing conviction and extraordinary joy abounded:

> The Word of the Lord was quick and powerful, and sharper than a two-edged sword;" many sinners were cut to the heart and fell prostrate under an awful guilt and condemnation of sin. This was not confined to any one class. The moral, genteel and well raised, the giddy and profane, the wicked, the drunkard and the infidel, as well as the proud and vain with all their gaudy attire, were brought down by the Spirit of the ALMIGHTY, and they appeared to have forgotten everything in this world in view of their soul's eternal salvation.[171]

Sometimes as many as 500 people collapsed on the ground crying for God to save them or were so struck down by God that they appeared lifeless.[172] And everywhere "a most solemn and interesting spirit of prayer manifested." As Levi Purviance recalled, "In crowds, tents, and wagons, you could hear fervent prayer. . . . It was difficult to get away from prayer; for more than a half mile I could see people on their knees before God in humble prayer."

The meeting at Cane Ridge lasted six days, but it profoundly altered the frontier. The astonishing revival swept into the Carolinas, Georgia, Virginia, western Pennsylvania, and Ohio.[173] The "excitement spread with the people, and the young converts joined the churches of their choice and the good work of reformation went on with irresistible force, and appeared like carrying everything before it. Many were fully persuaded that the glorious Millennial Day had commenced and that the world would soon become the Kingdom of our Lord Jesus Christ."[174]

Again and again those closest to the revival's story were quick to point to the power of united prayer that lay behind the spiritual eruption. In a report on the great move of God in the *GENERAL STATE of RELIGION In the PRESBYTERIAN CHURCH in the UNITED STATES*, the minutes of the Presbyterian General Assembly in 1803, we read:

> The Assembly considers it as worthy of particular attention, that most of the accounts of revivals communicated to them, stated, that the institution of praying societies, or seasons of special prayer for the out-pouring of the Spirit, generally preceded the remarkable displays of divine grace, with which our land has been recently favoured. In most cases, preparatory to signal effusions of the Holy Spirit, the pious have been stirred up to cry fervently and importunately, that God would appear to vindicate his own cause. The Assembly sees in this a confirmation of the word of God, and an ample encouragement of the prayers and hopes of the pious, for future and more extensive manifestations of divine power. And they trust that the churches under their care, while they see cause of abundant thankfulness for this dispensation, will also perceive, that it presents new motives to zeal and fervour, in application to that throne of grace, from which *every good and perfect gift cometh.*[175]

M'Nemar records many letters that state the same testimony about the power of united prayer. Several of his accounts sound like the following letter from four Kentucky pastors:

> We view Christ as the only center of union, and love the only bond. Let us labour after this spirit; and when we obtain it, then we shall all be united in one body. ****** Some are groaning for the wounds of the Presbyterian cause; some for the Methodist; some for the Baptist, &c., each believing that it is the cause of Christ for which they are groaning. And some are as heartily groaning for the wounds of the Christian cause without respect to name or parties. If we should unite our groans and cries to the Father of our mercies for the general release, and the coming of the Lord's kingdom with power, God would hear and answer us. O let us unite in the common cause. ***** Then will Zion shake herself from the dust, shine forth as the sun in his brightness, and be terrible as an army

with banners. Then shall she be a cup of trembling to all the people around about her, and shake terribly the nations. Then shall that
man of sin be destroyed, and righteousness shall flow down as a
mighty stream. These things, dear brethren, are not vain imagina-
tions, for God is now about to take the earth. Thy kingdom come.
Even so come, Lord Jesus. Brethren, yours in the Lord,

R. Marshall, J. Dunlavy
B. Stone, J. Thompson
Danville, October 18, 1804
To the Moderator of the
Synod of Kentucky[176]

The *Western Missionary Magazine* was begun in 1801 for the
same purposes as James Robe's *Christian History* in the 1730s and *The
Connecticut Evangelical Magazine*—to disperse "intelligence" for general encouragement and to inform prayer groups.[177] Like M'Nemar,
Western Missionary Magazine recorded testimonies on revival and
prayer. For example, an 1802 letter from the western New York and
eastern Ohio area noted that before the revival shook their region,
God gave them a foretaste of what was to come while they wrestled
in prayer:

> The divine presence . . . [initially was] manifested on the . . . first
> Tuesday of October, at West-Liberty, the charge of the Rev. James
> Hughes, in their meeting for concert prayer, many were affected
> toward the conclusion of the social exercise in the evening; an
> appointment was made to meet again at candle lighting, when more
> attended than had been before. Mr. Wylie from Eerie Presbytery
> preached a sermon; it was indeed a solemn evening; many were
> much engaged and seriously exercised, the pious present were
> much quickened and revived.[178]

The letter goes on to say that by the Sabbath following, a revival
shook the whole region from Cross Roads, Raccoon, and Three Springs,
and then exploded with greater power at a large Sacrament meeting on
the last Sabbath of the month. From there the awakening extended to
Upper Buffalo.[179]

Again from the Ohio presbytery came a report that seems pat-
terned after the others.[180] For over ten years Christians had prayed in
concert—with annual Sacraments—until blessing came. The report

begins by describing "sad declensions" of Christianity in 1799. It was a time when

> the graceless became more bold in sin and impiety, the floods of vanity and carnality appeared likely to carry all before them; most of the pious became weak and feeble in the cause of Christ, much buried in, and carried away with the things and pursuits of the world, and in some places a spirit of contention and animosity crept in, which appeared to lead into a great degree of contempt for ordinances, and government in the church and in families. . . . [It was at this juncture that the] meeting for the concert of prayer, for the outpouring of the Spirit and Revival of religion, on the first Tuesday in every quarter of the year, was cordially entered into by the Ohio Presbytery, and practised [sic] generally throughout their bounds. . . .
>
> About the latter end of the year 1801 [revival came]. Desire and prayer for this great favour increased through the following winter in many of our congregations; and in the spring and first part of the summer of 1802, there was a considerable rising of expectation . . . and indeed we were blessed. . . . [In anticipation of] the administration of the Lord's Supper, on the 4th Sabbath of September, 1802 . . . [there was an] uncommon engagedness in pleading for the divine presence on that occasion. *It is thought not improper to mention, for the encouragement of others in the future*, that an agreement was made and attended to by them, to spend a certain time about sun-setting, on each Thursday, in secret prayer, each by themselves, to plead with God for his gracious presence, and the outpouring of his Spirit on that occasion. This was done for some weeks before the Sacrament.[181]

The week preceding the Sacrament, there were numerous sessions of fervent prayer—with spiritual agitation, cries, and groanings among the people generally, and the powerful sense of God's presence in the prayer societies. On the weekend of the Sacrament, there was a powerful outpouring from God, the effects of which continued for months.

M'Nemar's *Revival* includes a poem echoing the promise of Zechariah 4:6: "Not by might, nor by power, but by my Spirit." It sums up what was generally understood as the divine pattern to the revival. Pastors from Ohio, giving up on fruitless, exhausting ministerial toil, turned instead to fervent and united prayer. They then waited expectantly on God for what they knew would come:

Five preachers form'd a body in eighteen hundred three,
From Antichrist's false systems to set the people free:
His doctrine and his worship in pieces they did tear—
But ere the scene was ended these men became a snare.

As witnesses for Jesus, they labor'd night and day,
To convince the blinded Pharisees that Christ was on his way;
But souls bound for the kingdom did strangely turn aside,
And for a little season took these to be their guide.

The word of God came unto them in eighteen hundred four—
"Your work is now completed; you're called to do no more.
My kingdom soon must enter, I cannot long delay;
And in your present order, you're standing in the way."

These preachers took the warning, and all with one accord,
Agreed such institutions must fall before the Lord;
And wisely they consented to take their righteous doom,
To die and be dissolved, to make the Savior room.

In their LAST WILL AND TESTAMENT, they published a decree,
For Christians in Ohio, Kentuck' and Tennessee,
To meet next October and swell the solemn prayer—
"Thy kingdom come, Lord Jesus, thy kingdom enter there!"

The meeting was observed, the solemn prayer was made;
We waited for an answer, which was not long delay'd;
The precious SEED of Canaan, long growing in the east,
Was planted in Ohio, ere next April feast.

The long expected kingdom at length began to spring,
Which to many has appeared a strange mysterious thing;
But we'll trace it thru' the summer, the hottest scene of all,
And try to find its fruit in the next ensuing FALL.[182]

In order to show that the Southern and Western revivals were not unique when it comes to concerted prayer, *Western Missionary Magazine* reprinted an article from *The Connecticut Evangelical Magazine* titled "PRAYER, A Weapon peculiar to those who fight under Christ, the Captain of our salvation."[183] After citing biblical examples of God answering the united prayers of his people, the article concludes:

We are taught . . . that it is altogether suitable, that in times of extraordinary difficulty and danger, the people of God should have recourse to extraordinary prayer. . . . Infidels, some of them, *have no God*; these therefore *cannot pray*. Others have a God, whom they own, but in works they deny him; for there is not the will to pray to him. Prayer makes no part of their religion. Here, then, is their weak place. Here Christians, you must make the attack. They despise this peculiar piece of armour, with which the Captain of your Salvation has furnished you; they think it of no use to you; therefore they will make no preparation to resist it. This gives the disciples of Christ great advantage over the followers of Voltaire. While these meet together to *concert* measures to "*crush the wretch*,"[184] (to use their own blasphemous word) let Christians form *concerts* of prayer, to beseech the God and Father of our Lord Jesus Christ to pull down the kingdom of Satan and build up the kingdom of his dear Son, and spread the sweet savor of his name through the world! Prayer-meetings, and explicit concerts in prayer, are things highly becoming the church of a prayer-hearing God. This matter is set in a clear point of light in President Edwards's "Humble Attempt to promote explicit agreement and visible union of God's people in extraordinary prayer for the revival of religion," &c. Every Christian ought to read this book. If prayer is such an all-important means in advancing the kingdom of the Redeemer, why is it not suitable that the subjects of this kingdom should take great pains to stir up one another to this duty—and has it not been found, by experience, that explicit agreement has greatly increased the spirit of prayer? In many places such explicit agreement, between a few Christian friends, has issued in a general revival of religion.[185]

Clearly, then, we can see that "America's Pentecost," like the modern missionary movement conceived on both sides of the Atlantic before it, was deeply influenced if not integrally linked to both Edwards's articulation of history's *telos*[186] and the divine means he saw to realize it. An Edwards-like postmillennialism dominated expectations in the 1800 revival, even as it dominated the vision of God's ascendant glory dawning on the nations of the earth for a growing throng of missionaries.[187] These visions and convictions drove people to united prayer in explicit agreement for the outpouring of God's Spirit and the advancement of Christ's kingdom, and then moved people into action.

America was not alone in facing serious problems. In the 1790s the situation in Great Britain was exceedingly grim, too. As the reviving effects of the 1800 awakening in America reached England, a holy jealousy emerged: "If God can work there, why not here?" While the call for the Concert was making its way throughout the United States, Alexander Pringle, minister in Perth, Scotland, issued the cry for prayer in Great Britain. In 1796 Pringle published a circular letter that was widely read.

> For some years past, through the tender mercies of God, a considerable revival has taken place among different denominations, both in Britain and America. The Spirit seems to have been poured out. . . . Meetings for prayer and spiritual conference have become frequent in various places. A deep concern for the general revival of religion in churches already planted, and for the extension of the Redeemer's kingdom to the ends of the earth, has occupied their minds. . . . They have cheerfully devoted a portion of their time, weekly or monthly, to the purpose of jointly wrestling at the throne of grace, for a more general revival of religion at home, and for the spread of the gospel into the lands covered with the shadow of death. Their number, which at first was small, has now greatly increased. The little cloud, which was like a man's hand, is now covering the face of the whole heavens in some churches. In Scotland, we have also a few who have already gone forth to the help of the Lord against the mighty. They are willingly offering themselves to the work, and statedly present their spiritual sacrifices of prayer and praise, at the altar of God, in unison with their Christian brethren of other churches. But why do the multitude of the friends of Christ, in this part of the island, yet sit still and abide in their tents? Why are we among the last to invite the King of Zion back again to his house and throne in the Protestant churches; and to invoke him to arise to take the heathen for his inheritance, and the uttermost parts of the earth for his possession? Are we less concerned for the glory of Immanuel? Are we less interested in the success of his work than our brethren? No, these are matters of common concern to all saints. But perhaps the true cause of this is much abated. For a series of years past, the power of religion has certainly been greatly on the decline among us. We are fallen from our first love. This is indeed a melancholy truth; yet I dare not impute our present inactivity wholly to this cause. Want of information and excitement is perhaps the great reason why the bulk of serious Christians among us have not stood forth, among the first in the laudable work. Though societies for prayer, for the success of the gospel at home and abroad

have been erected, and are increasing in England, in Wales, and in America, for a few years past; yet it is only of late that they have been brought forward to public notice, have openly declared their specific object, and invited all the friends of Christ to join them.[188]

In the years succeeding the 1800-1805 "Pentecost," there were ebbs and flows of reviving grace. In response to "communications" from America during one such flow, James Stewart, chaplain in the Church of England, Liverpool, summed up how English Christians felt: "In America, you fish with a net:—here, we fish with a hook."[189] Stewart, like Pringle, determined to do something about it. He began an intense campaign to promote the Concert of Prayer all over England. He "made several tours" through Scotland, Ireland, and England conversing with leaders at home and corresponding with leaders abroad.[190] He wrote to his fellow Englishmen: "Let all sincere Christians unite in earnest prayer for the general outpouring of the Holy Spirit. This will be the most likely mode to bring down an extensive blessing on mankind."[191] He explained to his readers that the "union for prayer is the special manner, by his gracious and powerful influence, that the kingdom of our Lord Jesus Christ is to be established." Like Edwards, Stewart insisted, "The holy Scriptures predict a day when the Holy Spirit shall be given in a very abundant manner and that this blessing will be preceded by earnest prayer."[192] To Stewart, this "extensive blessing" meant a global and all-inclusive outpouring from God:

By general outpouring of the Holy Spirit, is intended a grant as wide in extent as it is abundant in measure. A grant which may include all bishops, pastors, ministers and teachers at home, all missionaries and Christians abroad; a grant which may enliven, purify, and establish those Christian churches whose foundations are already laid; and plant, enlarge, and extend others not yet begun: a grant which may increase the zeal, and love, and holiness of all true Christians, and give spiritual life and light to sinners now dead in trespasses and sins: a grant which may bring the divine blessing upon the labours of the Christian press throughout the world; and give wisdom, simplicity, and success to every religious and benevolent institution; a grant which may comprehend both Jew and the Gentile; or to sum all in one sentence, such a grant of the Divine influences of the Holy Spirit, as "Shall fill the earth with the knowledge of the Lord, even as the waters cover the sea."[193]

Like McCready in Kentucky, Edwards in Northampton, and M'Culloch in Cambuslang, Stewart wrote covenants outlining the agreement for all to sign.[194] In the covenant were "daily supplications," "weekly meetings,"[195] and meetings for everyone to gather "monthly on a Monday evening nearest to the full moon, at six o'clock."[196] For pastors Stewart offered twenty-four weeks worth of lecture titles on the subject of united prayer for "the interests of the Redeemer's kingdom in general." For heads of households, he offered an assortment of scripted prayers for those who needed help leading their families in such praying.[197] The Scottish Kirk sent a copy of Stewart's work to every minister in the Church of Scotland, and the *Calcutta Christian Observer* published the same, recommending it to its readers in India.[198]

What was the motive for such united, concerted prayer? The promised millennium, of course. "Surely," wrote Stewart, "such a motive [as the millennial reign of Christ] will unite all Christians in prayer. With such an animating motive to excite the Church of Christ, it may perhaps be unnecessary to adduce any other argument" to persuade people to join.[199]

As the nineteenth century progressed, the legacy of the Concert of Prayer persisted though the formal scheme became diffused. There are sterling examples such as Andrew Murray, who was born in Scotland but who pastored in South Africa and promoted the Concert of Prayer in Africa. Murray witnessed powerful revivals. But one thing seems generally true: the Concert of Prayer—the original design of a single Holy Spirit-led movement uniting all true seekers after the glory of Christ—dissipated more and more into Concerts of Prayer. The Concert became more or less dismembered or disparate prayer unions using a similar strategy of praying but essentially unconnected to each other.

There is evidence to suggest that a global concert was still held out as a goal. In 1861 David Slie wrote *The Holy of Holies, or, World's Tri-Daily Concert of Prayer*.[200] Slie was from Rochester, New York, which had experienced the revival of 1757 deeply, transforming the city for generations to come. Slie pushed the private prayer side of the Concert of Prayer. He argued that even private prayer, synchronized to happen at the same time of day with other people's private prayers, was "entering into agreement and union with the hosts of heaven, angels and victorious saints, and our Savior who lives to intercede for us, and the Holy Spirit who groans for us with words inexpressible before the Father of Lights."[201] Revelation 4—5, said Slie, "encourages a strategy of pray-ers, coordinating their personal prayer times with many others, thus cooperating in a prayer concert, as saints answering the summons of God together, agreeing that the uttermost parts of the earth must be the possession of God."[202]

> Under the promise that the "earth shall be full of the knowledge of the Lord, as the waters cover the sea," it is reasonable to expect, that a spirit of prayer and supplication will be poured out *speedily* upon the praying hosts at large—SO THAT THEIR FAITH SHALL DAILY REPRESENT THE WANT OF THE ENTIRE WORLD BEFORE THE THRONE. . . . INDEED, THE PRESENT unmistakable dawnings of the MILLENNIUM, call at *this hour*, and onward, for a world's unceasing concert of prayer and praise, as the fulfillment of the prophecy, which says, "From the rising of the sun, even to the going down of the same, MY NAME shall be great among the Gentiles; and in *every* place, incense shall be offered unto my name, and a pure offering."[203]

Such a Concert, wrote Slie, "may be considered the most effectual method of promoting and perpetuating *pure* revivals of religion and holy living in general."[204] Furthermore, the pray-ers would be the group that paved the way for the coming of Christ.[205]

I cite three other nineteenth-century Concerts. The first is a relatively localized story, while the effect of the latter was global.

On October 10, 1821, a young lawyer by the name of Charles Grandison Finney (1792-1875) met his Savior in a grove of trees just north of the village of Adams, New York.[206] Like the patriarch Jacob, Finney had wrestled with God all day and refused to let him go until God blessed him. God did. So profoundly was Finney converted that his life completely changed, and he knew that his life would be dedicated to spreading the Gospel. He immediately set about sharing his faith with a confidence that his old life and career were ended and a new one was beginning. The town of Adams was astonished by the change. The pilgrimage Finney began in that little wood is well chronicled. Few people impacted the nineteenth century as much as Finney, either socially or evangelistically. His ministry was centered on preaching and prayer, especially concerted prayer made "in agreement." Whereas Edwards played a key role in the enormous firestorm of the Great Awakening, Finney was at the heart of many later brushfires of revival.

Within three months of his conversion, Finney had his initial first-hand experience of a reviving work of God. It is certain that the revival impressed the young Christian, helping to set the tone for the rest of his ministry. The revival in Adams, New York, was not, however, a result of Finney's preaching. In fact, he wasn't present when it began. His brother was. It started at a prayer meeting.

After recording the conversions of his mother and father in his *Memoirs*,[207] Finney wrote that he stayed in their neighborhood for another night or two, sharing the Gospel with as many as he met.[208] The following I quote in its entirety, as it gives us a glimpse of how the Concert of Prayer might have looked in many small towns at this time and of the resident power it possessed.

> I believe it was the next Monday night, they had a monthly concert of prayer in that small town. There were there a Baptist church that had a minister, and a small Congregational church without a minister. The town was very much of a moral waste, however; and at this time religion was at a very low ebb. My youngest brother attended this monthly concert of which I have spoken, and afterwards gave me an account of it. The Baptists and Congregationalists were in the habit of holding a Union Monthly Concert. But few attended, and therefore it was held at a private house. On this occasion they met, as usual, in the parlor of a private house. A few of the members of the Baptist church, and a few Congregationalists, were present. The deacon of the Congregational church was a thin, spare, feeble old man by the name of Montague. He was quiet in his ways, and had a good reputation for piety; but seldom said much upon the subject. He was a good specimen of a New England deacon. He was present, and they called upon him to lead the meeting. He read a passage of Scripture according to their custom. They then sang a hymn, and Deacon Montague stood up behind his chair and led off in prayer. The other persons present, all of them professors of religion and younger people, knelt down around the room. My brother said that Deacon Montague began as usual in his prayer, in a low, feeble voice; but soon began to wax warm and to raise his voice, which became tremulous with emotion. He proceeded to pray with more and more earnestness, till soon he began to rise upon his toes and come down with his heels; and then to rise up on his toes and drop upon his heels again, so that they could feel the jar in the room. He continued to raise his voice, and to rise upon his toes and come down upon his heels more emphatically. And as the Spirit of prayer led him onward, he began to raise his chair

together with his heels, and bring that down with still more emphasis. He continued to do this, and grew more and more engaged till
he would bring the chair down as if he would break it to pieces. In
the meantime the brethren and sisters that were on their knees,
began to groan, and sigh, and weep, and agonize in prayer. The dea-
con continued to struggle until he was about exhausted; and when
he ceased, my brother said there was nobody in the room that could
get off from the knees. They could only weep and confess, and all
melted down before the Lord. From this meeting the work of the
Lord spread forth in every direction all over the town. And it thus
spread at that time from Adams as a center, throughout nearly all
the towns in the country.[209]

As his *Lectures on Revivals of Religion*[210] clearly indicate, concerted,
united prayer by people in agreement was central to Finney's understanding of the work of God.[211] Just perusing the book's table of con-
tents gives one an unmistakable impression of the place of importance
fervent and united prayer held in Finney's scheme: "Prevailing Prayer,"
"The Prayer of Faith," "Spirit of Prayer," "Be Filled with the Spirit,"
"Meetings for Prayer," and "Necessity and Effect of Union" (in prayer).
Like James Stewart, Finney had no doubt that sincere Christians united
in earnest, believing prayer is "the most likely mode to bring down an
extensive blessing on mankind."[212]

Chapter 16 of *Lectures*, "The Effect of Union," is on the issue of
agreement in prayer. Finney believed that if God's people want revival
and agree to seek it, then revival will come. Finney insists that 1) we
should agree in our desires for revival; 2) we must agree in the motive
behind our desire for revival; 3) we must agree in desiring revival for
good reasons; 4) we must agree in faith for revival; 5) we must agree as
to the time when we desire the blessing of revival to come; etc.[213]

Expounding at one point on Matthew 13:19, Finney writes:
"[Jesus] states in the strongest possible case by taking the number
two as the least number between whom there can be an agreement,
and says that 'where *two* of you are agreed on earth, as touching anything that they shall ask, it shall be done for them of my Father which
is in heaven.' It is the fact of their *agreement* upon which he lays the
stress."[214]

The Concert of Prayer became a way of life for many Christians and
churches during the nineteenth century. In 1845 Dr. Samuel Miller
(1769-1850), a godly man and one of the two principal scholars at

Princeton Seminary,[215] wrote a book "addressed to the Members of the Presbyterian Church in the United States" titled *Letters on the Observance of the Monthly Concert of Prayer*.[216] Miller recounts the history of the Concert and its origins with Edwards. He writes: "There is reason to believe that this laudable concert in devotion, though slow in making its way, and though sometimes languishing, has never been wholly abandoned since the original agreement. . . . One church after another, and one religious denomination after another, not only in the United States but in various parts of Christendom, fell in with it, until we may safely say, it now pervades the greater part of the evangelical world. Even in Asia, in Africa and in the islands of the sea."[217]

The occasion for Miller's letter was the "falling off" of the observance. For him and the presbytery it was "an indication of the spiritual state of the church, deeply to be deplored."

> Surely, everyone who claims to be a Christian will be seen bowing before the throne of grace, and pleading for mercy for the church and the world. But is it found in experience to be? Alas! Would that it were! But no; in many cases not half, and in some not a third of the communicants of our churches make their appearance in these exercises of special devotion. A considerable number of those who are never absent from their seats in the ordinary services of the sanctuary on the Lord's day, are seldom seen in the place where special prayer is wont to be made for the revival of religion, and the enlargement of the kingdom of him, whom they profess to regard as the Lord, and the only hope of the world. How shall we account for this melancholy?[218]

THE REVIVAL OF 1857

The 1857 revival, or the Laymen's Prayer Revival, made prayer meetings such as the Fulton Street prayer meeting famous.[219] For years analysis of the 1857 revival has focused on the city of New York and men like Jeremiah Lanphier, who began the famous lay prayer meetings at the Dutch Reformed Church on the lower end of Manhattan.[220]

The facts about where the revival began and where the lay prayer meetings came from tell a grander tale. The story is rooted not in New York but in Boston.

Historic Park Street Church, located on the north end of the Boston Commons, was born as a result of a Concert of Prayer among three other Boston-area churches in 1800. Four decades later, concerned over the declension in Christian faith in the city, a group of people at Park Street Church began a prayer concert on March 3, 1840, for the outpouring of God's Spirit.[221] The group agreed to meet every day for prayer and kept annual minutes. While the group members attended larger monthly meetings of the Concert of Prayer in Boston at the time, this particular prayer meeting was a Park Street Church meeting for the purpose of intensifying the prayer effort. In their second year's minutes they record the following:

> Two years have now elapsed since the daily meeting for prayer was commenced, and we have entered this morning upon the third year. It had its origin with a few brethren, who were impressed with the importance and necessity of more special and united prayer for the revival of religion in [Boston]. By the suggestion of one of these brethren, at the close of the *monthly concert* in March 1840, a few agreed to meet in this vestry the next morning for prayer, and to consider the proposal to establish this meeting. The proposal was then adopted. . . . It was agreed that the special object of the meeting should be to pray for the influences of the Holy Spirit upon the city. This important object has, to a good degree, been the burden of the prayers daily offered here. At each meeting, a short portion of the Scriptures has been read, from three to five prayers offered, a few verses sung, and from ten to fifteen minutes allotted to the communication of appropriate religious intelligence and remarks. The number attending the meeting during the year has varied from thirty to three hundred.[222]

The prayer concert targeted specific churches in Boston: Park Street, Essex Street, Salem Street, Central Church, Bowdoin Street, Pine Street, Green Street, Old South, and Garden Street.[223] Over four years they tracked the progress of membership, baptisms, church plants, etc.

After two years of praying, all the churches began reporting significant growth and numerous conversions. From the minutes of 1842 we read: "All our churches are enjoying at the present time, to a greater or lesser degree, the reviving influences of the Holy Spirit. Other evangelical churches are also enjoying, with us, this rich blessing." These blessings were "unquestionably connected with this [prayer] meeting," remarked one pastor.[224] They charted each church's progress carefully.[225]

By the third year, while the attendance at the prayer meeting began to drop, the statistics on church attendance and the general impact of evangelical Christianity remained impressive. The members were grateful that for the first time in years, attendance in and around evangelical Boston churches exceeded that at the Unitarian places of worship.[226]

In the fourth year (1844), the prayer meeting died. As a warning to Christians everywhere, the prayer meeting's final minutes record a haunting revelation: "The average attendance [at the prayer meeting during] the present year has been less, it is believed, than any former year. . . . *The number added [to our churches over] the past year is about seven times less than the year previous, and less than on any year since the meeting commenced.*"[227] The Park Street prayer meeting was a hopeful enterprise and a disappointment. While these Christians sought God regularly and earnestly in union, agreeing to bless the churches of their city by asking God to pour out his Spirit on them, the churches flourished. When they stopped praying, progress stopped. One cannot but be reminded of the four churches of Ipswich mentioned earlier. Fortunately, the story doesn't end here.

Six years later, two men, each members of the Park Street Church meeting, decided to start another prayer meeting. They determined that the new meeting would comply more closely with the "union prayer meetings" (i.e., Concerts of Prayer) prevalent in England.[228]

In autumn the first meeting was begun at the Old South Church in the heart of Boston. "To this meeting" came "not only Congregationalists [Park Street Church is Congregational], but our Baptist, Methodist, Episcopalian, and Presbyterian brethren. . . . The spirit that . . . prevailed [was] the furthest removed from sectarianism; and the utmost liberty, consistent with Christian order, [was] enjoyed in the remarks which any individual might deem it proper to make."[229] Reminiscent of Zinzendorf's covenant with the disparate Moravians,

> All evangelical denominations united in the meetings, and during the . . . years which it has existed the most delightful harmony has prevailed. There is a general understanding that no controverted points in theology shall be discussed, and that all denominational peculiarities shall be avoided. If, occasionally, a stranger, not knowing the meeting is composed of all denominations of Christians, introduces some denominational matter, no notice is taken of it, and the meeting goes on without interruption. Occasionally, a Methodist present may be heard to say "Amen." With this excep-

tion, one could hardly tell to what denomination of Christians those present belonged.[230]

The goal of the prayer meeting was simple: "to pray for the revival of religion, in the outpouring of the Spirit on the inhabitants of this city."[231] Every morning, except Sunday, at eight—before the workday began—the members gathered to pray for one hour.[232]

It has been remarked by strangers who have attended the meeting for the first time, that the atmosphere of the Old South Chapel was peculiar. They had hardly entered the room before they were convinced that the place was pervaded with the sacred influences of the Holy Spirit. Hundreds who have spent a few days in Boston have said, as they left, that they never before attended such meetings; and, with tears in their eyes, they blessed God that they had had the opportunity. Nearly every morning, some stranger rises and says, in substance, "I have heard of this meeting, but never before had the privilege to attend it. I thought you had good meetings, and I rejoice to be here. I feel that I have benefited, and I shall go home and tell my brethren about it. I hope these meetings will continue; for you cannot tell, brethren, what an influence you are exerting all over the country. We look to you for information; and when the Spirit of the Lord is with you, and we hear of conversions, we are encouraged."

Similar remarks have been made by hundreds, and, for aught we know, by thousands, who, having caught the spirit of the meeting, have gone home to labor and pray with increased energy and zeal in the cause of their Master. All seem to be of one heart and one mind. There is a remarkable blending together of those who attend. . . . The rich and the poor are there together, all one in Christ Jesus. The most humble laborer in the vineyard of the Lord, from any quarter of the wide world, is welcome.

The leader of the meeting seldom reads more than eight or ten verses of Scripture, and if he comments at all upon them, he is very brief. The singing is led by anyone who chances to be present. A hymn is given out at the commencement, and after that, verses of familiar hymns are voluntarily struck up by any who feel disposed. This is one of the most interesting exercises of the meeting, and one in which nearly the whole congregation participates.[233]

In the very first year a surge of spiritual activity was reported among the churches participating. The effects grew more glorious from year to year.

In 1856, recalling the quarterly fasts of the original Concert of Prayer proposal, the Old South Prayer Meeting added quarterly solemn fast days to their prayer repertoire in order to more earnestly call upon God to pour out his power. The familiar cry went up: "Thy kingdom come, thy will be done on earth."[234] The prayer was heard:

> Let Satan's kingdom fall like lightning, enter every dwelling place, every habitation of men in this city . . . carry forward the work of grace through all the land, among the nations of the earth, upon the land and upon the sea. Let the fullness of the sea be converted to thee. Great God, we pray thee to move by the power of thy Holy Spirit upon all flesh, and let all flesh together rejoice in the salvation of our God. . . . Let Old South Church be the furnace to melt people and mould them into the image of Jesus Christ, that they may go forth, and let their light shine, and bring forth fruit unto God.[235]

By the spring of 1857, the participants had observed five fast days. Members filled the Old South Church to overflowing in both the morning and the afternoon.[236] By 1857, then, these hundreds and thousands of evangelical Christians in Boston had prayed every day, all year long, for over six years for the outpouring of God on their land. This meeting predates any others I have found and exceeds others in depth and solemnity at the time leading up to the 1857 revival. For over a year, Christians had fasted all day in five great solemn meetings of extraordinary prayer. Missionaries on furlough heard about the meetings and made their way to Boston to join them. Others from around the country brought the design back to their hometowns. A great, united, concerted cry was arising to God from Boston.

One of America's greatest preachers, Lyman Beecher, who by the late 1850s was an old man, became a regular attendee at the daily meetings and the quarterly fast days. Of him it was recorded: "The Rev. Dr. Beecher, senior, who attended [the fasts], and whose expertise in the Church of Christ among us has been long and extensive, remarked to the writer that he had never been present on any similar occasion where there was so great and so uniform solemnity of feeling and expression."[237]

With reports from ministries in the city of Boston combined with other reports filtering back from all over the country about the stirrings of God's Spirit, the January 1, 1857, minutes reflect an exhilarating confidence and rising hopefulness.[238] The pray-ers noted that if the present work of God continued, it would "practically engross the church of God on the earth, [and] how soon would the entire face of our world be altered! How soon might the 'the glorious Gospel of the blessed God' pervade it! . . . Thus shall 'the little ones become a thousand, the small one a nation,' and God 'will hasten it in its time.' But 'he will be sought unto to do it.'"[239]

About the time of the revival, the prayer at Old South became remarkably urgent:

> [T]here was an increased spirit of prayer among the attendants. . . . The faith of God's people seemed to be growing stronger every week. They carried the entire city to the throne of grace. Without regard for denominations, they wrestled with God, and seemed continually burdened with souls. . . . Soon, a cloud no bigger than a man's hand was seen. For seven years, every morning, prayer had been sent up to the Most High for the salvation of souls, and now the blessing seemed to be at hand. . . . [I]t was not long before the chapel was filled to overflowing, including the pulpit, gallery, both aisles, and all the passageways. The room below was opened, and both were filled to their utmost capacity . . . sometimes the whole audience would be bathed in tears. The place seemed filled with the blessed influences of the Holy Ghost.[240]

But what does this have to do with New York City and Jeremiah Lanphier? Well, if we were to stop here, the story of this Concert of Prayer is impressive enough, but New York made it even more significant.

In the winter and spring of 1857, Charles Finney was preaching in Boston.[241] In April Finney's famous friend, Lewis Tappan (1788-1873), traveled from New York to Boston to be with him.[242] Tappan was raised in Northampton, Massachusetts, attended Jonathan Edwards's former church, and was a devout evangelical Christian. He grew to be a successful merchant, founder of the *Journal of Commerce* and of what was to become Dun and Bradstreet, and was one of the richest men in America. He was, with Finney, a leader in the movement to abolish slavery, having mapped out the court case and raised funds and support, for example, for the defense of Africans in the infamous *Amistad* case. He had been the first president of the American Anti-slavery Society. A close advisor and supporter of Finney's, he helped Finney found Oberlin College.

While in Boston, Tappan visited the Old South prayer concert, at the time meeting at Boston's Tremont Temple for one of its large quarterly fasts. He was thrilled by it, so much so that he determined to form meetings like it upon his return to New York City.[243]

That spring *The Congregationalist* magazine published a report under the heading "UNION PRAYER MEETING at Old South Church."

> On the 4th of May, 1857, after conference of brethren belonging to the several churches in Brooklyn, N.Y., it was unanimously agreed to begin a Union Morning Prayer Meeting, in some central place, and invite the members of various evangelical churches as their circumstances would permit. . . .
>
> The responsibility of these meetings in Boston and Brooklyn rest chiefly upon laymen, although they are approved by ministers, many of whom attend them. Laymen lead the meetings. . . . These facts are stated to encourage Christians in other places—in all our cities, towns and villages—to establish similar morning prayer meetings.[244]

Lanphier started one such meeting at the Dutch Church near the financial district in lower Manhattan. When one examines the procedures, guidelines, and organizational structure of the Lanphier meetings in New York City, except for the time of the meeting, they are the same as those of the Old South Prayer Meeting in Boston.[245] There is little doubt where the Lanphier model came from. Likewise, there can be little doubt as to the effect the revival of 1857 had on the nation. J. Edwin Orr estimated that out of a population of thirty million, one million people came to Christ in the United States between 1857 and 1858. From the East Coast to the Midwest to the deep South, churches and communities were transformed. For nearly eight years Christians in Boston had pleaded with God in concert for such a shower of grace upon the nation. Others joined them, and God answered.

One additional note regarding the New York prayer meeting and the ensuing 1857-1858 revival. Few people take the condition of the country into consideration when telling the story of this revival. When Lanphier launched his meeting near Wall Street with a handful of people, it was September. A month later when the Dutch Church was full, the Bank of Philadelphia, one of the largest in the country, had just collapsed. This failure sent shock waves through the financial district. By winter tens of thousands of people were filling New York churches with prayer. In January the stock market crashed, and by midwinter the country was in depression. On top of all this, the nation was watching the horizon as the terrible dark clouds of civil war gathered. These were huge contributing factors, *but so was the prayer concert!*

This, then, is a glancing view of how an elegantly simple vision among a few pastors in Cambuslang, Scotland, and the might of a New England intellect combined into a humble attempt to promote the glory of God and advance Christ's kingdom. For generations to come, we will consider ourselves blessed because of the glorious enterprise called the Concert of Prayer.

Four

Back to the Future?

Today many evangelical Christians cite Jonathan Edwards and his *Humble Attempt* as a historical model worth emulating. In certain quarters, Edwards has never been more richly esteemed. At first blush, his call for visible union and extraordinary prayer is appealing. But should our future be found by going back to the design of Jonathan Edwards, William M'Culloch, and others?

I'm delighted with the emphasis we see today on prayer. Bill Bright's "Fasting and Prayer" conferences, for example, have reintroduced fasting to modern Christians. Bright has consistently and compellingly called for millions to fast. He leads a satellite linkup once a year that enables tens of thousands of people to pray and fast together no matter where they are in the United States. I have been a part of each of Dr. Bright's events. Everywhere I travel, I meet people whose lives have been recast by forty-day fasts. The hearts of major leaders have been woven together by these fasts.

Presently, "Lighthouses of Prayer" are proliferating in our nation. Championed by people such as Ed Silvoso, Paul Cedar, and Al VanderGriend, Lighthouses turn private homes into centers for prayer for one's neighbors living to the left, to the right, and across the street. Dozens of evangelical denominations, including my own, are hopping on board the Lighthouse train. The plan is helping many churches implement "prayer evangelism." Prayer evangelism became especially popular in anticipation of a new millennium, since people everywhere are open to considering transcendent issues. This time in history presents an extraordinary opportunity to pray for one's neighbors, bless them, and present the Gospel.

There are many, many other schemes. "Prayer Walking" is getting Christians out on the streets to pray up and down their neighborhoods. This idea is at the heart of the annual "March for Jesus" celebrated in thousands of cities and towns around the globe. Men and women, boys and girls take to the streets to bless the city and fill it with praise. By logical extension, prayer-walking pilgrimages called "Prayer Journeys" are popular. Ad hoc groups, missionary teams, and church teams travel to nations where the Gospel is absent or impotent. There they pray on site, calling down God's grace. This is "praying on site with insight," as Steve Hawthorn[1] would say.

"See You at the Pole" is an occasion every September when millions of high school students gather at their school's flagpole to pray blessing upon their school. Its rise has been nothing less than phenomenal. It was for this event in 1999 that kids and chaperones were assembled at Wedgewood Baptist Church in Fort Worth, Texas, when a madman entered, shooting and bombing.

Since the late 1980s "Prayer Summits" have abounded. Popularized by Joe Aldrich and the late Terry Dirks of International Renewal Ministries, Prayer Summits bring pastors of common faith from across denominational lines to meet for three or four days with no agenda other than prayer. These meetings have affected tens of thousands of ministers. Hundreds of these summits have been held on most of the continents of the globe. Profound spiritual breakthroughs are commonplace. Truly, the summits have been life-changing for thousands. Brokenness over sin, reconciliation, personal spiritual reformation, and the beginning of deep friendships are routine.

And then there was October 1997. For nearly a decade Promise Keepers has been changing the nature of relationships in modern Evangelicalism. I was backstage at "Stand in the Gap" when 1.3 million men gathered on the great mall in Washington, D.C., from every corner of America. My role, a modest one, was to pray over each speaker just before they went out on the platform. But for over a year there had been fasting, prayer meetings, and intense intercessory prayer. Prayer walks blanketed Washington, D.C. Steve Hawthorn saw to it that every street and building in the city was prayed over two-and-a-half times! From every race and denominational stripe men came to seek the face of God. What a sight to behold—over a million men on their faces before Christ—asking God to forgive their sins. This "Sacred Assembly" was the largest religious gathering in the history of the United States.

These movements and remarkable events and dozens of others like them constitute a wonderful mosaic. Personally, I have been humbled to play a role. God is at work, and his people are seeking more of him. But taken separately or as a whole, are they the heirs of the Concert of Prayer?

PRAYER AND THE WORD OF GOD

The evolution of practical theology in this era is demanding rediscovery of prayer, too. Whereas the Word of God has been preeminent in twentieth-century Evangelicalism, especially in light of the Fundamentalist controversies early this century, prayer is now reemerging as one of the two pillars of local church ministry, evangelism, and revival. The Bible studied, rightly handled, and prophetically preached is the mark of the modern Evangelical. Our conviction regarding this Word must not be compromised at any cost. Woe to us if our commitment to the Scriptures is ever marginalized. Skilled exposition of the text of Scripture is paramount.

Time and time again the great historical figures of the church remind us of the dilemma faced by the apostles while the church was born. Will we choose rightly as they did?

In Acts 6, after the church had been birthed in an explosion of new believers, we read of "rumblings of discontent" (NLT) regarding food distribution. Those representing Greek-born widows complained that the women were not treated fairly. The problem, laden with racism, prejudice, and willful neglect of the powerless, threatened to blow apart the newborn gospel enterprise. When the apostles were clamorously confronted with the problem, they reacted in a way few people expect of leaders: They refused to get mixed up in it. Calling the whole church together, the Twelve responded resolutely: "It would not be right for us to neglect the ministry of the word of God in order to wait on tables."[2] In other words, "We refuse to solve this problem, but we have a suggestion." Pastors have been fired for lesser things. Essentially, the apostles told church members to solve it themselves.

To give the church members help, the apostles created a new category of officers (since called "deacons") to handle the task and established basic criteria for their selection ("full of the Spirit and wisdom"). From that point on it was up to church members to choose deacons from among themselves and see that the problem was addressed. The apostles insisted that they be left alone for the most important things— "prayer and the ministry of the word"—the two pillars upon which the whole gospel enterprise rests. This incident is the first example in the church age of leaders deflecting the tyranny of the urgent in order to concentrate on first things first.

The apostles understood by example and experience the primacy of "prayer and the ministry of the word." For one, they had just experienced Pentecost. When Jesus stood on the Mount of Olives giving his final words before reentering glory, he said clearly: "[S]tay in the city until you have been clothed with power from on high."[3] Jesus explicitly ordered them not to embark on the work of his kingdom until they had been empowered by the Holy Spirit to do so. Obediently, the disciples waited . . . in prayer.

> Then they returned to Jerusalem from the hill called the Mount of Olives, a Sabbath day's walk from the city. When they arrived, they went upstairs to the room where they were staying. Those present were Peter, John, James and Andrew; Philip and Thomas, Bartholomew and Matthew; James son of Alphaeus and Simon the Zealot, and Judas son of James. They all joined *together* ("*with one mind*")[4] *constantly in prayer,* along with the women and Mary the mother of Jesus, and with his brothers. (Acts 1:12-14)

So prayer was the precursor to Pentecost. This is a story told many times, but when the Holy Spirit was poured out upon the first church in Acts 2, it was in the context of a prayer meeting. With tongues of fire dancing on their heads and overflowing their hearts—manifesting the power and the presence of God—the Christians made a ruckus, Peter preached, and thousands were swept into the kingdom. Someone once said, "The disciples prayed for ten days, Peter preached for ten minutes, and three thousand were saved. The same would not have happened had the disciples prayed for ten minutes and Peter preached for ten days."

Furthermore, Acts 2:42ff. says that praying became the ubiquitous fruit of Pentecost. Prayer was happening everywhere, coming from everybody, and the church grew exponentially. Again in Acts 4, with the first persecution, the disciples' immediate response was to pray together earnestly that God would make them bold witnesses and that he would stretch out his hand to perform miraculous signs and wonders. God shook the place where they were praying and filled them again with his Holy Spirit.

But the apostles knew that prayer and the ministry of the Word were foundational and nonnegotiable because they had seen it exemplified in the life of Christ, too. The Bible records that Jesus' greatest triumphs were coupled with much praying. After Jesus prayed, he was able to accomplish extraordinary things. Prayer was present throughout his ministry and was the instrumentality whereby God poured out his very life and power and authority into his Son. We are told:

> Very early in the morning, while it was still dark, Jesus got up, left the house and went off to a solitary place, where he prayed.(Mark 1:35)

Jesus often withdrew to lonely places and prayed (Luke 5:16).

> During the days of Jesus' life on earth, he offered up prayers and petitions with loud cries and tears to the one who could save him from death, and he was heard because of his reverent submission. (Heb. 5:7)

After Jesus prayed, the Holy Spirit descended on him like a dove.

> When all the people were being baptized, Jesus was baptized too. And as he was praying, heaven was opened and the Holy Spirit descended on him in bodily form like a dove. And a voice came from heaven: "You are my Son, whom I love; with you I am well pleased." (Luke 3:21-22)

It was only after forty days of fasting and prayer that Jesus, filled with the Holy Spirit's power,[5] inaugurated his public ministry, preaching in open forums with hitherto unheard-of authority, calling his first disciples.[6]

Jesus, who "would not entrust himself to [people], for he knew all men,"[7] still deemed it essential to climb a mountain and pray all night before he chose twelve men from among his throng of disciples and bestowed upon them the title of "apostles."[8]

It was after a night of praying that Jesus walked on the Sea of Galilee, met his terrified disciples as they sailed in the storm, and then stilled the raging wind and seas.[9]

It was when he took Peter, John, and James onto a mountain to pray that Jesus was transfigured.

As he was praying, the appearance of his face changed, and his clothes became as bright as a flash of lightning. . . . Moses and Elijah appeared in glorious splendor . . . [and] a [glory] cloud appeared and enveloped them. . . . A voice came from the cloud, saying, "This is my Son, whom I have chosen; listen to him." (Luke 9:29-35)

From this mountain Jesus descended and cast out demons.

It was after praying—with sweat drops of blood—that Jesus fully resolved, and was enabled and emboldened, to endure the cross of Calvary for the forgiveness of our sins:

And being in anguish, he prayed more earnestly, and his sweat was like drops of blood falling to the ground. (Luke 22:44)

The Crucifixion itself was nothing if it was not an ongoing prayer meeting between Jesus and the Father. The first words out of his mouth from the cross were intercession:

"Father, forgive them, for they do not know what they are doing." (Luke 23:34)

Then, at the height of his suffering, the Lamb of God cried the lament of the psalmist:

About the ninth hour Jesus cried out in a loud voice, *"Eloi, Eloi, lama sabachthani?"*—which means, "My God, my God, why have you forsaken me?" (Matt. 27:46)

Finally, at the moment of his death, Matthew records that Jesus cried out with a "loud voice" (Greek: *phone megale*): "Father, into your hands I commit my spirit."[10] As this prayer erupted from his lips, enormous spiritual power was unleashed. The earth quaked, the rocks beneath Jesus' cross split, the tombs near Jerusalem opened, and righteous people who were dead were raised to life.

This coupling of prayer and manifest power did not go unnoticed by his disciples; it was the reason the disciples came to him and requested, "Lord, teach *us* to pray."[11] So when the apostles were pressed by the problems of an exploding church, the centrality of prayer was primary in their minds. By example and experience they knew when the tyranny of the urgent was thrust upon them.

THE HOLY SPIRIT

One of the prominent features of the Reformation was the conviction that reliance on the Holy Spirit for the accomplishment of all spiritual work is the heart of ministry and Christian life. This conviction determined how Christian work was done from the sixteenth century on.

> All those whom God hath predestined unto life, and those only, he is pleased, in his appointed and accepted time, effectually to call, *by his word and Spirit*, out of that state of sin and death in which they are by nature, to grace and salvation by Jesus Christ; enlightening their minds spiritually and savingly to understand the things of God; taking away their heart of stone, and giving unto them an heart of flesh; renewing their wills, and by his almighty power determining them to that which is good; and effectually drawing them to Jesus Christ.[12]

J. I. Packer, under whom I studied theology, calls Reformation theology "a theology of the Holy Spirit." God must do the work of God. Only God can reveal God to veiled and corrupt minds, raise the dead, change reprobates "from glory to glory" into the image of Christ. Only God can make an heir out of an enemy. "Apart from me you can do nothing,"[13] says Jesus. The promises of God are fulfilled, "'Not by might, nor by power, but by my Spirit,' says the LORD Almighty."[14] This emphasis on the work of God explains why the legacy of the Reformation produced great men and women of prayer "who wrestled with God like Jacob" and why Edwards and others saw that their efforts were hopeless apart from the hand of God.

Anglican C. S. Lewis illustrates this post-Reformation reliance on the Holy Spirit in *The Chronicles of Narnia*. In *The Lion, the Witch and the Wardrobe* we are introduced to four siblings who discover in the back of an old wardrobe closet an entrance into the enchanted land of Narnia. They find Narnia to be a wondrous land full of intelligent, articulate, and deeply spiritual animals. It is also a land under a curse of perpetual winter—a winter without hope or joy. A wicked queen is responsible for the curse. She is a usurper, a witch with extraordinary power. She rules without mercy.

Lastly, Lewis introduces a lion—a great, magnificent, mysterious beast who comes from beyond space and time and who is spoken of in hushed and reverent terms. His name is Aslan, the Christ-figure who lays down his life for Narnia, but rises from the dead more powerful and majestic than ever. With spell-breaking authority, the resurrected Aslan proceeds to reverse the effects of the curse. One needn't see the lion physically to know that he is near. Whenever Aslan is near, people see signs of spring—thawing streams, flowers poking through the snow, and the budding of the crocuses.

Toward the end of the story, Aslan leads a group of liberators in a rout of the queen's forces. In a climactic scene, Aslan liberates Narnia's castle. With the queen in flight, he leads his troop into the courtyard and finds it strewn with statuary—creatures turned to stone by the spell of the queen. The question arises: How will Aslan free the creatures turned to stone? We soon find out.

He strides toward the first statue, draws near, lowers his regal head, and *breathes on it*. As the breath of Aslan touches the stone, the statue ripples into flesh, and as the released creature's lungs fill with the breath of Aslan, it wakes to life and begins to dance and shout to the praise of the great lion. Soon the whole courtyard is alive with the praises of Aslan.

Exquisitely, C. S. Lewis illustrated Reformation thinking about how people who are spiritually dead are made alive by God. The passage recalls God's promise in Ezekiel 36:26-27:

> I will give you a new heart and put a new spirit (*ruach*, Hebrew for "breath," "wind," "spirit") in you; I will remove from you your heart of stone and give you a heart of flesh. And I will put my Spirit in you and move you to follow my decrees and be careful to keep my laws.

Foreshadowing Pentecost, God promises a day to come when a new relationship will be established between himself and his people. "There is a day approaching when instead of giving you laws you cannot keep, I will breathe my Spirit into you and change your heart. My Spirit will constrain you and empower you to do that which you cannot do on your own—obey and thus please me."

Lewis echoes, too, John 20 in which Jesus, just risen from the dead, suddenly appears to his disciples and says, "'Peace be with you! As the Father has sent me, I am sending you.' And with that he breathed on them and said, 'Receive the Holy Spirit.'"

Recall John 3. One night a religious scholar and ruler named

Nicodemus risked his position and reputation to meet with Jesus. Nicodemus sat at the pinnacle of Jewish society, a scrupulously religious member of the Sanhedrin, the ruling council for all Israel. If Nicodemus wasn't going to heaven, no one was. Nicodemus told Jesus that by word and supernatural works Jesus had proved that he was a teacher "come from God." It is likely that Nicodemus was convinced that Jesus would be impressed that a member of the ruling counsel of Israel was impressed with Jesus.

Jesus, however, laid Nicodemus bare: "No one can see the kingdom of God unless he is born again."

Nicodemus was chagrinned and incredulous, but Jesus pressed on:

> I tell you the truth, no one can enter the kingdom of God unless he is born of water and the Spirit [Greek: *pnuema*: "wind," "breath"]. You should not be surprised at my saying, "You must be born again." The wind blows wherever it pleases. You hear its sound, but you cannot tell where it comes from or where it is going. So it is with everyone born of the Spirit.

Jesus tells Nicodemus that his decision about him was of the flesh and as far as he could go. Nicodemus now stood in need of something beyond the sphere of the flesh—a miracle. "Flesh gives birth to flesh, but the Spirit gives birth to spirit." Spirit-birth is beyond man. And the Spirit who gives birth cannot be controlled or domesticated. No one can tell him what to do or when to do it. Like the wind, the Spirit's effect can be measured, but you don't know where it came from or where it is going. In the same way, Nicodemus stood in need of the breath of God to blow upon his soul and remake his life. And the moment was urgent: There was no guarantee the Spirit would blow in his direction again.

The Holy Spirit was Nicodemus' only hope of life, and he was helpless to influence it. He could only surrender.

Shortly after God's promise in Ezekiel 36 that he would take from his people their hearts of stone, give them hearts of flesh, and put his Spirit in them, God illustrated the point dramatically:

> The hand of the LORD was upon me, and he brought me out by the Spirit of the LORD and set me in the middle of a valley; it was full of bones. He led me back and forth among them, and I saw a great many bones on the floor of the valley, bones that were very dry. He asked me, "Son of man, can these bones live?"

I said, "O Sovereign LORD, you alone know."

Then he said to me, "Prophesy to these bones and say to them,
'Dry bones, hear the word of the LORD! This is what the Sovereign
LORD says to these bones: I will make breath enter you, and you will
come to life. I will attach tendons to you and make flesh come upon
you and cover you with skin; I will put breath in you, and you will
come to life. *Then you will know that I am the LORD.*'"

So I prophesied as I was commanded. And as I was prophesying, there was a noise, a rattling sound, and the bones came
together, bone to bone. I looked, and tendons and flesh appeared
on them and skin covered them, *BUT there was no breath in them.*
(Ezek. 37:1-8)

Ezekiel was to learn the greatest lesson any preacher or witness can
know. Regardless of the prophet's faithful obedience and the wonderful
noise and activity Ezekiel's preaching produced, his audience remained
dead.

What happens next is a most eloquent expression of why God will
not allow us to succeed apart from prayer. First, God does not say to
Ezekiel, "Stand aside. I'll show you how." Ezekiel remains the instrument. God's plan is to work his redemptive purposes through human
vessels (i.e., "jars of clay"). Nevertheless, there is no mistake: "The
power is from God and not from us"(2 Cor. 4:7):

Then he [the Lord] said to me, "Prophesy to the *breath*; prophesy,
son of man, and say to it, 'This is what the Sovereign LORD says:
*Come from the four winds, O breath, and breathe into these slain, that
they may live.*'" So I prophesied as he commanded me, and breath
entered them; they came to life and stood up on their feet—a vast
army. (vv. 9-10)

And the punch line?

This is what the Sovereign LORD says: "O *my* people, *I* am going to
open your graves and bring you up from them; *I* will bring you back
to the land of Israel. *Then you,* my people, will know that *I* am the
LORD, when *I* open your graves and bring you up from them. I will
put *my* Spirit in you and you will live, and *I* will settle you in your
own land. Then you will know that I the LORD have spoken, and I
have done it, declares the LORD." (vv. 12-14)

In other words, "This work is my work, and I will share my glory with no one!" says the Lord Almighty. As John Piper observes:

> God aims to exalt Himself by working for those who wait for Him. Prayer is the essential activity of waiting for God: acknowledging our helplessness and His power, calling upon Him for help, seeking His counsel. So it is evident why prayer is so often commanded by God, since His purpose in the world is to be exalted for His mercy. Prayer is the antidote for the disease of self-confidence that opposes God's goal of getting glory by working for those who wait for Him.[15]

Piper's statement illustrates the intensity with which men and women must hold fast to the centrality of the Holy Spirit in every spiritual work. The bottom line is what Paul wrote the Corinthians: "The kingdom of God is not a matter of talk but of power" (1 Cor. 4:20).

Charles Spurgeon is worthy of citing at length on this point. While preaching on the subject of revival to a packed house of thousands of people, he explained:

> Dear Friends, we do not know what God may do for us if we do but pray for a blessing [of the Holy Spirit]. Look at the movement we have already seen; we have witnessed Exeter Hall, St. Paul's Cathedral, and Westminster Abbey, crammed to the doors, but we have seen no effect as yet of all these mighty gatherings. Have we not tried to preach without trying to pray? *Is it not likely that the church has been putting forth its preaching hand but not its praying hand?* O dear friends! Let us agonize in prayer, and it shall come to pass that this Music Hall shall witness the sighs and groans of the penitent and the songs of the converted. It shall yet happen that this vast host shall not come and go as now it does, but little the better; but men shall go out of this hall praising God and saying—"It was good to be there; it was none other than the house of God, and the very gate of heaven." Thus much to stir you up to prayer.
>
> . . . [A]ll the stories we have heard [about past revivals] should correct any self-dependence which may have crept into our treacherous hearts. Perhaps we as a congregation have begun to depend upon our numbers and so forth. We may have thought, "Surely God must bless us through the ministry." Now let the stories which our fathers have told us remind you, and remind me, that *God must do it all*; it may be that some hidden preacher, whose name has never been known, some obscure denizen of St. Giles will yet start up in

this city of London and preach the Word with greater power than bishops and ministers have ever known before. I will welcome him; God be with him; let him come from where he may; only let God speed him, and let the work be done. Mayhap, however, God intends to bless the agency used in this place for your good and for your conversion. If so, I am thrice happy to think such should be the case. *But place no dependence upon the instrument.* No, when men laughed at us and mocked us most, God blessed us most; and now it is not a disreputable thing to attend the Music Hall. We are not so much despised as we once were, but I question whether we have so great a blessing as once we had. We would be willing to endure another pelting in the pillory, to go through another ordeal with every newspaper against us, and with every man hissing and abusing us, if God so pleases, if he will but give us a blessing. *Only let him cast out of us any idea that our own bow and our own sword will get us the victory. We shall never get a revival here unless we believe that it is the Lord, and the Lord alone, that can do it!*

Having made this statement, I will endeavor to stir you up with confidence that the result may be obtained that I have pictured, and that the stories we have heard of the olden time, may become true in our day. Why should not every one of my hearers be converted? Is there any limitation in the Spirit of God? Why should not the feeblest minister become the means of salvation to thousands? Is God's arm shortened? My brethren, when I bid you pray that God would make the ministry quick and powerful, like a two-edged sword, for the salvation for sinners, I am not setting you a hard, much less impossible task. We have but to ask and to get. Before we call God will answer; and while we are yet still speaking he will hear. God alone can know what may come of this morning's sermon, if he chooses to bless it. From this moment you may pray more; from this moment God may bless the ministry more. From this hour other pulpits may become more full of life and vigor than before. From this same moment the Word of God may flow, and run, and rush, and get to itself an amazing and boundless victory.

Only wrestle in prayer, meet together in your houses, go to your closets, be instant, be earnest in season and out of season, agonize for souls, and all that you have heard [about past revivals] shall be forgotten in what ye shall see; and all that others have told you shall be as nothing compared with what ye shall hear with your ears, and behold with your eyes in your own midst.[16]

Similarly, when the disciples faced their first internal crisis in Acts, they knew beforehand what could not be compromised. Leaders in the movement of God who have known the priorities of Word and prayer (i.e., the Spirit) were useful to heaven. Leaders who forget this lesson dissipate, blunt, or obstruct the work of Christ. In a word, a prayerless ministry is fruitless because it is godless.

Furthermore, crises like those of Acts 6 should be expected—especially in the wake of great spiritual blessing—because the kingdom of darkness does not want Christians to pray and conspires to thwart prayer. Samuel Chadwick once remarked, "The one concern of the devil is to keep the saints from prayer. He fears nothing from prayerless study, prayerless work, prayerless religion: he laughs at our toil, mocks at our wisdom, but he trembles when we pray." The Reformers coined a verse: "Satan trembles when he sees the weakest saint upon his knees."

We should not find it surprising, then, that at the very time Edwards was mobilizing the Concert of Prayer, he faced his most painful personal and ministry crisis. Neither should we find it surprising that at the time promoters of the Concert were trying to get it rooted in American soil, Edwards ended up out in the hinterlands of western Massachusetts for essentially the rest of his life.

Prayer means spiritual power, the power of Jesus (the Vine) through his people (the branches), and we should rejoice for men and women within the body of Christ who today are reordering their lives and ministries so that prayer is always coupled with the ministry of the Word and with all other ministry.

For a generation Billy Graham has declared emphatically, "There are three things necessary for a successful crusade: the first is prayer, the second is prayer, and the third is prayer." I was Prayer Chairman for the Northern New Jersey Crusade in 1991. On one conference telephone call with Dr. Graham and Ron Hutchcraft about Graham's decision to accept our invitation to New Jersey, his expressed concern wasn't finances, church mobilization, or the growth of our organization. Rather, he asked repeatedly if the people of God were praying. He understood what is so easily neglected.

Along with the tide of praying activities, we should be encouraged by the enormous volume of material produced today about prayer, reminding us of the priorities of Jesus, the pentecostal power of the early church, and testimonies about churches that pray. Books such as *Fresh Wind, Fresh Fire* by Jim Cymbala present local churches and pastors with compelling stories, an emphasis on the Holy Spirit, and the reminder of first things first. Also wonderful are the numbers of Christian leaders who are finding each other in order to seek God.

But let us return once again to the question before us regarding the Concert of Prayer—this call to "extraordinary prayer." As laudable as today's emphases are, particularly the return to the prominence of the Holy Spirit's work, the Concert was not just a means to encourage people to pray or remind them of the Spirit's preeminence. All those who signed on in the 1700s were already prayer warriors of unusual dedication. They did not need a new technology or, at worst, a gimmick or a tickler to encourage a discipline they had already mastered.

The Concert of Prayer proved to be a means to combat spiritual declension. We certainly can relate to the issues of spiritual decline. There is a general sense that spiritual life is sagging badly in Western societies today, calling for an urgency to seek God for help. In an age of moral crises in the presidency; unspeakable violence in our schools, families, and workplaces; a rise in neopaganism and the abandonment of truth and morals, there is a deepening awareness that the challenge before the church is monumental, even irresolvable.

As we have seen, historical moments like our own have helped the church realize that its task is, indeed, beyond its ability. Times like our own have driven Christians to earnest prayer. If you take the periods after the Great Awakening when evangelicals such as Andrew Fuller, James McCready, David Austin, and James Stewart adopted the Concert, you will find that the day was exceedingly dark.

I like the way David Henderson described Andrew Fuller's post-Awakening England. Quoting Charles Dickens, Henderson writes: "It was the best of times, it was the worst of times."[17] England was "a land of great paradoxes . . . [of] great advancement and learning, and . . . unspeakable cruelty and ignorance among the masses."[18] The gin trade was flourishing (vastly more devastating than today's cocaine plague), the slave trade commonplace, and vices rampant. There were mass hangings of men, women, and children (down to the age of ten) in public parks—many for trivial crimes. Rates of illegitimacy were unspeakably high, highwaymen at large endangered travel and commerce, the poor lived in squalid cities, children worked twelve- to fourteen-hour shifts in the mines and factories, gambling exploited the weak, political corruption robbed Britain of justice, and a stagnant church faced an era when the Gospel was brushed aside by the Enlightenment. All of this and more added up to reasons enough for despair. As we heard

Isaac Backus lament, times were equally grim in America. In response, Christians joined together and turned to God in the Concert.

Today Christians feel themselves pushed to the margins of the American agenda. We watch with deep concern as children are taught from "Rainbow Curricula," as AIDS sweeps away thousands, as the venereal disease epidemic grows exponentially, as the disparity between rich and poor reaches historic levels, and cities decay. All the while the church seems desperately unprepared to fulfill its divine objectives. We are driven to wrestling with God for our nation, church, and families.

Harkening back to another desperate time, Spurgeon was moved by the great intercessions of John Knox:

> The famous Welch was . . . a great intercessor for his country; he used to say that he wondered how a Christian could lie in his bed all night and not rise to pray. When his wife, fearing that he would take cold, followed him into the room to which he had withdrawn, she heard him pleading in broken sentences, "Lord, wilt Thou not grant me Scotland?"[19]

We, too, must plead with God for our nation. As Moses, with his face in the ground and refusing water or food, pled with God not to abandon Israel after that nation worshiped the golden calf, we must go to unusual lengths in our pleading. But this does not define the Concert of Prayer.

Praying with other Christians is important, too. The Pietistic emphasis on small-group prayer societies is a lesson from history that all of us need to recapture, especially in the light of the death of the local church prayer meeting. Today's small group ministry gurus have not discovered something new. As we have seen, small prayer groups were critical to the powerful workings of God over the past 300 years. It's a joy to meet with other Christians. It builds us up, keeps us accountable, and provides avenues of service to God. But the Concert of Prayer was not a glorified small-group strategy.

Then there is the issue of unity, which is not just a nice thing (as opposed to divisiveness and a critical spirit). There is enormous spiritual power in unity. Repeatedly generations of evangelical leaders pointed not only to the prayer meeting of Pentecost but to Jesus' promise in Matthew 18:19 as a fundamental promise: "I tell you that if two of you on earth agree about anything you ask for, it will be done for you by my Father in heaven."

Unity among Christians is desirable. Lessons from the centuries teach that God acts powerfully when the differences between Christians are diminished and their commonalities highlighted. In this condition, Christians are able to present a unified front against the problems facing God's kingdom. We are able to complement each other's strengths and weaknesses.

In the days of John Cleaveland, the idea of a parish was particularly strong. One simply did not breech or absorb the boundaries of another man's parish. Parishes were akin to the European fiefdoms where earls and princes were granted by the king regions over which they would rule. Castles stood at the center of towns to protect subjects. The castles were symbols of power and authority. In theory everything belonged to the king, but the reality was that one ruler did not dare to interfere with another's rule. This was a picture of the way ministers saw their parishes. In 1742 Nathaniel Appleton warned against itinerant preachers:

> Ministers leaving their own particular charges, and going place to place, without any regular Call or Desire, intruding themselves into other Men's Parishes; whereby they are in Danger of exciting and gratifying their own Pride, stirring up itching Ears of the People, and leading them away from their Love and Esteem of their own faithful Ministers.[20]

Like Promise Keepers and Prayer Summits, the Concert of Prayer was a means by which this idea was broken down. Even though the earliest Concert was among principally Congregational, Baptist, and Presbyterian churches, the gatherings for prayer reached out across parish boundaries and united disparate saints. The Concert's forerunner, the Moravian prayer societies, had done the same. This development was healthy.

As in the case of Ipswich, too, union prayer meetings maintained a formidable shield against error within the church. Christians praying together buttressed orthodoxy and fostered an evangelical spirit among themselves. United prayer also gave the four churches of Essex a sense of identity that transcended the parochial concerns of each parish. Unity among Christians is powerful and beautiful. The Concert of Prayer preached "visible union" and succeeded in securing it. But unity was not the goal of the Concert.

Similar to today's strategies, the Concert of Prayer also became a great networking mechanism. It brought talented and able men and women together who would never have met otherwise. It galvanized their relationships. We plotted the Whitefield connection among the evangelicals of the 1740s, 1750s, and 1760s. They fashioned a network whereby pulpits were filled, colleges established, and orphanages funded. Correspondence among the leaders was extensive, and important things got done. A network of gifted leaders was a wonderful fruit of the Concert, but that was not its goal.

The Concert of Prayer also increased attendance at evangelical churches. It caused ministries to grow and churches to be built. In the wake of mighty movements of God, the prayer movement showed itself to be an excellent *modus operandi* for church growth. In the most wonderful examples, millions of people were added to the church's ranks in a matter of a few years. But to reduce the Concert to a means of church growth or an incubator in which multiple new endeavors for evangelism are hatched is to ignore its *raison d'être*. Likewise, seeking God for revival and working for successful evangelism are not the same thing.

What then was the Concert of Prayer? It was a movement based on a broad consensus regarding clear theological interpretations of biblical revelation about the nature of history and God's design for the future. It was born out of convictions that say with certainty that, regardless of how bright or dark the hour we live in, God is about to do something greater than he's ever done before. Furthermore, it said that God would not move forward with his ever-increasing and ever more marvelous plans until Christians agreed with him and agreed with each other about what he was going to do. A great and lucid vision of Christ's earthly reign was before their eyes—with every nation, people, tribe, and tongue united as one company before the throne of God, Christ the Son, and the sevenfold Spirit. It was a compelling vision that would not let Christians rest or let go of God until the rule of God held sway in every aspect of life.

This vision was the soil out of which blossomed the abolition of slavery, child labor laws, world missions, mass evangelism, countless revivals, orphanages, public hospitals, mental institutions, colleges, Sunday schools, and housing laws. This vision drove William Booth to establish the Salvation Army and to "invade" city centers to drive out the gin trade and capture whole communities for the sake of righteousness. Lord Teignmouth, former governor-general of India, could be the first president of the British and Foreign Bible Society and a member of the Clapham Sect—a classic prayer society—fighting and praying diligently against slavery.

To these leaders, the vision of the reign of Christ was no pipe dream. Their faith in a glorious future "was the substance of things not seen."[21] People like William Fuller could mourn in his diary regarding the salvation of the lost, but then decry the injustice of the English capitalists and their cruelty toward the East Indies:

> Oh for the time when neither the scepter of oppression nor heathen superstition shall have any sway over them! Lord Jesus, set up Thy glorious and peaceful kingdom all over the world. Found earnest desires this morning in prayer that God would hear the right as to them, and hear our prayers, in which the churches agree to unite *for the spread of Christ's kingdom.*[22]

This hope and conviction was vital since each time the Concert was begun, participants often saw little empirical evidence that the kingdom of God was advancing anywhere. Yet to them the promise of God's greater workings was so real that they could agree with each other "as touching any thing that they shall ask" (Matthew 18:19 KJV) and have confidence that the Father was going to grant the kingdom to them. Wrote Edwards to M'Culloch:

> I think we, and all others, who have lately united by explicit agreement in extraordinary Prayer for general Revival of Religion and the coming of Christ's Kingdom, may, without presumption, be greatly encouraged . . ."if any two of you shall agree on earth as touching any thing you shall ask, it shall be done of my Father which is in heaven;" and, "Before they call, I will answer; and while they are yet preaching, I will hear."[23]

To the Concert and the overall work of the Gospel, the positive perspective Christians held toward history was of incalculable worth and fundamental. Richard Lovelace, in his chapter "Prospects for Renewal" in *Dynamics of Spiritual Life* (a still invaluable resource), quotes nineteenth-century Calvin Colton to emphasize the importance of theological optimism:

> Christians now have only to take advantage of [the certainty that Christianity will be supreme with respect to humankind, and] . . . plant their feet upon this ground, start from this point, and, by one united and vigorous onset, march directly to the conquest of

the world, in the use of the simple and naked weapons of evangelical truth.[24]

This positive view of history made praying urgent, passionate, and
expectant:

> [P]rayer must not be a few cold wishes offered to God as a matter
> of course, or expressed at the conclusion of . . . devotions, merely
> for the sake of making a good finish; but the humble, fervent, ago-
> nizing, and believing intercession of souls travailing in birth for the
> salvation of sinners, and which will not let God rest until he "estab-
> lish Jerusalem, and make her a praise in the earth."[25]

This perspective produced a whole generation of Christians who in
turn, with urgency, passion, and expectancy, became the answer to their
own prayers.

How people feel about the future has a great deal to do with their
praying. At the time when I became Prayer Chairman of the Northern
New Jersey Billy Graham Crusade, I was a leader in a Concert of Prayer
in New Jersey. Mobilizing people to pray was exceedingly hard *until* the
certainty of Dr. Graham's crusade settled in on the Christians of our
region. When they could precisely visualize the impact the crusade
would have on their churches and their neighborhoods, the urgent
delight to pray in concert skyrocketed. Agreement in prayer was powerful because everyone had a comprehension of what a crusade would
do. People's hearts were delighted with the prospects of a divine visitation, and they could articulate what that visitation would look like. My
own parochial experience with a Billy Graham crusade attested to the
power of an articulated, hopeful vision. However, a hopeful vision for
the reign of Christ does not exist today.

In many respects, the relative absence of an optimistic vision is due,
in part, to prevalent eschatologies. While postmillennialism sounds
incredible[26] and is not a significant view, the image of amillennialism
comes across like a shrug of the shoulders, and the predominant strain
of premillennialism sounds like a Bronx cheer at history and
humankind. The image of the church surviving the sinking ship of history, saving as many rats as possible, hardly motivates anyone to claim
the ship as a prize for the eternal King.[27]

Today's predominant premillennialism, and I am in its camp, would
not have compelled Carey to India, Booth into London, or McCready

into the hills of Kentucky. I doubt, too, it would have kept Charles Simeon in Cambridge or inspired the Moravians in their missionary expeditions. Perhaps they would all have moved into the suburbs, homeschooled their kids, and waited for Jesus to return.

The common vision and worldview held by our forefathers made them world Christians. They envisioned every society and every part of society transformed. People like Charles Finney could preach salvation, call for the formation of a "Benevolent Empire," decry slavery, and preach for women's suffrage all in one breath, because his worldview demanded it.

I do not suggest that eighteenth- and nineteenth-century Evangelicals were unanimous about every fine detail of what God was about to do. We heard Whitefield and Carey express reservations about some of Edwards's interpretations, and we witnessed David Austin expanding Edwards's and Bellamy's interpretations into dangerous political realms. In the introduction to *Humble Attempt* itself, the signatories left room for differing opinions on certain matters. But there was broad consensus, and the towering stature of Edwards was the chief reason. Even amillennialists and premillennialists, though each was an evangelical minority from 1750 to 1850, were swept up into an optimistic faith. However these men and women differed, the larger picture was never in doubt: Christ was coming in power to rule the nations and exalt the church, and Christians everywhere were the divinely appointed means in the advancement of this certain end.

Do we need to revisit the past to find our way into the future? I am convinced that we do. To embrace the Concert of Prayer is to reexamine our theologies of history and the Holy Spirit, determine that we will agree on a God-sized vision, articulate it, and hold it. Then as one people, we wrestle with God, refusing to let him go until he blesses us, and we offer ourselves to him to be the answer to our prayers.

Given the climate of today, I cannot image an Edwards-type figure capable of casting a new vision for this generation. But I am convinced it is within our reach if we would be serious about the consequences of not having one and the power inherent within one. Though he is an immensely rich resource and a sterling example, Edwards warns us that the past may not provide all the answers needed to ascertain what God has yet to do:

> . . . by conceiving of revival wholly in terms of some particular past revival . . . [is to] "limit God, where he has not limited himself . . . for whosoever has well weighed the wonderful and mysterious

methods of divine wisdom in carrying on the work of the new creation—or in the progress of the work of redemption, from the first promise to the seed of the woman to this time—may easily observe that it has all along been God's manner to open new scenes, and to bring forth to view things new and wonderful . . . to the astonishment of heaven and earth. . . ."[28]

At the dawn of a new century and millennium, the absence of a compelling vision, our lack of unity and agreement, combined with general prayerlessness, much less extraordinary praying, makes for a disappointing stew. The void allows and encourages a cacophony of visions and plans—doing what's right in our own eyes. Going back to the Concert of Prayer is a well-advised step into our future, pregnant with promise. If we did so, we would not be the first to try. Standing with one foot in the twenty-first century and surveying the enormous challenges and opportunities before us, we can be reminded of leaders who faced similar scenes at the end of the nineteenth century. In 1885 in Northfield, Massachusetts, Dwight L. Moody gathered some of the top evangelical leaders from Western Christianity. As they surveyed the troubled landscape of historic, biblical Christianity and then considered the gargantuan task of spreading the kingdom of Christ over the nations of the earth, they looked back for both inspiration and a model. To Christians everywhere they issued a clarion call titled, "An Appeal to Disciples Everywhere."[29]

To Fellow Believers of every name scattered throughout the world, Greetings:
Assembled in the name of our Lord Jesus Christ, with one accord, in one place, we have continued for ten days in prayer and supplication, communing with one another about the common salvation, the blessed hope, and the duty of witnessing to a lost world.
It was near to our place of meeting that, in 1747, at Northampton,[30] Jonathan Edwards sent forth his trumpet-peal, calling upon disciples everywhere to unite the whole habitable globe. That summons to prayer marks a new era and epoch in the history of the church of God. Praying bands began to gather in this and other lands; mighty revivals of religion followed; immorality and infidelity were wonderfully checked; and, after more than fifteen hundred years of apathy and lethargy, the spirit of missions was reawakened. In 1784, the monthly concert was begun, and in 1792, the first missionary society formed in England; in 1793, William Carey sailed for India. Since then, one hundred missionary boards

have been organized, and probably not less than one hundred thousand missionaries, including women, have gone forth into the harvest-field. The Pillar has moved before these humble laborers, and the two-leaved gates have opened before them, until the whole world is now accessible. The ports and portals of Pagan, Moslem, and even Papal lands are now unsealed, and the last of the hermit nations welcomes the missionary. Results of missionary labor in the Hawaiian and Fiji Islands, in Madagascar, in Japan, probably have no parallel even in apostolic days; while even Pentecost is surpassed by the ingathering of ten thousand converts in one mission station in India within sixty days, in the year 1878. The missionary bands had scarcely compassed the walls and sounded the gospel trumpet, when those walls fell and we have but to march straight on and take possession of Satan's strongholds.

(God has thus, in answer to prayer, opened the door of access to the nations.) Out of the Pillar there comes once more a voice, "Speak unto the children of Israel, that they go forward." And yet the church of God is slow to move in response to the providence of God. Nearly a thousand millions of the human race are yet without the Gospel; vast districts are wholly unoccupied. So few are the laborers, that, if equally dividing responsibility, each must care for at least one hundred thousand souls. And yet there is abundance of both men and means in the church to give the Gospel to every living soul before this century closes. If but ten millions, out of four hundred millions of nominal Christians, would undertake such systematic labor as that each one of that number should, in the course of the next fifteen years, reach one hundred other souls with the gospel message, *the whole present population of the globe would have heard the good tidings by the year 1900!*

Our Lord's own words are, "Go, ye, therefore, and disciple all nations;" and, "This Gospel of the kingdom shall be preached in all the world for a witness unto all nations; and then shall the end come." Peter exhorts us both to "look for and hasten the coming of the day of God;" and what if our inactivity delays His coming? Christ is waiting to "see of the travail of His soul;" and we are impressed that two things are just now of great importance: first, the immediate occupation and evangelization of every destitute district of the earth's population; and, secondly, a new effusion of the Spirit in answer to united prayer.

If at some great centre like London or New York, a great council of evangelical believers could meet, to consider the wonder-working of God's providence and grace in mission fields, and how fields now unoccupied may be insured from further neglect, and to arrange and adjust the work so as to prevent needless waste and friction among workmen, it might greatly further the glorious object of a world's evangelization; and we earnestly commend the suggestion to the prayerful consideration of the various bodies of organizations. What a spectacle it would present both to angels and men, could believers of every name, forgetting all things in which they differ, meet, by chosen representatives, to enter systematically and harmoniously upon the work of sending forth laborers into every part of the world-field!

But, above all else, our immediate and imperative need is a new spirit of earnest and prevailing prayer. The first Pentecost crowned ten days of united, continued supplication. Every subsequent advance may be directly traced to believing prayer, and upon this must depend a new Pentecost. We therefore earnestly appeal to all fellow-disciples to join us and each other in importunate daily supplication for a new and mighty effusion of the Holy Spirit upon all ministers, missionaries, evangelists, pastors, teachers, and Christian workers, and upon the whole earth; that God would impart to all Christ's witnesses the tongues of fire, and melt hearts before the burning message. It is not by might nor by power, but by the Spirit of the Lord, that all true success must be secured. Let us call upon God till He answereth by fire! What we are to do for the salvation of the lost must be done quickly; for the generation is passing away, and we with it. Obedient to our marching orders, let us "go into the world, and preach the Gospel to every creature," while from our very hearts we pray, "Thy kingdom come."

Grace, mercy, and peace be with you all.

Done in convention at Northfield, Mass., August 14, 1885, [Dwight L.] Moody presiding.

> Committee:
> Arthur T. Pierson, Philadelphia,
>> Presbyterian, Chairman.
> A. J. Gordon, Boston, Baptist.
> L. W. Munhall, Indianapolis, Methodist.
> Geo. F. Pentecost, Brooklyn, N.Y.,
>> Congregationalist.
> William Ashmore, Missionary to Swatow,
>> China, Baptist.
> J. E. Studd, London, England,
>> Church of England.
> Miss E. Dryer, Chicago Avenue Church.

A similar call has gone out in our day, May 1999, issued by nearly 200 evangelical leaders in the United States. It ran as a full-page advertisement in *USA Today* (see Appendix 3). Perhaps the 1999 call will falter. Perhaps we will find the appropriate courage, passion, theology, and divinely imparted dreams to drive it. Did Moody *et al.* find theirs? Though world missions have thrived over the past century and the pleasure of the Lord has been evident, there have been no corresponding revivals of international consequence in the West. The church in Europe has been laid waste, the church in the British Isles is close behind, and that of the United States is making sounds as if she will follow. The American church has less influence upon our culture today than at any time since the 1790s. Fortunately, the cultural context is not nearly so grave as then. Members of the 1885 Northfield Convention would have mixed emotions if they could look back over the last 100 years. Only part of their dreams were realized, another part is dissolving. They did, however, have the wisdom to look back. We have reasons to rejoice over the twentieth century. But we also have reasons to mourn—and then look back to unspeakably rich eras and learn. May God stir our hearts, grant to us new dreams and visions for our generation and beyond, and pour out a "spirit of grace and supplication" to fit them.

Appendix 1

Call to Prayer from Scotland

A MEMORIAL *from several Ministers* in Scotland, *to their Brethren in different Places, for continuing a* Concert for Prayer, *first entered into in the Year* 1744.[1]

Whereas it was the chief Scope of this *Concert*, to promote more abundant Application to a Duty that is perpetually binding, *Prayer that our Lord's Kingdom may come*, join'd with *Praises*:

I. And it contain'd some circumstantial Expedients, apprehended to be very subservient to that Design, relating to stated Times for such Exercises, so far as this would not interfere with other Duties; particularly a Part of *Saturday-Evening*, and *Sabbath-Morning*, every Week; and more solemnly of some One of the *first Days* of each of the Four great Divisions of the Year, that is, of each *Quarter*; as the first *Tuesday*, or first convenient Day after: And the Concert, as to this Circumstance, was extended only to *two Years*; it being intended, that before these expired, Persons engaged in the *Concert* should reciprocally communicate their Sentiments and Inclinations, as to the *prolonging* of Time, with or without Alteration, as to the Circumstance mention'd: And it was intended by first Promoters, that others at a *Distance* should propose such circumstantial *Amendments* or *Improvements*, as they should find proper: It is hereby earnestly entreated, that such would communicate their Sentiments accordingly, now that the Time first proposed is near expiring.

II. To induce those already engaged to adhere, and others to accede to this Concert; it seems of Importance to observe, that *Declarations of Concurrence*, the communicating and spreading of which are so evidently useful, are to be understood in such a *Latitude*, as to keep at the greatest Distance from *entangling* Men's Minds: Not as binding to Men to set apart any fixed Days from secular Affairs, or even to fix on any Part of such and such a precise Day, whether it be convenient or not; nor as *absolute* Promises in any Respect: But as *friendly, harmonious Resolutions*, with

Liberty to alter Circumstances as shall be found expedient. On account of all which Latitude, and that the circumstantial Part extends only to a few Years, it is apprehended, the *Concert* cannot be liable to the Objections against *periodical* religious Times of human Appointment.

III. It is also humbly offered to the Consideration of Ministers, and others furnished with Gifts for the most publick Instructions, Whether it might not be of great Use, by Blessing God, if short and nervous scriptural *Persuasives* and *Directions to the Duty in View, were compos'd and published* (either by particular Authors, or several joining together; which last Way might some Times have peculiar Advantages) *and that from Time to Time*, without too great Intervals; the better to keep alive on Men's Minds a just Sense of the Obligation to a Duty so important in itself, and in which many may be in Danger to faint and turn remiss, with such repeated Incitements: And *whether it would not also be of great Use, if Ministers would be pleas'd to preach frequently on the Importance and Necessity of Prayer for the Coming of our Lord's Kingdom*; particularly near the Quarterly Days, or on these Days themselves, where there is publick Worship at the Time.

IV. They who have found it incumbent on them to publish this *Memorial* at this Time, having peculiar Advantages for spreading it, do entreat that the Desire of *Concurrence* and *Assistance* contain'd in it, may by no Means be understood as restricted to any particular *Denomination* or *Party*, or to those who are OF such or have such Opinions about any former Instances of remarkable religious Concern, but to be extended to *All*, who shall vouchsafe any Attention to the Paper, and have at Heart the Interest of *vital Christianity*, and the *Power of Godliness*, and who, however different about other Things, are convinc'd of the Importance of fervent *Prayer*, to promote that common Interest, and of Scripture-Persuasives to promote such Prayer.

V. As the first printed Account of this *Concert* was not a *Proposal* of it, as a Thing then to begin, but a Narration of it, as a Design *already* set on Foot, which had been brought about with much Harmony, by Means of private *Letters*; so the farther Continuance, and, 'tis hop'd, the farther Spreading of it seems in a promising Way of being promoted by the same Means; as importunate Desires of the *renewing the Concert* have been transmitted already from a very different Corner abroad, where the Regard to it has of late increased: But notwithstanding of what may be done by private Letters, it is humbly expected, that a *Memorial* spread in this Manner, may, by God's blessing, farther promote the good Ends in View; as it may be usefully refer'd to in Letters, and may reach where they will not.

VI. Whereas in a valuable Letter, from the Corner just now mentioned as a Place where regard to the *Concert* has lately increased, it is proposed, that it should be continued for *Seven Years*, or at least for a much longer Time than what was specified in the first Agreement; those concern'd in this *Memorial*, who would rather receive and spread *Directions* and *Proposals* on this Head, than to be the first Authors of any, apprehend no Inconvenience, for their Part, in agreeing to the *Seven Years*, with the *Latitude* above describ'd, which reserves Liberty to make such circumstantial Alterations, as may be hereafter found expedient: On the contrary it seems of Importance, that the Labour of spreading a *Concert*, which has already extended to so distant Parts, and may, it is hoped, extend farther, may not need to be *renewed* sooner, at least much sooner; as it is uncertain but *that* may endanger the *dropping* of it; and it seems probable, there will be less Zeal in spreading of it, if the Time propos'd for its Continuance be too inconsiderable.——Mean Time, Declaration of Concurrence for a *lesser* Number of Years may greatly promote the good Ends in View: Tho' it seems very expedient, that it should exceed what was first agreed on; seeing it is found on Trial, that Time, instead of being too long, was much too short.

VII. If Persons who formerly agreed to this *Concert* should now *discontinue* it; would it not look too like that *Fainting in Prayer*, against which we are so expressly warn'd in Scripture? And would not this be the more unsuitable at *this Time*, if any within the *British* Dominions, when they have the united Calls of such *publick Chastisement* and *Deliverances*, to more Concern than ever about *publick Reformation*, and consequently about that which is the *source* of all thorough Reformation, the *regenerating* and *Sanctifying* Influence of the almighty *Spirit* of GOD?

—*August* 26, 1746.

At the end of the memorial Jonathan Edwards added, "The Ministers in *Boston* fore-mention'd[2] (to whom most of the Copies of this *Memorial* were sent) who, I suppose, have had later and more full Intelligence than I have had, say, concerning the Proposal, in a Letter,—*The Motion seems to come from Above, and to be wonderfully spreading in* Scotland, England, Wales, Ireland, *and* North-America."

Appendix 2

William Carey's *Enquiry*

Excerpts from *An Enquiry into the Duty of Christians in general, and what Means ought to be used, in order to promote this Work.*[1]

If the prophecies concerning the increase of Christ's kingdom be true, and if what has been advanced, concerning the commission given by him to his disciples being obligatory on us, be just, it must be inferred that all Christians ought heartily to concur with God in promoting his glorious designs, for *he that is joined to the Lord is one Spirit.*

On the first, and most important of those duties which are incumbent upon us, is *fervent and united prayer.* However the influence of the Holy Spirit may be set at naught, and run down by many, it will be found upon trial, that all means which we can use, without it, will be ineffectual. If a temple is raised for God in the heathen world, it will not be *by might, nor by power,* nor by the authority of the magistrate, or the eloquence of the orator; *but by my Spirit, saith the Lord of Hosts.* We must therefore be in real earnest in supplicating his blessing upon our labours.

It is represented in the prophets, that when there shall be *a great mourning in the land, as the mourning of Hadadrimmon in the valley of Megiddon, and every family shall mourn apart, and their wives apart,* it shall all follow upon a *Spirit of grace, and supplication.* And when these things shall take place, it is promised that *there shall be a fountain opened for the house of David, and for the inhabitants of Jerusalem, for sin, and for uncleanness,*—and that *the idols shall be destroyed,* and *the false prophets ashamed* of their profession (Zech. 12:10, 14—13:1, 6). This prophecy seems to teach that when there shall be an universal conjunction in fervent prayer, and all shall esteem Zion's welfare as their own, then copious influences of the Spirit shall be shed upon the churches, which like a purifying *fountain* shall cleanse the servants of the Lord. Nor shall this cleansing influence stop here; all old idolatrous prejudices shall be rooted out, and truth prevail so gloriously that false teachers shall be so ashamed as rather to wish to be classed with obscure herdsmen, or the meanest peasants, than bear the ignominy attendant on their detection.

The most glorious works of grace that have ever took [sic] place have been in answer to prayer; and it is in this way, we have the greatest reason to suppose, that the glorious out-pouring of the Spirit, which we expect at last, will be bestowed.

With respect to our own immediate connections, we have within these few years been favoured with some tokens for good, granted in answer to prayer, which should encourage us to persist, and increase in that important duty. I trust our *monthly prayer-meetings* for the success of the gospel have not been in vain. It is true a want of importunity too generally attends our prayers; yet unimportunate, and feeble as they have been, it is to be believed that God has heard, and in a measure answered them. The churches that have engaged in the practice have in general since that time been evidently on the increase; some controversies which have long perplexed and divided the church, are more clearly stated than ever; there are calls to preach the gospel in many places where it has not been usually published; yea, a glorious door is opened, and is likely to be opened wider and wider, by the spread of civil and religious liberty, accompanied also by a diminution of the spirit of popery. . . . If an holy solicitude had prevailed in all the assemblies of Christians in behalf of their Redeemer's kingdom, we might probably have seen before now, not only an *open door* for the gospel, but *many running to and fro, and knowledge increases*; or a diligent use of those means which providence has put in our power, accompanied with a greater blessing than ordinary from heaven. . . . We must not be contented however with praying, without *exerting ourselves in the use of the means* for obtaining of those things we pray for. We're *the children of the light*, but *as wise in their generation as the children of this world*, they would stretch every nerve to gain so glorious prize, nor ever imagine that it was to be obtained in any other way.

Appendix 3

National Prayer Accord

This copy of the National Accord appeared as an advertisement in *USA Today*, April 26, 1999.

DECLARATION OF DEPENDENCE

For more than two centuries, our national motto has been "In God We Trust." These powerful words were originally intended to express our dependence upon God for His favor and blessing. The Holy Scriptures teach us that the ills and misfortunes of any nation are a reflection of the spiritual condition of Christ's Church. Historically speaking, there have been many times when facing adversity or difficulty, the Church and our nation have entrusted themselves afresh to God. This has often been expressed by joining our hearts in united prayer regardless of denominational background. Psalm 33:12 says, "**Blessed is the nation whose God is the Lord.**"

We, the undersigned, want you to know that our greatest desire is to see our nation truly blessed by the Lord God. Therefore, we are publishing this "Declaration" as an expression of our concern for the Church in America and our love for our nation. This desire is neither politically nor economically motivated; rather, it comes from a fervent desire that our nation and our people continue to enjoy the benefits of God's favor. To disregard Him or the counsel of His Word, the Bible, is to risk becoming the object of His discipline.

Therefore, we, the undersigned, have urged our churches to unite in a national accord of prayer with us by distributing "A Nationwide Call to Prayer to the Church in America" in our churches. Additionally, we are urging all other churches and Christians who perhaps have not yet seen this "Call" to also distribute it in their churches. Finally, we invite all churches and all Christians to join us in this national accord of prayer by observing the National Day of Prayer on May 6, 1999. May the Lord bless you and our nation as we unite our hearts in prayer before Him.

A Nationwide Call to Prayer to the Church in America

A CALL FOR EXTRAORDINARY PRAYER

In recognition of:

- Our absolute dependence upon God
- The moral and spiritual crises facing our nation
- Our national need for repentance and divine intervention
- Our great hope for a general awakening to the lordship of Christ, the unity of His Body, and the sovereignty of His Kingdom
- The unique opportunity that the dawn of a new millennium presents to us for offering the Gospel of Christ to everyone in our nation

WE STRONGLY URGE all churches and all Christians of America to unite in seeking the face of God through prayer and fasting, persistently asking our Father to send revival to the Church and spiritual awakening to our nation so that Christ's Great Commission might be fulfilled worldwide in our generation.

A CALL FOR UNITED ACTION

Therefore, we humbly yet strongly request all churches and all Christians to join together, at a minimum, in the following five patterns of prayer:

- By *daily* spending time with the Lord in prayer and in the reading of His Word so as to yield ourselves fully to the control and empowerment of the Holy Spirit,
- By *weekly* humbling ourselves before God by designating a day or part of a day (Friday, if possible) for united prayer with fasting as the Lord leads,
- By **monthly** designating in individual churches one service for concerted prayer, emphasizing this call, with special focus on its neighborhood applications,
- By **quarterly** assembling in multi-church prayer events emphasizing this call, with special focus on its citywide applications,
- By **annually** participating in the nationwide prayer events emphasizing this call, with special focus on its national and global applications.

Keep this call in your Bible for daily prayer. If you would like more information regarding this call, national prayer events, ongoing strategic plans, or prayer resources, visit the National Prayer Committee website at *www.nationalprayer.org*.

SIGNATURES

Dr. Billy Graham - Billy Graham Evangelistic Association
Dr. Bill Bright - Founder, Campus Crusade for Christ
Bishop George McKinney - Church of God in Christ
Dr. John Perkins - Christian Community Development Association
Dr. Paul Cedar - Chairman, Mission America

CHURCH LEADERS

A. L. Berry, The Lutheran Church
George Battle, African Methodist Episcopal Zion
Lynford Becker, Mennonite Brethren Churches
Maurice Bingham, Church of Christ Holiness, USA
Ron Black, General Association of General Baptists
Richard Blank, Southern Methodist Church
Stuart Briscoe, Elmbrook Church
Dave Butts, Christian Church/Church of Christ
Roderick Caesar, Bethel Gospel Tabernacle Fellowship
Clifford Christensen, Conservative Congregational Christian Conference

Ed Davis, Evangelical Presbyterian Church
John DelTurco, Christian Church of North America
David Engelhard, Christian Reformed Church in North America
George Estes, Board of Missions Presbyterian (Cumberland)
Rev. Jerry Falwell, Thomas Road Bible Church
Jeff Farmer, Open Bible Churches
Edward Foggs, Church of God
H.Eddie Fox, World Evangelical Methodist Council
James Gee, Pentecostal Church of God
Paul Gilchrist, American Evangelical Orthodox Church
Prince Gibson, National Baptist Convention of America
Bill Hamel, Evangelical Free Church
David Hansley, Convention of Original Free Will Baptists
Jack Hayford, Church on the Way
James B. Henry, First Baptist Church, Orlando
E.V. Hill, National Baptist Convention USA
Clyde Hughes, International Pentecostal Church of Christ
Todd Hunter, Association of Vineyard Churches
Cecil Johnson, Church of God, Mountain Assembly, Inc.
Richard Kohl, Evangelical Congregational Church
Ted Lanes, Assemblies of God International Fellowship
James Leggett, International Pentecostal Holiness Church
Nathaniel Linsey, Christian Methodist Episcopal Church
Don Long, International Church of Four Square Gospel
Kirk Looper, Seventh Day Baptist General Conference
Max Lucado, Oak Hills Church of Christ
Hugh Magers, Episcopal Church Center
Ed Mitchell, CBA of America
P. J. Moore, Conservative Lutheran Association
John Moran, The Missionary Church, Inc. U.S.
Charles Mylander, Friends of the Southwest
Robert Overgaard, Sr., Church of the Lutheran Brethren
Bob Reccord, Southern Baptist Convention
Robert Ricker, Baptist General Conference
Adrian Rogers, Bellevue Baptist Church
David Ross, Advent Christian General Conference
Donald Roth, Evangelical Mennonite Church
Robert Schmitz, Midwest Congregational Christian Fellowship
Robert Schuller, Crystal Cathedral
John Sills, The Evangelical Church of North America
Chester Smith, Congregational Holiness Church
Bennett Smith, Progressive National Convention
Reilly Smith, The Brethren Church
W. T. Sneal, National Missionary Baptist Convention of America
Richard Snyder, Free Methodist Church of North America
Jack Stone, Church of the Nazarene
Roger Swanson, United Methodist Church
Daniel Tipton, Church of Christ in Christian Union
Joseph Tkach, Worldwide Church of God
Thomas Trask, Assemblies of God
Robert Uhrig, Christian Union

George Veach, Elim Fellowship
Lamar Vest, National Association of Evangelicals
Paul Walker, Church of God
Rick Warren, Saddleback Community Church
Robert Watson, The Salvation Army
Daniel Weiss, American Baptist Churches
Oswill Williams, Church of God of Prophecy
Ed. Williamson, Evangelical Methodist Church
Pat Wilson, Pentecostal Church of God
Harry Wood, The Wesleyan Church
Melvin Worthington, National Association of Free Will Baptists
Wayne Yarnall, Primitive Methodist Church
Philip Yntema, North American Baptist Conference

CHRISTIAN MINISTRY LEADERS

Lonnie Allison, Billy Graham Center
Don Argue, Northwest College
Bill Atwood, The Ekklesia Society
Robert Bakke, National Broadcast Concert of Prayer
Reinhard Bonnke, Christ for All Nations
Vonette Bright, Women Today International
David Bryant, Concerts of Prayer International
Luis Bush, AD 2000 and Beyond Movement
Bobbye Byerly, World Prayer Center
Patricia Chen, First Love Ministries International
Evelyn Christenson, AD 2000 Women's Track
Robert Coleman, Trinity Evangelical Divinity School
Charles Colson, Prison Fellowship
Loren Cunningham, Youth with a Mission
Martin De Haan, RBC Ministries
James Dobson, Focus on the Family
Shirley Dobson, Focus on the Family
Stephen B. Douglass, Campus Crusade for Christ
Ted W. Engstrom, World Vision
Paul Fleischmann, National Network of Youth Ministries
Leighton Ford, Leighton Ford Ministries
Tom Fortson, Promise Keepers
Millard Fuller, Habitat for Humanity
Dave Gibson, Mission America
Mary Glazier, Wind Walkers International
John Guest, John Guest Evangelistic Team
Brandt Gustavson, National Religious Broadcasters
Jane Hanson, Aglow International
James Heidinger, Good News Movement
Sterling W. Huston, Billy Graham Evangelistic Association
Jerry Kirk, Coalition for Protection of Children and Families
Cleon Laughlin, Evangelistic Missionary Fellowship
Larry Lewis, Mission America
Steve Macchia, Vision New England
John C. Maxwell, INJOY
Bill McCartney, Promise Keepers

Paul McKaughan, Evangelical Fellowship of Mission Agencies
Jesse Miranda, AMEN
James Montgomery, Dawn Ministries
Harold L. Myra, Christianity Today
Dellanna O'Brien, Women's Missionary Union
Lloyd John Ogilvie, U.S. Senate Chaplain
Luis Palau, Luis Palau Evangelistic Association
Roger Parrott, Bethaven College
Dan Peterson, Great Commission Prayer Movement
Tom Phillips, International Students, Inc.
Pat Robertson, Christian Broadcasting Network
Robert A. Seiple, U.S. State Department
Dal Shealy, Fellowship of Christian Athletes
Ron Sider, Evangelicals for Social Action
Mary Lance Sisk, Love Your Neighbor Ministries
Richard E. Stearns, World Vision
Thomas Wang, Great Commission International
John Williams, Jr., Evangelical Friends
Ralph Winter, U.S. Center for World Missions
Ravi Zacharias, Ravi Zacharias International Ministries

WOULD YOU LIKE MORE INFORMATION? CONTACT US.

MISSION AMERICA
5666 Lincoln Drive, Suite 100
Edina, MN 55436 or
e-mail: *missionamerica@compuserve.com*

NATIONAL DAY OF PRAYER TASK FORCE
P. O. Box 15616
Colorado Springs, CO 80935-5616 or
e-mail: *ndptf@aol.com*

AMERICA'S NATIONAL PRAYER COMMITTEE
For more information on the national prayer movement, visit our website at *www.nationalprayer.org* or call toll free 1-877-NOW-HOPE.

NATIONALLY BROADCAST CONCERT OF PRAYER
To find out how you can link up by radio, TV or internet to a national prayer meeting contact: *www.concertofprayer.org*

NOTES

INTRODUCTION

1   "To God Be the Glory," by Fanny J. Crosby and William H. Doane.

2   To my embarrassment, I later discovered that only seventy people from my own congregation showed up. David Bryant later explained that a weak turnout from the host church is common.

3   See David Bryant, "Special Report: The Most Hopeful Sign of Our Times: A Growing Prayer Movement Points America Toward Spiritual Revival," *National & International Religion Report*, Stephen M. Wike, Publisher. Copyright 1992 by Media Management, P.O. Box 21433, Roanoke, VA 24018.

4   In 1992 *Intercessors for America*, a twenty-year-old prayer movement headquartered in Washington, D.C., emblazoned across its newsletter (November 1992, Vol. 19, No. 11) a picture of Jonathan Edwards and four inches of large-font copy quoting from his treatise calling for Concerts of Prayer. Over the copy was written: "Walking Out the Vision of America's Christian Founders."

CHAPTER 1: FIRST THINGS FIRST

1   J. I. Packer, *Knowing God* (Downers Grove, Ill.: InterVarsity Press, 1973), p. 24.

2   E. Stanley Jones, "How to Pray," *The Christian Advocate*, 1945.

3   Os Guinness, *The Dust of Death* (Wheaton, Ill.: Crossway Books, 1994), p. 385.

4   See Isaiah 56:7; Matthew 21:13; Mark 11:17.

CHAPTER 2: EDWARDS, PRAYER SOCIETIES, CAMBUSLANG, AND THE CONCERT OF PRAYER

1   Jonathan Edwards was tutored by his grandfather, Solomon Stoddard, who pastored his church for sixty years. Stoddard was convinced about the cycles of renewal and decline in the church, having seen five "harvests," as he called them, in his Northhampton church (1679, 1683, 1696, 1712, and 1718). In a sermon entitled "On the Outpouring of the Spirit of God" (printed by B. Green of Boston) written in 1712, the same year as one of those "harvests," Stoddard taught the following:

Doctrine: There are some special Seasons wherein God doth in a remarkable manner revive Religion among his people.

Use: Q. How is it with a people when Religion is revived?

Saints are quickened. It contributes much to the flourishing of Religion, when righteous men flourish in Holiness. . . .

Sinners are converted. God makes the Gospel at times to be very powerful. . . . There is a mighty Change wrought in a little Time.

Many that are not Converted do become more Religious. . . . When God works savingly upon some . . . the Reputation of Religion is advanced, and People are disposed to keep the external convenant.

Observation: This reviving is sometimes of longer, and sometimes of shorter Continuance. God is very Arbitrary [unpredictable] in this matter. The people of God are praying and waiting for this Mercy . . . but God will take his own time for this Mercy.

2   For an overview of the early 1740s move of God in Jonathan Edwards's town, see "The State of Religion at Northampton in the County of Hampshire, About 100 Miles Westward of Boston," published in *The Christian History*, Vol. 1, (January 14, 21, 28, 1743), and also in S. E. Dwight's *Life of President Edwards*.

3   Father of the future vice president, Aaron Burr, Jr., renowned pastor and one of the founders of Princeton University.

4   This work will be referred to as *Humble Attempt* from this point forward.

5   One of the reasons for the lack of scholarly attention to this piece has to do with how scholars view the work. Stephen Stein, for example, writes that Edwards's apocalyptic writings, of which *Humble Attempt* is a part, are an "embarrassment to some students of American thought. . . . Few people in the twentieth century share his enthusiasm for the Apocalypse; even fewer will find Edwards's interpretation persuasive or intellectually respectable. Those committed to contemporary apocalypticism will probably judge his reflections inappropriate for devotional literature." Stephen J. Stein, ed., *The Works of Jonathan Edwards,* Vol. 5, *Apocalyptic Writings* (New Haven and London: Yale University Press, 1977), p 1. In his Acknowledgments, Stein wonders out loud what value there was in his efforts to examine Edwards's apocalyptic ideas.

6   Among the top candidates for his most important work are Edwards's account of the Northampton revival, *Faithful Narrative of the Surprising Works of God,* because it became a benchmark for pastors and leaders with regard to reporting and testing true awakening and because through its twenty printings it prepared the American colonies for the outbreak of the Great Awakening (see J. I. Packer, *Jonathan Edwards and the Theology of Revival,* from *Increasing in the Knowledge of God*, papers read at the Puritan and Reformed Studies Conference, 1960, p. 15), and The *Life of David Brainerd*, which was found in the suitcase of virtually every missionary for a hundred years after Edwards's death. As we shall see, however, *Humble Attempt* left a remarkable legacy of its own.

7   "Universal."

8   Stein, ed., *Humble Attempt*, in *Apocalyptic Writings*, Vol. 5, p. 38.

9   Ibid., pp. 446-47.

10   Ibid., pp. 444-45. From Edwards's letter to a correspondent in Scotland (printed originally in *The Christian Monthly,* ed. James Robe, No. 8 [November 1745], pp. 234-54). John M'Laurin of Glasgow was probably the unnamed correspondent. Edwards forwarded three copies of the invitation to COP to his close friend Joseph Bellamy (1719-90), president of Yale: "I have lately received a pacquet from Scotland, with several Copies of a memorial, for the continuing of propagating an agreement for joint prayer, for the general Revival of Religion; those of which I have I send you desiring you to dispose of them where they will be most serviceable. For my part I heartily have complied with that which is fallen in with by all from the rising to the setting sun." (Letter from Jonathan Edwards to Joseph Bellamy. Northampton, January 15, 1746, p. 47. Jonathan Edwards MSS, folder XXXIX. 7. C. Yale College Archives.)

11   See Arthur Fawcett, *The Cambuslang Revival* (London: Banner of Truth, 1971), p. 58ff. See also J. Woodward, *Account of the Rise of the Religious Societies,* 3rd ed. (London), 1701.

12   Stein, ed., *Apocalyptic Writings*, Vol. 5, p. 37. Stein wonders about this openly.

13   Little of what Spener wrote could be considered original. He was indebted to theologian Johann Arndt (1555-1621) and others. In fact *Pia Desideria* was first written as a preface to the republishing of Arndt's book *True Christianity.*

14   Spener's *Pia Desideria* (1675) was his formal call to revival within a declining Lutheran church, but the prototype to *Pia Desideria* was first proposed in 1669 and then instituted the following year as the *collegia pietatis* ("pious assembly").

15   *Christian History,* Vol. 5, No. 2 (published by Christian History Institute), 1986, p. 13.

16   Lecky in his *History of Morals* writes of Wesley's conversion on May 24, 1738: "What happened in that little room was of more importance to England than all the victories of Pitt by land or sea." See John Greenfield, *Power from on High* (Edinburgh: Marshall, Morgan and Scott, 1927).

17   As a leader of the prayer societies movement, Horneck was widely influential. "In 1673, Horneck (Church of England) of London, preached a number of what he called 'awakening sermons.' As a result several young men began to meet together weekly in order to build up one another in the Christian faith. They gathered in small groups at certain fixed locations, and their places of meeting became known as Society rooms. In these gather-

ings they read the Bible, studied religious books and prayed; they also went out among the poor to relieve want at their own expense and to show kindness to all. This activity was recognized by the Church of England, rules were laid out to govern it, and the work grew so that by 1730 nearly one hundred of these Societies existed in London, and others—perhaps another hundred—were to be found in cities and towns throughout England. The Societies movement became, in many senses, the cradle of the Revival, and a knowledge of it is essential to an understanding of Whitefield's early ministry and of John Wesley's organization." (Arnold A. Dallimore, *George Whitefield: The Life and Times of the Great Evangelist of the Eighteenth-Century Revival*, Vol. 2 [Westchester, Ill.: Cornerstone Books, 1979], p. 29.) Horneck's influence guided the establishment and management of the Holy Club of which Whitefield and Wesley were members (Ibid., p. 88).

18   Woodward, *Religious Societies*, p. 23-29.

19   Ibid.

20   Since many of the things Spener wrote about in *Pia* were not original to himself, it is no surprise that much of what he espoused could be found prior to 1675, and not in Europe alone but in England as well. For example, religious societies meeting for prayer and Bible reading were also found in England during the seventeenth century. When Robert Baillie was in London for the Westminster Assembly, he wrote home to Scotland on August 10, 1645: "Truly the godly here are a praying people," noting further that their practice was to meet in small groups in private homes. (Robert Wodrow, *Analecta, or Materials for a History of Remarkable Providences &c,* Vol. 3, Maitland Club edn. [Glasgow, 1842], pp. 444-46.)

21   Ibid.

22   Ibid.

23   "Henry Scougal (1650-1678), the saintly Professor of Theology in King's College, Aberdeen, . . . was made constant president among his fellow-students at their private meetings for prayer. Fervent Presbyterians and pious Episcopalians were at one here." (Fawcett, *Cambuslang*, quoting Henry Scougal, *The Life of God &c* [Edinburgh, 1747], p. 274.)

The first organized effort to forward missionary activity beyond the seas was undertaken by the [Scottish] Society for Propagating Christian Knowledge [S.S.P.C.K.] "[b]eginning in a small prayer society of lawyers, and inspired by an Episcopalian minister. . . . In 1709 Queen Anne gave the society Letters of Patent" (ibid., p. 213). David Brainerd, Jonathan Edwards's would-be son-in-law, was among the first of their missionaries commissioned.

24   "In the diary of Alexander Johnstone . . . we have the chronicle of this overseer of roads in east Stirlingshire. A prominent elder in Bothkennar Church, he sat in the General Assembly. On Wednesday, September 3, 1723, his entry reads: 'Met with the society for prayer, who had appointed this day from ten in the morning to six at night, to be spent in religious duties . . .' [included were the names of men from the different professions and some social leaders of the community]." (Fawcett, *Cambuslang*, p. 67, quoting from *Records of the Scottish Church History Society*, Recs. Vol. 4, pp. 266-72.)

In 1731 in his prayer society, Wodrow paid tribute to John Dundas of Philipstown, "Clerk to this Church twenty-eight years." In 1698 Dundas describes his society:

> This private meeting laid the first foundation of that noble design of reformation of manners in King William's time. . . . About ten years later, they gave the first beginnings to the Society for Propagation of Christian Knowledge and Reformation of the Highlands and Islands, which has come to so great a length. How great a matter doth some times a little good fire kindle! They concerted subscriptions, they formed the charter to be expeded by [the] Queen, and brought the matters to an excellent bearing; and all as a little weekly society for prayer and conference upon Christian purposes! There were but eight or ten members, lauers. . . . Now and then, some of the Ministers of Edinburgh met with them, and all they did was in concert with them, joyned in prayer (quoted by Fawcett, ibid., p. 55).

25   Spener's vision for Pietism emphasized an energized laity.

26   Letter of Samuel Rutherford, "The Deliverance of the Kirk of God," regarding a contro-

versy in the General Assembly concerning the lawfulness of home meetings for Bible study and prayer.

27   "When in 1740 the Associate Presbytery (the Seceders) was formed in Scotland, among their first orders of business was the formation of prayer societies with complete rules governing their operation" (Fawcett, *Cambuslang*, p. 70).

28   For a brief overview of Pietism's spread in America, see Donald Durnbaugh, "The Flowering of Pietism in the Garden of America," *Christian History*, Vol. 5, No. 2, p. 23ff.

29   Ibid., p. 19.

30   Tennent was eventually persuaded by other Great Awakening heroes (including Edwards) to let the college die and join the founding of a more appropriate—and accredited—institution: The College of New Jersey, or Princeton.

31   *The Christian History*, May 28, 1743, Vol. 43, No. 13, p. 97.

32   Dr. Increase Mather in a treatise entitled *Pray for the Rising Generation*, printed in 1678, writes as follows:

> Prayer is needful on the Account, in that CONVERSIONS are becoming *rare* in the Age of the World. They that have their thoughts exercised in discerning Things of this Nature, have had sad Apprehensions with Reference unto this Matter; That the Work of Conversion hath been at a great Stand in the World. In the last Age, in the Days of our Fathers, in other Parts of the World, *scarce a Sermon preached but* some *evidently converted*, and sometimes *hundreds in a sermon*. Which of us can say we have seen the like? *Clear, sound* CONVERSIONS ARE NOT FREQUENT IN SOME CONGREGATIONS. The Body of the *rising Generation* is a *poor, perishing*, unconverted, and (except the Lord pour down his Spirit) an *undone Generation*." (Ibid., pp. 97-98)

Showing that his concern for the spiritual state of New England was persistent and long-lived, Mather also wrote *The Glory Departing from New England*, printed 1702.

33   *Private Meetings Animated and Regulated* (Boston: T. Green, 1706), pp. 4-23. (Widener Microforms: Microfiche W 2571 [1263] Microfiche [New York: Readex Microprint, 1985] 11 x 15 cm. Early American Imprints, 1st ser., no. 1263.)

34   *Private Meetings Animated and Regulated* was reprinted under the title *Proposals Concerning Religious Societies. Humbly Offered unto GOOD MEN, in several Towns of the County: For the Revival of DYING RELIGION.* Boston, printed by S. Kneeland, for John Phillips, and sold at his shop over against the south side of the Town House, 1724 (Widener Microforms: Microfiche W 2571 [2558]. Microfiche [New York: Readex Microprint, 1985] 11 x 15 cm. Early American Imprints, 1st ser., no. 2558.)

35   Mather, *Private Meetings*, p. 5.

36   Ibid., p. 8. We gain insight into Mather's understanding of the relationship between prayer societies, fervent prayer, and the spreading of the Gospel from a book written by Scotsman Robert Millar. One of the early pioneers of the Society for Propagating Christian Knowledge (founded by a prayer society that supported some of the earliest missionaries in the American colonies), Millar wrote in 1723 about the society's missionary aims and methods. He titled his book *The History of the Propagation of Christianity and Overthrow of Paganism . . . the present State of the Heathens Is Enquired into; and Methods for Their Conversion Offered.* At the top of his list of methods of conversion is fervent prayer "by joining in solemn days of humiliation and prayer for that end." Robert Wodrow sent a copy of the book to Cotton Mather. (Fawcett, *Cambuslang*, p. 215; citing *The Correspondence of Robert Wodrow*, ed. T. M'Crie, 3 vols. [Edinburgh: Wodrow Society, 1842], p. 154.)

See also Increase Mather's understanding of the role of earnest prayer: *A Discourse Concerning Faith and Fervency in Prayer, and the Glorious Kingdom of the Lord Jesus Christ on Earth, Now Approaching* (Boston, 1710), cited by Ruth Bloch in *Visionary Republic: Millennial Themes in American Thought, 1756-1800* (Cambridge, Mass.: Harvard University Press, 1985).

37   Ibid., pp. 9, 11, 19. To help us visualize further the groups' dynamics and to emphasize the power of the laity in this movement of prayer, Mather quotes Giles Ermin as Ermin

records in 1681 the deportment of his prayer society in *Well-Catechized and Humble Christians Excellent in Practical Piety*:

> [Those in the prayer society] kept their Station, did not aspire to be *preachers*, but in *Gifts of Prayer*, few Clergy-men must come near them. I have known some of them, when they did keep their *Fasts* (as they often did), they divided the work of Prayer: The First began with *Confession*; the Second went with *Petitions* for *themselves*; the Third with *Petitions* for *Church and Kingdom*; the Fourth with *Thanksgiving*. . . . These were Old *Jacob's* Sons—they could Wrestle and Prevail with God.

38 Thomas Prince, *Extraordinary Events the doings of GOD, and marvellous in pious Eyes, Illustrated in a Sermon at the South Church in Boston, N.E., On the General Thanksgiving, Thursday, July 18, 1745*. Occasioned by taking the City of Louisbourg on the Isle of Cape Breton. Printed for D. Henchman in Cornhil, 1745, pp. 25-26.

39 Along with Prince, Webb was one of the original American signatories of Jonathan Edwards's call to Concerts of Prayer in *Humble Attempt*.

40 John Webb, *A SERMON Preach'd June 18, 1734, Being a Day of Prayer with Fasting observed by the NEW NORTH CHURCH in BOSTON. (A SERMON on a Day of Prayer, for the Reviving of GOD's Work)* (Boston: S. Kneeland and T. Green, 1734. Widener 2571 [3850]), pp. 25, 31, 32). Prince's *Christian History*, 1744, pp. 391-92, records that John Webb's ministry, like that of others, grew substantially—literally by a thousand members—in the wake of Whitefield's work in Boston. The fact that Webb and Edwards cooperated in the COP seems unsurprising when one places the thoughts of Webb's above sermon alongside the words of Edwards in *Humble Attempt*. Edwards writes:

> And I hope, that such as are convinced it is their duty to comply with and encourage this design [for Concerts of Prayer] will remember we ought not only to go speedily to pray before the Lord, and seek his mercy, but also to go constantly. We should unite in our practice those two things, which our Savior unites in his precept, praying and not fainting. If we should continue some years, and nothing remarkable in providence should appear as though God heard and answered, we should act very unbecoming believers, if we should therefore begin to be disheartened and grow dull and slack in seeking of God so great a mercy. It is very apparent from the word of God, that he is wont often to try the faith and patience of his people, when crying to him for some great and important mercy, by withholding the mercy sought for a season; and not only so, but at last succeed those who continue instant in prayer, with all perseverance, and "will not let him go except he blesses. . . ." Whatever our hopes may be, we must be content to be ignorant of the times and season, which the Father hath put in his power: and must be willing that God should answer prayer, and fulfil his own glorious promises, in His own time. (*The Works of President Edwards*, Vol. 2 [New York: Burt Franklin, 1968], p. 312.)

41 Fawcett, *Cambuslang*, p. 32.

42 A snapshot description of Cambuslang can be found in Earl E. Cairns, *An Endless Line of Splendor* (Wheaton, Ill.: Tyndale, 1986), p. 60ff.

43 Various spellings of his name can be found: M'Culloch, McCulloch, MacCullock, MacCullough, M'Cullock.

44 Fawcett, *Cambuslang*, pp. 38-39; quoting A. P. Stanley, *Lectures on the Church of Scotland* (London, 1872), p. 137.

45 Fawcett, ibid.

46 Ibid., p. 92. "One of his congregation reflected: 'Hearing a minister [M'Culloch] on a fast day, after sermon, read some papers relating to the success of the Gospel abroad; I was greatly affected at the thought that so many were getting good, and I was getting none.'"

47 *Glasgow Weekly History* was first published by M'Culloch in 1741 for the purpose of faithfully recording the accounts of spiritual awakening and publishing his correspondence with Edwards. After fifty-two issues, the newsletter ceased publication in 1743.

48 The Andover-Newton and the Yale (Beinecke) Archives of JE MSS have numerous letters between Jonathan Edwards and M'Culloch throughout the 1750s. Others within

M'Culloch's circle of pastors began writing Edwards, too. Especially regular in their correspondence were James Robe, William M'Laurin, and particularly John Erskines.

49 Fawcett, *Cambuslang*, p. 94, quoting the *Glasgow Burgh Records*, May 23 and June 27, 1739.

50 Ibid., p. 97, citing Janet Hamilton, *Poems of Purpose, &c* (Glasgow, 1870), pp. 194-96.

51 Ibid., p. 96, citing *Scots Magazine*, October 1740, p. 487.

52 Ibid., p. 68. M'Culloch wrote to James Robe at Kilsyth: "Under the late Dearth the People suffered greatly, the poor were numerous, and many . . . were at the Point of starving." The cold was so bad that the peat moss commonly used for fuel was too hard to dig.

53 See Arnold Dallimore, *George Whitefield*, Vol. 2 (Wheaton, Ill.: Crossway Books, 1979), p. 120-37.

54 M'Culloch wrote Whitefield: "It is a matter of great Joy and Thankfulness to God, who sent you here, and gave you so much Countenance, and so remarkably crown'd your Labours when here at Glasgow with Success." (Fawcett, *Cambuslang*, p. 102, quoting *Glasgow Weekly History*, No. 13.)

55 William M'Culloch, *Narrative of the Extraordinary Work at Cambuslang in a Letter to a Friend with Proper Attestations by Ministers, Preachers, and Others* (Boston: S. Kneeland and T. Green, 1742), pp. 4-5, found in *The Christian History* (Boston: S. Kneeland and T. Green, 1743), printed for Thomas Prince.

Not only would M'Culloch have been influenced by the work and correspondence of Jonathan Edwards, but the history of the Scottish kirk had models, too:

> The extraordinary work which began in Scotland on June 21st, 1630, already referred to, was evidently granted in answer to prayer. The day preceding was the Sabbath, on which the sacrament of the Lord's supper was administered; and many of the communicants, being convinced of the necessity of a revival of God's work, did not that evening retire to rest, but joined in little companies, and spent the whole night in devotional exercises, especially for the outpouring of the Spirit. The Lord heard their prayer, and gave a signal answer the very next day, in the conversion of five hundred souls under the preaching of Mr. Levingston. In the Friendly Isles a revival, perhaps never surpassed since the days of the apostles, was obtained in answer to prayer." (Robert Young, *The Importance of Prayer Meetings, in Promoting the Revival of Religion* [New York: Lane & Tippet, for the Methodist Episcopal Church, 1846], p. 44.)

56 Fawcett, *Cambuslang*, p. 106.

57 Ibid., quoting M'Culloch, Mss *Examination of persons under Spiritual Concern at Cambuslang, during the Revival in 1741-2; By the Rev'd William MacCulloch, Minister at Cambuslang*, Vol. 2, p. 266.

58 Dallimore, *George Whitefield*, p. 122. Dallimore adds: "A similar work was taking place in Kilsyth. Robe reported that on Sunday, May 16 (1742):

> An extraordinary power of the Spirit . . . accompanied the word preached. There was a great mourning in the congregation. . . . Many cried out, and these not only women; but some strong and stout hearted men: After the dismission of the congregation an assay was made to get the distressed into my barn . . . the number of them and their friends attending them was so many, that I was obliged to convene them in the Kirk. . . . When I assayed to speak with them, I could not be heard, such were the bitter cries, groans, and the voice of their weeping. (Quoting James Robe, *The Revival of Religion at Kilsyth, Cambuslang and other places in 1741* [Glasgow, 1840], p. 38.)

Of note, too, are the testimonies heard from pastors in other towns surrounding Cambuslang. In *A faithful Narrative of the extraordinary Work of the Spirit of God, at Kilsyth, and other Congregations in the Neighborhood* by James Robe we hear similar stories. Of particular note is the emphasis on the part the prayer societies played in the awakenings. See notes below.

59 *A Faithful Narrative of the Surprising Works of God.*

60 M'Culloch, *Narrative of the Extraordinary Work at Cambuslang*, bound within *The Christian History* (Boston: S. Kneeland and T. Green, 1743), for Thomas Prince. It was during this

period that M'Culloch began writing to Thomas Prince in Boston so that the information about extraordinary works of God in England could be reprinted in New England.

61   "At the request of M'Culloch and other ministers Whitefield agreed to return to Cambuslang . . . in a month's time. The local Societies for Prayer—now gloriously alive— began immediately to beseech God that there might be a still greater measure of blessing. And their prayers did not go unfulfilled" (Dallimore, *George Whitefield*, p. 127).

62   A Letter to John Cennick in *The Works of George Whitefield*, Vol. 1 (London, Edinburgh, 1771; Republished London: Banner of Truth, 1976), pp. 409-10. "Societies for Prayer that had almost become extinct were revived, and in view of the solemn truths that had taken hold of upon them, people prayed with an earnestness they had not previously known" (Dallimore, ibid., p. 122). James Robe (Glasgow) reports that in the wake of Cambuslang, the societies for prayer, once long abandoned in his parish, were revived: "Formerly there were only two praying societies in the church; by year's end there were 18 (many flocking into them)" (Fawcett, *Cambuslang*, p. 131).

M'Culloch wrote that the success of the awakening was dependent upon "pressing jointly, *the Necessity of Repentance towards God, of Faith in the Lord Jesus Christ, and the Holiness in all manner of Conversation*; that it came after such *Preparatives* as an extensive Concern about Religion gradually increasing; together with extraordinary *fervent* Prayer in large Meetings particularly relating to the *success* of the gospel" (M'Culloch, *Narrative of the Extraordinary Work at Cambuslang*, p. 7).

63   Dallimore, *George Whitefield*, pp. 135-36.

64   Robe, *History*, pp. 17-21.

65   Ibid., pp. 44-45.

66   Ibid., May 7, 1743, No. 10, p. 77.

67   Ibid., p. 313.

68   Fawcett, *Cambuslang*, p. 119; Fawcett continues by quoting the *Glasgow Weekly History*, No. 39, pp. 1-2: "None ever saw the like since the Revolution in Scotland, or even anywhere else. . . . Some have called them fifty Thousand; some forty Thousand; the lowest estimate I hear of . . . makes them to have been upwards of thirty Thousand." Fawcett adds, "It is easy to grasp the significance of this when one recalls that the total population of Glasgow in 1740 was estimated by the magistrates to be only 17,034." M'Culloch closed his account of the day: "May our exalted Redeemer go on from Conquering to Conquer, 'till the whole Earth be filled with his Glory'" (quoting *Glasgow Weekly History*, No. 39, pp. 6-7).

69   Before calling for a similar Communion service with Whitefield in the open fields at Kilsyth, James Robe sought the advice and prayer support from "several Societies for Prayer" (*Glasgow Weekly History*, p. 131).

70   Fawcett writes, "One cannot read the testimonies gathered together by M'Culloch without being struck by the eager concern expressed for the conversion of others, and the outreachings in prayer and desire to the whole world. . . . One young man's 'heart's Desire and prayer to God' was 'that the Lord may send a Revival of Religion, in the life and power of it, to all the Corners of the Land.' . . . When Alexander Bilsland was at the Cambuslang communion in August 1743, many passages of Scripture came to his mind, particularly that text in Isaiah 54:5: 'Thy Maker is Thy Husband, the Lord of Hosts is his Name; the God of the Whole Earth shall he be called': 'Upon which my heart was melted down with love to God; and with difficulty I got My Self restrained from Shouting aloud for Joy.' He went on: 'What made Me rejoice most of all at that time, was the last part of that text, "The Lord God of the whole Earth shall he be called," by which I got a large view of the Extent of the Redeemer's Kingdom to become universal over the Whole Earth: which prospect was most agreeable and delightful to Me.'" (Fawcett, *Cambuslang*, pp. 210-211, quoting from M'Culloch's MSS., Vol. 1, pp. 9, 132-133.)

Regarding M'Culloch's own interest in the global spread of the Gospel, he was a fervent supporter of the S.S.P.C.K. (Fawcett, ibid., p. 217, citing William M'Culloch, *Sermons on Several Subjects*, ed. R. M'Culloch [Glasgow, 1793], Preface, pp. 18-19.)

71   M'Culloch, *Narrative of the Extraordinary Work*, Attestation I, p. 7ff.

72   Fawcett, *Cambuslang*, pp. 122-23, quoting from John Erskines, *Signs of the Times Considered, or the high PROBABILITY that the present APPEARANCES in New England, and the West of Scotland, are a PRELUDE of the Glorious Things promised to the CHURCH in the latter Ages* (Edinburgh, 1742), p. 18. See also Harry Stout, *The Divine Dramatist* (Grand Rapids: Wm. B. Eerdmans, 1991), p. 154.

73   Prince, *The Christian History*, letter from M'Culloch to Edwards, p. 361.

74   That is, to "revive true religion in all parts of Christendom . . . and fill the whole earth with his glory." (*The Works of Jonathan Edwards* [London, 1817], p. 423ff.)

75   *Humble Attempt*, section III, in *Works of President Edwards*, Vol. 2, p. 445.

76   Stein, ed., *Apocalyptic Writings*, Vol. 5, p. 77. See also John Gillies, ed., *Sermons and Essays by the Late Rev. Mr. John M'Laurin* (Philadelphia: Knox, 1811), p. viii., cited by Fawcett, *Cambuslang*, pp. 224-27.

77   Wesley's letter to Lord [Erskines] Grange, March 16, 1745, *The Letters of the Rev. John Wesley*, standard edn., ed. N. Curnock, Vol. 2 (London, 1909), p. 33. In the letter Wesley thanks Lord Grange for his correspondence because "it shows a truly Christian spirit. I should be glad to have also the note you mention touching the proposal for prayer and praise. Might it not be practicable to have concurrence of Mr. Edwards in New England, if not of Mr. Tennent also, herein? It is evidently one work with what we have seen here. Why should we not all praise God with one heart?"

Erskines would become, too, an admirer of Jonathan Edwards. When Edwards was ejected from his Northampton charge, Erskines, along with John M'Laurin (of Glasgow) and William M'Culloch, organized financial support for him from among his Scottish ministerial friends. Erskines offered to secure for Edwards a pastorate within the Church of Scotland. (*The Works of Jonathan Edwards* [London, 1817], p. 158.) The above exchange of letters is a clear demonstration of the ecumenical nature of the COP: Scotch Presbyterian Erskines wrote to Anglican Wesley, who recommended that Congregationalist Edwards be notified.

78   Stein, ed., *Apocalyptic Writings*, Vol. 5, p. 445. Edwards's letter to an unknown correspondent in Scotland (printed originally in Robe, ed., *The Christian Monthly*, No. 8 [November 1745], 234-54). John M'Laurin of Glasgow was probably the unnamed correspondent.

79   S. E. Dwight, *The Life of President Edwards*, Vol. 1 (New York: G.&C.&H. Carvill, 1830), pp. 242-45.

80   None of these memorials has to date been found.

81   See Edwards's comments on prayer societies in C. C. Goen, ed., *The Great Awakening*, Vol. 4 (New Haven, Conn.: Yale University Press, 1962), p. 544, and Stein, ed., *Apocalyptic Writings*, Vol. 5, p. 445.

82   See Stephen Stein, *William and Mary Quarterly*, 3rd ser., Vol. 37, No. 2, April 1980, p. 263-70. These "bids" seem to mirror a later development—"awakening notes" submitted in revival meetings requesting prayer for persons under conviction.

83   Stein, ed., *Apocalyptic Writings*, Vol. 5, p. 1-15.

84   Perry Miller, "The End of the World," in *Errand into the Wilderness* (Cambridge, Mass.: Harvard University Press, 1956), p. 233. See also Stein, ibid., p. 8.

85   When Jonathan Edwards invited George Whitefield to come to Northampton to preach, Edwards expressed his hope that the glorious works being reported surrounding Whitefield's ministry pointed to "the dawning of a day of God's mighty power and glorious grace to the world of mankind." He also encouraged Whitefield to keep preaching "that the work of God may be carried on by a Blessing of your Labours . . . until the Kingdom of Satan shall shake, and his proud Empire fall throughout the Earth and the Kingdom of Christ, that glorious Kingdom of Light, holiness, Peace and Love, shall be established from one end of the Earth to the other!" (Edwards's Letter of Invitation to George Whitefield, *William and Mary Quarterly*, 3rd ser., Vol. 29, 1972, pp. 488-89. See Stein, ed., *Apocalyptic Writings*, Vol. 5, p. 25.)

These works of God were described by Edwards "as forerunners of those glorious times so often prophesied of in the Scripture, and that this was the first dawning of that light, and beginning of that work which, in the progress and issue of it, would at last bring on the church's latter-day glory." (Goen, *Awakening,* Vol. 4, *Works of Jonathan Edwards,* p. 560.)

86   This preoccupation explains part of the embarrassment certain scholars feel toward Jonathan Edwards's apocalyptic material.

87   *Personal Narrative,* quoted in Stein, *Apocalyptic Writings,* Vol. 5, p. 15.

88   The Greek word *telos* refers to the goal or final purpose. For example, Jonathan Edwards wrote, "The end of God's creating the world was to prepare a kingdom for his Son (for he was appointed heir of the world)." (J. I. Packer, *Jonathan Edwards and the Theology of Revival,* from *Increasing in the Knowledge of God,* papers read at the Puritan and Reformed Studies Conference, 1960.)

89   Gerald R. McDermott, *One Holy and Happy Society: The Public Theology of Jonathan Edwards* (University Park, Penn.: Pennsylvania State University Press, 1992), p. 47. McDermott has provided a marvelous study of how Jonathan Edwards's view of the millennium helped him fashion a dynamic vision for society (which became the basis for his critique of existing social conditions) and a vision for international-global relations.

90   The third stanza of William Bradbury's famous hymn "Sweet Hour of Prayer" alludes to the very special quality of prayer that gives one vision into what will be.

> Sweet hour of prayer, sweet hour of prayer,
> May I thy consolation share,
> Till from Mount Pisgah's lofty height
> I view my home and take my flight.

91   McDermott, *Society,* p. 45, citing Clarence H. Faust and Thomas H. Johnson, ed., *Jonathan Edwards: Representative Selections* (New York: American Book Co., 1935).

92   S. E. Dwight, ed., *Memoirs of the Rev. David Brainerd,* Vol. 10, pp. 399-400. The closer Brainerd came to death, the more the two men talked of the millennium: "The more the symptoms of its approach increased, still the more did his [Brainerd's] mind seem to be taken up with this subject." Along with his concerns for Zion, Brainerd complained to Jonathan Edwards about the lack of compliance with the proposed Concert of Prayer that was designed to be, in its essence, a united effort imploring God to establish the glories of Zion.

93   In the Yale and Andover-Newton Jonathan Edwards Archives, letters to and from Erskines are the most numerous of any overseas source during the last fifteen years of Jonathan Edwards's life.

94   So great was Erskines's admiration of Jonathan Edwards that when Edwards was ejected from his Northampton pulpit, Erskines, along with John M'Laurin (of Glasgow) and William M'Culloch, organized financial support for him from among his Scottish ministerial friends. Erskines offered to secure for Edwards a pastorate within the Church of Scotland. (*The Works of Jonathan Edwards* [London, 1817], p. 158.)

Regarding an eventuality that will prove enormously important, in "April, 1784, Andrew Fuller, a minister in the Northamptonshire Association, brought to the attention of the Northamptonshire Baptist leaders a 'parcel of books from Dr. John Erskines of Edinburgh, [and with it] a copy of Jonathan Edwards's [*Humble Attempt*]—a stirring call to prayer" (Fawcett, *Cambuslang,* p. 229).

For a discussion of the relationship between Jonathan Edwards and Erskines, see Stein, *Apocalyptic Writings,* pp. 70-74.

95   See Mather, *Private Meetings,*, p. 33.

96   See McDermott, *Society,* p. 48.

97   Dwight, *Memoirs,* Vol. 1, p. 70. Also see Stein, *Apocalyptic Writings,* p. 10. Stein tells us that during the French and Indian Wars, Jonathan Edwards "followed developments closely because the outcome had implications for the view of history he had shaped in his reflections on Revelation" (p. 32).

98   Stein, ibid., p. 4.

99   Lowman's *Paraphrase and Notes on the Revelation* was the single most-cited work in *Notes on the Apocalypse* (see McDermott, *Society*, p. 56).

100   Stein notes, "By his day many a respected Puritan colonial pastor had been impressed with the likes of John Cotton, Roger Williams, the historian Edward Johnson, the poet Michael Wigglesworth, and father and son Increase and Cotton Mather and others, and filled their pulpits, papers and diaries with apocalyptic discourse, many maintaining that most of the vials of Revelation had been poured out, and the beginning of the millennium was imminent. They thought of themselves as living players in the script of Revelation. The last shoe to drop was the fall of the Pope. Queen Anne's War (1702-1713), in which Jonathan's father was a chaplain to American troops, against the Catholic French in Canada, and later the French and Indian Wars and the providential happenings at the victory of Louisbourg—at each advancement of liberty and victory and revival, the fever pitch of excitement could only have grown" (Stein, *Apocalyptic Writings*, p. 5).

See the depth of this anti-Roman Catholic conviction surrounding the Canadian French in Timothy Edwards's letter to Mrs. Esther Edwards, September 10, 1711, in Sereno E. Dwight, ed., *The Works of President Edwards with a Memoir of His Life*, Vol. 1 (New York, 1829-30), p. 15.

101   Letter to a correspondent in Scotland, Northampton, November 20, 1945 (printed originally in *The Christian Monthly*, Robe, ed., No. 8, [November 1745], pp. 234-54) was written after the American victory at Cape Breton. Jonathan Edwards seems to have been singularly impressed with the victory as proof of the power of fervent prayer and as a presage of God's consummate victory over the Antichrist. The Roman papacy, wrote Edwards, was a "viper of some loathsome, poisonous, crawling monster" (cited in Stein, ibid., p. 11).

102   McDermott, *Society*, p. 58, citing Robert Middlekauf, *The Mathers: Three Generations of Puritan Intellectuals* (New York: Oxford University Press, 1971), p. 337, 348.

Imminentism was prevalent even after the 1740s. Charles Chauncy and Jonathan Mayhew disagreed on the timing of Christ's bodily return, but both spread hopes for the speedy culmination of history. Mayhew expected a fundamental transformation of the world in the near future. In the 1750s, books by Anglican Richard Clark, Scottish Presbyterian David Imrie, and seventeenth-century English Presbyterian Christopher Love used numerology, extrabiblical sources, and a personal revelation to predict the beginning of the millennium in the following decade. Reprints of two seventeenth-century premillennialist Puritans, William Torry and Ezekiel Cheever, further encouraged the belief that the millennium could soon begin. Even Joseph Bellamy, Jonathan Edwards's friend and disciple, [expected the millennium soon] (McDermott, ibid., p. 57, note #64).

103   Stein, ed., *Humble Attempt*, in *Apocalyptic Writings*, Vol. 5, pp. 394, 410-11. See also pp. 77, 129. See further McDermott, *Society*, p. 50.

104   J. I. Packer, analyzing Jonathan Edwards's *Religious Affections*, suggests that Jonathan Edwards knew quite well that revivals, even powerful ones, are a part of the historical trauma the church can expect to battle through. Paraphrasing Edwards's thoughts, Packer writes:

> Revival means renewal of life, and life means energy. It is true that revival delivers the church from the problems created by apathy and deadness, but it is equally true that it is a torrential overflow of disorder and undisciplined spiritual vitality. In a revival, the saints are suddenly roused from a state of torpor and lethargy by a new and overwhelming awareness of the reality of spiritual things, and of God. They are like sleepers shaken awake and now for the moment see where they are; in one sense, they now see everything, as they never saw it before; yet in another sense, because of the very brightness of the light, they can hardly see anything. They are swept off their feet; they lose their sense of proportion. They fall into pride, delusions, unbalance, censorious modes of speech, extravagant forms of action. Unconverted persons are caught up in what is going on; they feel the power of truth, though their hearts remain unrenewed; they become "enthusiasts," harsh and bitter, fierce and vainglorious, cranky and fanatical. Then, perhaps, they fall into spectacular sin, and apostasize alto-

gether; or else remain in the church to scandalize the rest of men by maintaining, on dogmatic perfectionist grounds, that while what they do would be sin in others, it was not sin in them. Satan (who, as Jonathan Edwards somewhere observes, was "trained in the best divinity school in the universe") keeps step with God, actively perverting and caricaturing all that the Creator is doing. A revival, accordingly, is always a *disfigured* work of God, and the more powerful the revival, the more scandalizing disfigurement we may expect to see. . . . "A work of God without stumblingblocks is never to be expected," he wrote grimly in 1741; ". . . we shall probably see more instances of apostasy and gross iniquity among professors. . . ." (J. I. Packer, *Jonathan Edwards and the Theology of Revival*, from *Increasing in the Knowledge of God*, papers read at the Puritan and Reformed Studies Conference, 1960.)

105 These outpourings are meant to "prove the reality of Christ's kingdom to a skeptical world and serve to expand its bounds among Christ's erstwhile enemies." (Packer, ibid., p. 24. See also McDermott, *Society,* p. 50.)

Commenting on the role each of these extraordinary works of God plays in the ultimate design of heaven, Jonathan Edwards wrote:

> When God manifests himself with such glorious power, in a work of this nature . . . he appears determined to put honour upon his Son, and to fulfill his oath that he has sworn to him, that he would make every knee to bow . . . to him. God hath had it much on his heart, from all eternity, to glorify his dear and only-begotten Son; and there are some special seasons that he appoints to that end, wherein he comes forth with omnipotent power to fulfil his promise . . . to him. Now these are times of remarkable pouring out of his Spirit, to advance his kingdom; such is a day of his power. (Edwards, *Works*, Vol. 1, p. 380.)

106 Edwards, *Humble Attempt*, in *Works of President Edwards*, Vol. 2, p. 445.

107 Edwards, *Works of President Edwards*, Vol. 1, p. 62.

108 Ibid., pp. 61-62, citing Cotton Mather ("at various points in his career"), Edward Johnson, Chief Justice Samuel Sewall, and Joseph Morgan, among many.

109 Ibid., p. 61; Stein ed., *Humble Attempt*, in *Apocalyptic Writings*, Vol. 5, p. 333. Emphasis added.

110 Stein, ed., ibid., p. 181.

111 Ibid., p. 66-67.

112 Ibid., p. 40, 41.

113 McDermott, citing ibid., p. 339.

114 Edwards, *Works of President Edwards*, Vol. 2, p. 291.

115 Ibid., p. 469.

116 *Works*, Dwight, ed., Vol. 1, p. 102.

117 Ibid., p. 151-52. See McDermott, *Society*, p. 45.

118 Edwards, *Works*, Vol. 1, p. 426.

119 To Jonathan Edwards

> . . . the union of praying Christians will be beautiful . . . because unity itself is "amiable" and consistent with God's plan. . . . When the church throughout the world, diverse as it is, acts as one family, it is a mark of glory for its Head. By the act of united prayer the fractured church manifests the reality of the "Body of Christ." . . . Spiritual union will lead to better relations among the separated parts of the church. Thus for Jonathan Edwards the concert of prayer was both a means to an end and an end in itself. . . . The proposal does not rest upon the assumption that God is more likely to hear prayers because they are offered at the same time. United prayer is beneficial for other reasons, principally because it promotes the unity of scattered Christians and nurtures confidence among them. Visible acts of worship, including corporate prayer, glorify God and encourage the saints by building mutual affection among the participants (Stein, Vol. 5, pp. 42, 43).

120 Zechariah 8:20-23: "This is what the Lord Almighty says: 'Many peoples and the inhabi-

tants of many cities will yet come, and the inhabitants of one city will go to another and say, "Let us go at once to entreat the Lord and seek the LORD Almighty. I myself am going." And many peoples and powerful nations will come to Jerusalem to seek the LORD Almighty and to entreat him.' This is what the Lord Almighty says: 'In those days ten men from all languages and nations will take firm hold of one Jew by the hem of his robe and say, "Let us go with you, because we have heard that God is with you."'"

121 *Humble Attempt*, Stein, ed., Vol. 5, p. 314. One of the most remarkable biblical illustrations Jonathan Edwards uses to insist that joint prayer is integral to God's unfolding plan comes from his exposition of Revelation 8:

> God has respect to the prayers of his saints in all his *government* of the *world*; as we may observe by the representation made in Rev. 8 at the beginning. There we read of *seven angels* standing before the throne of God, and receiving of him *seven trumpets*, at the sounding of which, great and mighty changes were to be brought to pass in the world, through many successive ages. But when these angels had received their trumpets, they must stand still, and all must be silent, not one of them must be allowed to *sound*, till the *prayers of the saints* are attended to. The angel of the covenant, as all-glorious high priest, comes and stands at the altar, with much incense, to offer with the *prayers of all the saints* upon the golden altar, before the throne; and the smoke of the incense, with the *prayer of the saints*, ascends up with acceptance before God, out of the angel's hand: and *then* the angels prepare themselves to sound. And God, in the events of every trumpet, remembers those *prayers*: as appears at last, by the great and glorious things he accomplishes for his church, in the issue of all, in *answer* to those prayers, in the event of the *last* trumpet, which brings the glory of the *latter days*, when these prayers shall be turned into *joyful praises* (Rev. 11:15-17). *And the seventh angel sounded; and there were great voices in heaven saying, the kingdoms of this world are become the kingdoms of our Lord and of his Christ; and he shall reign forever and ever. And the four-and-twenty elders, which sat before God on their seats, fell upon their faces, and worshipped God saying, "We give thee thanks, O Lord God Almighty, which art and wast and art to come, because thou hast taken to thee thy great power, and hast reigned."* Since it is the pleasure of God so to honour his people, as to carry on all the designs of his kingdom in this way, viz. By the prayers of his saints; this gives us great reason to think, that whenever the time comes that God gives an extraordinary spirit of prayer for the promised advancement of his kingdom on earth—which is God's great aim in all preceding providences, and the main thing that the spirit of prayer in the saints aims at—then the fulfillment of this even is nigh. (*Humble Attempt* in *Works of President Edwards*, Burt Franklin, p. 471.)

122 Edwards, *Works*, Vol. 2, p. 312.

CHAPTER 3: HARVESTS, MISSIONS, AMERICA'S PENTECOST AND THE CONCERT OF PRAYER

1   "Stand Up, Stand Up for Jesus" by George Duffield, from Alfred Smith, ed., *Living Hymns* (Montrose, Penn: Encore Publications, 1972).

2   The combination of the Concert of Prayer proposal and Edwards's views on the millennium.

3   S. E. Dwight, *Life of President Edwards*, Vol. 1 (New York: G.&C.&H. Carvill, 1830), p. 246. Dwight goes on to say that a particular error first hindered the Concerts of Prayer. Certain people taught that prophecy foretold that the church would be almost completely destroyed before Christ's kingdom came. In this case, to pray for the millennium was to pray for the destruction of the church! Edwards argued that, no, those particular calamities were all but behind the church. The "general conviction" was that all that was left to usher in the millennial reign of Christ was the fall of popery.

4   Ibid., p. 245. Dwight adds: "[*Humble Attempt*] had great influence in securing the general adoption of the measures proposed [The COP]— a measure, which was pursued for more than a half century by many of the American churches, and only discontinued on the adoption of the more frequent Concert—the Monthly Concert—for United and Extraordinary Prayer, for the same great object, proposed at an Association of the ministers of the Baptist

Churches, in the counties of Northampton, Leicester, etc. held at Nottingham, in 1784, and observed the first Monday evening of each month; and now extensively adopted throughout the Christian world."

5 Ibid.

6 See letter from Jonathan Edwards to Joseph Bellamy. Northampton, January 15, 1746, p. 47. Jonathan Edwards MSS, Folder XXXIX. 7. C., Yale Archives. See also *Sermons and Essays by the Late Reverend Mr. John M'Laurin,* ed. John Gillies (Glasgow: James Knox, 1755), p. v: "[Jonathan Edwards] encouraged the societies for prayer which multiplied in Glasgow about this time. With his approbation there was a general meeting appointed once a month (which still subsists), consisting of a member of each society, with a minister for their Presses to enquire into the state of the societies and to send more experienced persons to assist the younger sort. And several years afterwards he was the chief contriver and promoter of the concert for prayer which hath been complied with by numbers both in Great Britain and America." (See too Gillies's footnote regarding *Humble Attempt.*)

7 Dwight, ed., *Life of President Edwards,* pp. 243-45: Letter to Rev. William M'Culloch, Northampton, September 23, 1747. Jonathan Edwards ends the letter hopefully by discussing what he perceives to be the fulfillment of biblical prophecies about the Lord's coming and then adds:

> I cannot think otherwise, that we have a great reason to suppose that the beginning of that glorious work of God's Spirit, which, before it is finished shall accomplish these things, is not very far off; and there is very much in the word of God, and in the present aspects of divine Providence, to encourage us greatly in our begun Concert for Extraordinary Prayer for the coming of Christ's Kingdom. Let us therefore go on with what we have begun in that respect, and continue instant in prayer, with all perseverance, and increase more and more in faith and fervency, and not keep silence, nor give God any rest, till he establish, and make Jerusalem a praise in the earth.

8 Seen as an evangelical leader of consequence, Mr. Sutton years later was the recipient of a written apology and confession of wrongdoing from one of the ringleaders of Jonathan Edwards's ouster from Northampton. (Jonathan Edwards, *History of Redemption,* ed. David Austin [New York: T. and J. Swords, 1793], preface, p. 10.)

9 Kittery, Maine, was the home of one of Jonathan Edwards's admirers, Lord William Pepperell. John Rogers (1692-1773) was the founding pastor of the second church in Kittery (or Eliot, which had been the northern half of Kittery until 1810) and pastor for fifty-four years. He was the son of Rev. John Rogers of Ipswich, Maine (who, we will see below, was party to the COP in Ipswich). "There were extensive revivals in [John Rogers's] parish in 1742 and 1815. Up to 1820, 338 persons had been added to this church since its foundation, 140 under the pastorate of Mr. Rogers [alone]." (Everett S. Stackpole, *Old Kittery and Her Families* [Somersworth: New England History Press, 1981], pp. 199-203.)

To press the point that Whitefield was responsible for not only revivals and awakenings but for networking evangelical pastors who would one day unite in the COP, Whitefield's last visit to Maine was on:

> Tuesday, September 25, or Wednesday, 26, 1770; having preached in the morning in Portsmouth, he preached in the afternoon in Mr. [John] Rogers's church at the Reach [Kittery/Eliot] on the other side of the river. The following day, Thursday, 27, he preached for the last time on Maine soil, strangely enough where he had first preached on his first visit, in the church of York First, now under the care of Rev. Isaac Lyman, Mr. Whitefield's old friend and supporter (Rev. Samuel Moody having died in 1747). Three days later, on Sunday, September 30, Mr. Whitefield died in Newburyport and was buried there. (Calvin Montague Clark, *History of the Congregational Churches in Maine,* Vol. 2 [Portland: The Congregational Christian Conference of Maine, 1935], p. 239.)

10 Brainerd was one of Edwards's favorite people. Brainerd's "dying advice to his own congregation [of Indians in Pennsylvania was] that they should practise agreeably to that proposal" for "united and extraordinary prayer, amongst Christ's ministers and people, for

the coming of Christ's kingdom." (Jonathan Edwards, ed., *The Life of David Brainerd* [Grand Rapids: Baker Book House, 1983], p. 324.)

11   Arthur Fawcett, *The Cambuslang Revival* (London: Banner of Truth, 1971), p. 277: Letter to Mr. M'Culloch, May 23, 1749.

12   See Dwight, *Life of President Edwards*, Vol. 1, p. 262: Letter to Mr. M'Culloch, October 7, 1748, wherein Jonathan Edwards writes of sending the proposal to New Jersey. John Belcher (1682-1757), an evangelical Christian, was providentially the royal governor of New Jersey in 1748. Without a favorable governor, the College of New Jersey (Princeton) could not have received a charter to begin. In John Belcher's letter from Burlington (New Jersey), May 31, 1748, we read about the charter to found New-Jersey College (p. 268).

With Belcher, we again witness the "Whitefield factor." Just prior to his meeting with Jonathan Edwards and preaching at his church, Whitefield and Belcher had met while Whitefield was preaching in New Jersey. The two became good friends: "A newspaper report stated, 'Mr. Whitefield has not a warmer friend anywhere than in the first man among us. Our Governor [Belcher] can call him nothing less than the Apostle Paul. He has shown him the highest respects and carried him in his coach from place to place; and could not help following him fifty miles out of town.'" (Arnold A. Dallimore, *George Whitefield: The Life and Times of the Great Evangelist of the Eighteenth-Century Revival*, Vol. 1 [Wheaton, Ill.: Crossway Books, 1979], p. 536, citing the *South Carolina Gazette*, No. 361.)

When Whitefield returned to England, he employed M'Culloch of Cambuslang in the raising of funds for Belcher's efforts to bankroll the College of New Jersey (ibid., Vol. 2, p. 285).

13   Dwight, ibid., Vol. 1, 268: Letter from Burlington, New Jersey, May 31, 1748.

14   Tennent had strong ties to Whitefield's ministry (Dallimore, *Whitefield*, Vol. 1, pp. 416-17, 434, 485, 492).

15   Again, Davenport was a host of Whitefield. Whitefield preached in his church prior to making his way to Edwards (see ibid., pp. 491, 492, 565-67; Vol. 2, pp. 184-87, 196, 215, 216).

16   Dwight, *Life of President Edwards*, Vol. 1, p. 279. Samuel Buell (1716-1798), a Presbyterian and a graduate of Yale (1741), was installed as pastor of East Hampton, Long Island, on September 19, 1746. Jonathan Edwards preached the installment sermon (Isaiah 62:4-5) on the union of a minister to his people "in order to their being brought to the blessedness of a more glorious union, in which Christ shall rejoice over them, as the bridegroom rejoiceth over the bride" (*Works*, Dwight, ed., Vol. 6, pp. 189-216). During the awakening in Northampton, 1741-42, Buell preached at Jonathan Edwards's church every day for several weeks with immense effect upon Northampton: "tears, faintings, groanings and many professed salvations—especially among the youth."

17   Ibid.

18   Dwight, *Life of President Edwards*, Vol. 1, p. 279. Upon graduation, Buell, an itinerant, preached his way through Connecticut and Massachusetts with great effect. Jonathan Edwards reported an awakening in Northampton after Buell had preached for a season there: "Almost the whole town seemed to be in great and continual commotion day and night: and there was, indeed, a very great revival of religion" (Samuel Buell, "A FAITHFUL NARRATIVE of the *Remarkable Revival of Religion* in the CONGREGATION of EAST-HAMPTON on Long Island, in *the year of our Lord*, 1764" [Sag Harbor: Aiden Spooner, 1808], introduction, pp. 6-7.)

Buell so admired Edwards that he stated that Jonathan Edwards "was, under heaven, his oracle" (Buell, p. 12). Not only did Buell study Jonathan Edwards's writings thoroughly and unite with him in the COP, but he held Edwards's position on Communion and baptism, views that had caused Edwards's dismissal from Northampton. "No person," wrote Buell, "ought to be a guest at the *Holy Supper*, without the wedding garment of imputed *righteousness* and inherent *holiness* derived from Christ our Lord *Redeemer*" (Buell, p. 59).

19   Dwight, ibid., Vol. 1, p. 265: Letter to Erskines, 1749.

20   Ibid., p. 262: Letter to M'Culloch, October 1748.

21   Ibid.

22   Jonathan Edwards writes to Joseph Bellamy, Northampton: "Please to accept one of my Books on Prayer for the Revival of Religion which I here send you, & send me word whether the proposal for united prayer be complied with in your Parts." (Letter, January 15, 1746, p. 47. Jonathan Edwards MSS, Folder XXXIX. 7. C., Yale Archives.)

23   The distinguished Bellamy (1719-1790) studied at Yale with Jonathan Edwards and pastored down the Connecticut River Valley in Bethlehem, Connecticut.

24   Sewall, Foxcroft, Benjamin Colman, Prince, and Webb were not only supporters of Jonathan Edwards's efforts but ardent supporters of Whitefield's ministry as well. For example, during October 1740, Whitefield preached in Sewall's meetinghouse. During his stay, "awakened souls—many more than he had time to deal with—came seeking him at his lodgings, but he had to leave them in order to preach at the Old South Church. Upon arriving, however, he found the crowd so great that he could not get in by the doors and was obliged to enter through a window" (Dallimore, *Whitefield*, Vol. 1, p. 533). In Boston when opposition to Whitefield became intense, all these men visited Whitefield and opened their pulpits to him (pp. 532-33; Vol. 2, p. 195. Also *The Christian History*, Vol. of 1744, p. 288).

So convinced that the prophecies of the last days were being played out and grieved that many were opposing the "signal Work of the Holy Ghost of late, to and fro in *New-England*, superior *to what* has been in many Years past" (the opponents were denouncing all the pamphlets of late), Foxcroft wrote the foreword for the republishing of Robert Fleming's *The Fulfilling of the Scripture. Or An Essay shewing the exact Accomplishment of the WORD of GOD, in his WORKS performed and to be performed. For confirming of Believers, and convincing Atheists of the present Time* (Boston: Rogers and Fowle, printed for Walter McAlpine near Mill-Bridge, 1743).

25   Stein, Vol. 5, p. 48; quoting Letter of May 6, 1749 (MS, Houghton Library, Harvard University).

26   Dwight, *Life of President Edwards*, p. 279: Letter to Mr. Robe, May 23, 1749.

27   Perhaps rather than ironic, we could imagine Edwards's dismissal to be demonic. If it is true that the Concert of Prayer was his unsurpassed legacy, it would seem reasonable that the powers of darkness would make every effort to thwart this work.

The issue was the Lord's table and who could partake. Because of the great influx of "awakened" souls, Edwards was ambivalent about offering them an ordinance he considered reserved for the truly saved. His father-in-law had encouraged an open table. For a while Jonathan Edwards went along with this policy, but this problem for his conscience was exacerbated when years later those awakened declined in their affections for the Gospel, appearing as unregenerate as before, but insisting that they have access to all ordinances. Edwards refused and was ultimately dismissed.

28   In a letter to Bellamy, Northampton, Jonathan Edwards speaks of the "grave confusion" in his church about "the controversy." (Letter of December 6, 1749 in Jonathan Edwards MSS, Folder XXXIX. 7, Yale Archives.)

29   Jonathan Edwards's difficulties with his former church did not end with his leaving Northampton. For years to come, certain families sought to discredit him. Knowing one of Edwards's chief benefactors to be Lady Pepperell of Kittery, Maine, Edwards's rivals pestered her with letters asking her not to support the work in Stockbridge. The Williams family, for example, who "had been strenuous opponents of Mr. Edwards at Northampton, and active in effecting his dismission, and were opposers to his settlement at Stockbridge," wrote letters to Lady Pepperell imploring her not to help in Edwards's efforts among the Indians. (Usher Parsons, *The Life of Sir William Pepperell* [London: Sampson Low, Son, & Co., 17; Boston: Little, Brown, & Company], pp. 250ff.)

But Edwards continued to be hopeful. His letters to Lady Pepperell include all kinds of speculation about the end of the age and what the signs of the times might mean. It seems that one of the primary reasons for the letter writing was the gathering of intelligence and signs of encouragement on that day's horizon.

Colonel William Pepperell was one of George Whitefield's greatest admirers. His home was opened to Whitefield (Dallimore, *Whitefield*, Vol. 2, p. 193). While the Cape Breton affair was unfolding, Whitefield's endorsement helped Pepperell muster an army for the expedition (Dallimore, p. 202).

30   The Concert of Prayer was renewed in June 1754. (See John Gillies, ed., *Historical Collections Related to Remarkable Periods of the Success of the Gospel and Eminent Instruments Employed in Promoting It*, Vol. 2, [Glasgow, 1754], p. 402.)

31   Dwight, *Life of President Edwards*, Vol. 1, p. 461.

32   Ibid., p. 496.

33   Fawcett, *Cambuslang*, p. 142.

34   Kuypers could only compare it to the Day of Pentecost (Letters of Kuypers to Gillies in Gillies, *Historical Collections*, appendix, p. 23).

35   Fawcett citing Hugh Kennedy, *A Short Account of the Rise & Continuing Progress of a Remarkable Work of Grace in the United Netherlands*. In several letters from the Reverend Mr. Hugh Kennedy, minister of the Gospel in the Scots Congregation in Rotterdam, 1750.

36   William Tennent II, quoted in "History of Revivals of Religion," *American Quarterly Register*, Vol. V, 1833, p. 212.

37   Aaron Burr, *The Watchman's Answer to the Question, What of the Night, &c. A SERMON Preached before the SYNOD OF NEW-YORK, Convened at NEW-ARK, in New-Jersey, September 30, 1756*, 2nd edn. (New York, 1757); Alan Heimert, *Religion and the American Mind. From the Great Awakening to the Revolution* (Cambridge, Mass.: Harvard University Press, 1966), p. 86. Burr died the year of the revival (1757), prompting the school to turn to Jonathan Edwards as its president.

38   Burr, *The Watchman's Answer*, p. 37.

39   Joseph Bellamy, *The MILLENNIUM or the THOUSAND YEARS OF PROSPERITY promised to the CHURCH OF GOD, in the OLD TESTAMENT and in the NEW, shortly to COMMENCE and to be carried on to PERFECTION under the auspices of HIM, WHO, IN THE VISION, was presented to St. JOHN*. The work was edited and republished in 1794 by David Austin, who bundled it with *Humble Attempt*—Part I: *The Millennium*, Part II: *Humble Attempt*, Part III: *Halifax on Present Evidences* (Boston, 1758; Elizabethtown: Shepard Kollock, 1794). Also found in *Works*, Vol. 1, p. 456ff.

40   Smith was a pastor in Leacock, Pennsylvania, who came to Christ under the preaching of Whitefield. He was a trustee of Princeton, the father of Stanhope Smith, the seventh president of Princeton, and John Smith, president of Hampden-Sydney College. For a fuller picture of the Smith family story, see Paul K. Conkin, *Cane Ridge: America's Pentecost* (Madison, Wis.: The University of Wisconsin Press, 1990), p. 50.

41   Heimert, *Religion and the American Mind*, p. 81.

42   Ibid., p. 82.

43   Ibid.

44   The original name for the area was Chebacco, an Indian title. (See D. Hamilton Hurd, *History of Essex County Massachusetts*, Vol. 2 [Philadelphia: J. W. Lewis & Company, 1888], p. 1153.)

45   [The first settlers] were largely men of wealth and learning, and some merchants[:] The peopl[ing] of this town is by men of good ranke and quality, many of them having the yearly revenue of large estates in England before they came to this wilderness [citing the records of the House of Commons, in memorable resolve of the 10th of March 1642: *Wonder-working Providence*]. They were thoughtful, conscientious, heroic, righteous, God-fearing; thoughtful, for they had clear views of the tenets of their religion and of civil life . . . God-fearing, for it was their purpose in all things to serve Him. . . . [Concerning the government of the town, the] object of our early ancestors was religious freedom, and when they had obtained the right and privilege to exercise it, they established governments to protect, sustain and foster it. The Bible was to them the Book of Books: it contained the principles of all municipal, moral and religious governments, and was absolute authority in all such matters (ibid., p. 570).

46   Ibid., p. 576.

47   Ibid.

48   Ibid., p. 579.

49   David Kimball, *A Sketch of the Ecclesiastical History of Ipswich. The Substance of a Discourse in Two Parts, Delivered in that Town, December 1820* (Haverhill, Mass.: Printed at the *Gazette and Patriot* Office, 1823), p. 35.

50   Ibid., p. 584.

51   Ibid.

52   Ibid.

53   Christy Wilson, Jr., *More to Be Desired Than Gold*, comp. Ivan S. Chow, ed. Helen S. Mooradkanian (South Hamilton, Mass.: Printed for Gordon-Conwell Theological Seminary, 1992), p. 83.

54   See Christopher M. Jedfrey, *The World of John Cleaveland* (London/New York: W. W. Norton and Company, 1979), p. 22.

55   Late in his life Aaron Burr, Sr., president and founding trustee of Princeton, was overheard saying to Dr. Scott of New Brunswick, New Jersey, that the principal reason Princeton College was founded was the expulsion of Brainerd from Yale. (Maclean, *History of the College of New Jersey* [Philadelphia: Lippincott & Co., 1877], p. 55, citing the diaries of Jonathan Dickinson, Elizabethtown, New Jersey.)

56   See the Biographical Sketch of John Cleaveland in the MSS Collection. Four folders. Essex Institute, Salem, Massachusetts.

57   We may sense the passion communicated by Whitefield during this visit: "Whitefield dined with the President, the Rev Thomas Clap, and afterwards preached twice at the College. Standing before this body of young men—men who would later fill the pulpits of Connecticut—he again felt the gravity of his task and sought to make the fullest use of his opportunity. 'I spoke very closely to the students,' he says, 'and shewed the dreadful ill consequences of an unconverted ministry. Oh, that God may quicken ministers! Oh, that the Lord may make them a flaming fire!'" (Dallimore, *Whitefield*, Vol. 1, p. 552, citing Whitefield's journals.)

58   Jedfrey, *John Cleaveland*, p. 22.

59   Ibid. At Harvard, meanwhile, Nathaniel Appleton was a busy apologist in like manner. Echoing Edward's concerns for union, Appleton preached:

>   FINAL APPEAL TO UNITY . . . instead of differing, and disputing about lesser Points, let us unite in the common Cause, against Sin and Wickedness, and for the promoting of the Kingdom of Christ, and the Salvation of Souls. And let us spare no Pain, nor Labour. Let us consider that our blessed Lord, had such Regard for precious souls that he left the Bosom of the Father, and the Realm of Light, and Glory above, and shed his own Blood, to purchase Salvation for them, and shall we think it hard to *spend* and *be spent* on the Service of Christ and Souls? . . . But if GOD should crown our faithful Endeavors with Success. . . . Oh! this will make us shine in the World, especially in the Eyes of those, who by our Ministry are won over to CHRIST. But we shall shine most gloriously hereafter, in the Kingdom of our Father. (From Nathaniel Appleton, *Faithful Ministers of Christ*, p. 38.)

60   See J. I. Packer, *Jonathan Edwards and the Theology of Revival*, from *Increasing in the Knowledge of God*, Papers read at the Puritan and Reformed Studies Conference, 1960:

>   A study of Jonathan Edwards on revival forewarns us against both these mistakes. . . . Edwards shields us from the romantic fallacy by constantly directing our attention to the problems which revival brings in its train. . . . No revival, though in itself a purging and purifying work of God, is ever free from attendant disfigurements. We need not read beyond the New Testament to appreciate that. Yet this must not blind us to the fact that revival is a real and glorious work of God, and a blessing much to be desired when the church's vitality is low (p. 26).

61   Jedfrey, *John Cleaveland*. In 1764 Cleaveland's credentials were publicly ridiculed by a Dr. Mayhew, D.D., pastor of the West Church of Boston. Mahew accused Cleaveland of

wrongdoing, noting that Cleaveland had been expelled from school. When news of the outburst reached Yale, its president sought to right the past wrong by awarding Cleaveland the title of A.M. the same year (Biographical Sketch, Essex Institute).

62   Biographical Sketch, Essex Institute.

63   "The first pastor of the Second Church in Ipswich was John Wise (1652-1725), among the first colonists to formally protest the taxation of the colonies without representation in England. At a town meeting [in 1687], pursuant to an order from the treasurer of the colony, acting under the command of Governor Andros, for the purpose of choosing a commissioner to join with the selectmen in assessing the inhabitants, the citizens, after having been forcibly and eloquently addressed by Mr. Wise, voted unanimously not to choose such commissioner, or take any steps whatever to collect the tax" (Hurd, *History of Essex*, p. 1164). The Second Church of Ipswich eventually became the Second Church of Essex when the town of Essex formed.

64   Ibid. "[S]oon after, signs of discontent and disaffection towards him began to be manifested, first like drops of a slight sprinkling from the outermost fringe of a cloud, the cloud gradually increasing in density till it became dark and frowning, and the rain began to fall pitilessly."

      "James Davenport, pastor of a controversial New Light congregation in Boston to whose ministry was attached certain fringe individuals, preached in Nathaniel Rogers's church and in his public prayer alluded to Pickering as a man blinded, asking God to open his eyes and cause the scales to fall from them" (ibid., p. 1166).

65   A.k.a., Ipswich/Essex.

66   Hurd, *History of Essex*, p. 1167. As these things often go, not long afterward a segment of Second Church unsympathetic to the New Lights split off and formed the South Church in Ipswich (p. 1168).

67   Ibid., p. 1169.

68   Ibid.

69   Ibid.

70   Biographical Sketch, Essex Institute.

71   Robert Crowell, *History of the Town of Essex from 1634 to 1868* (Published by the Town of Essex, Mass., 1868), p. 208. Of those who went from Cleaveland's church were three of his four sons. Once, after Gloucester had been attacked, Cleaveland prayed for his men " 'that the enemy might be blown'—'to hell and damnation,' loudly interrupted an excited soldier—'to the land of tyranny from whence they came,' continued the undisturbed chaplain, without altering his tone or apparently noticing the interruption" (p. 209).

72   Ibid., p. 182. Sometime after 1780, the COP would become known as the Quarterly Fast.

73   Ibid.

74   Chebacco was the original Indian name of the town.

75   Cleaveland's congregation first split away from the Second Church, forming the Fourth Church, but later merged again with Second Church, dropping the name Fourth Church.

76   John Cleaveland, *A SHORT and PLAIN NARRATIVE of the late WORK of GOD's SPIRIT at CHEBACCO in IPSWICH, in the YEARS 1763 and 1764: Together with Some Accounts of the Conduct of the Fourth Church of Christ in IPSWICH, in admitting MEMBERS—and their Defense of said Conduct* (Boston: Z. Fowle, 1767, Widener Microforms: Microfiche W 2571 [10581] Microfiche [New York: Readex Microprint, 1985] 11 x 15 cm. Early American imprints. First series; no. 10581).

77   Ibid., pp. 10-12.

78   Ibid.

79   Rev. Nathaniel Rogers pastored the First Church of Ipswich. John Rogers, of Kittery/Eliot, Maine, complied with the COP in his church and had Whitefield frequently in his pulpit.

      Jonathan Parsons was the first pastor of the first Presbyterian church organized in Massachusetts (1746) from disaffected members of the First Congregational Church,

Newburyport. Parsons was brought to Newburyport by Whitefield, and it was in Parsons's house that Whitefield died and in his church that Whitefield was buried.

Daniel Rogers of Exeter prayed at the funeral of George Whitefield and "openly confessed that, under God, he owed his conversion to the labours of George Whitefield. As he prayed over Whitefield's body, he cried out, 'O my father, my father!' then stopt and wept as though his heart would break, and the people weeping all through the place. Then he recovered and finished his prayer and sat down and wept." (Dallimore, *Whitefield*, Vol. 2, p. 510, quoting from John Gillies, *Memoirs of the Life of the Reverend George Whitefield* [London: E. & C. Dilly, 1772], p. 274.)

Others who offered help were Samuel Chandler, Ebenezer Cleaveland of Gloucester (John Cleaveland's brother), Jedediah Jewitt and James Chandler of Rowley, John Emerson of Topsfield, Moses Parsons of Byfield, George Leslie of Linebrook, Francis Worcester, living in Holles, Nathaniel Noyes of Southampton, and Mr. Nathan Ward of Plymouth in New-Hampshire.

80   "The whole number of those we admitted [to my church] in the Space of Seven or Eight Months was upwards of Ninety; but above two-thirds of the them were Females. I have heard that the Rev. Mr. Parsons of Newbury-port admitted about that Time upwards of Fifty; and the Rev. Mr. Jewett of Rowley, about Thirty; and the Rev. Mr. Chandler of Gloucester, a considerable Number, but I have not heard how many" (Letter from John Cleaveland to Parker Cleaveland, July 11, 1774, MSS in the Essex Institute).

When one considers that Ipswich was a town of perhaps 250 adults (1250 total people), the percentages are quite large. See also Jedfrey, *John Cleaveland*, p. 116: "Most of the villagers [of Ipswich] who joined the church in the eighteenth century joined during the revival years of 1727-1728, 1742-1743, or 1763-1764. The last of these began, according to Cleaveland, 'in the Spring and Summer of the Year 1763.' . . . It went on into the autumn of the following year. Church membership swelled in Chebacco (Essex) and the surrounding towns."

This "Work of God's Spirit" was not without its difficulties. See Heimert, *Religion and the American Mind*, pp. 334ff.

81   Letter from John Cleaveland to Parker Cleaveland, July 11, 1774, MSS in the Essex Institute, p. 4. See also Crowell, *History of Essex*, p. 182: "After noticing the Quarterly Fast, the conference and prayer-meetings of the church, as preceding this revival and probably the means in the hand of producing it . . ."

Dr. Cutler, as early as 1780, had united, with Messrs. Cleaveland [Second], [Joseph] Dana [South], and [Levi] Frisbie [First], in the observance of a Quarterly Fast and Concert of Prayer for the coming of Christ's kingdom. These meetings were held in rotation in the four churches, and the pastors alternately delivered a discourse prepared for the occasion. The venerable Mr. Cleaveland died in 1799; Mr. Frisbie, who had much of the missionary spirit, died in 1806, but their successors continued to observe the Quarterly Fast. Dr. Dana and Dr. Cutler lived to witness the ordination of many missionaries, for the home and foreign field, and rejoiced in the hope of a triumphant future for the Church of God on earth. (William P. Cutler and Julia P. Cutler, *Life Journals and Correspondence of Rev. Manasseh Cutler*, Vol. 2 [Cincinnati: Robert Clarke & Co., 1888], p. 367.)

82   Present-day Hamilton, Massachusetts.

83   Crowell, *History of Essex*, p. 182. This cooperation may have been foreseen seven years earlier. From Church Minutes dated December 6, 1763, we are told that after Jonathan Mayhew of Boston accused Cleaveland of wrongdoing, Cleaveland's congregation called upon three other churches to join them in a "solemn assembly and . . . keep a Day of humble Fasting and Prayer for the divine Direction and Blessing upon our sincere Endeavours for the Peace and Good Order among ourselves" (Cleaveland MSS Folder: "Church Minutes").

"In 1760 the second church in Ipswich, then under the pastoral care of the Rev. Mr. Cleaveland, agreed to spend one day every quarter of a year in congregational fasting and prayer for the outpouring of God's spirit upon them and upon all nations, agreeably to the concert of prayer first entered into in Scotland, some years before. The four churches in town soon entered into the design; and this was the origin of the quarterly fast, still kept up in Ipswich, and the towns dismembered from it" (Kimball, *Ecclesiastical History of Ipswich*, p. 34, footnote).

As to the thoroughly evangelical nature of the Concert of Prayer, see Joseph Dana's address to the Ipswich Concert, "A Sermon Delivered at Ipswich, on a Day of Prayer," August 4, 1807 (Newburyport: Ephraim W. Allen, 1808):

> What a loud alarm is here sounded in the ears of a busy world. Very loud, most certainly, to those who transgress the golden law of Christ, to acquire the riches, the pleasures, or the flattering distinctions, of this poor world. But loud and powerful to all who pursue earthly things in a manner not consistent with seeking *first* the kingdom of God and his righteousness. O that it might bring all such to a solemn pause! It is not a trifling question which calls for it. It is such a one as the SAVIOR OF THE WORLD has thought proper to state, with great solemnity. WHAT IS A MAN PROFITED, IF HE SHALL GAIN THE WHOLE WORLD, AND LOSE HIS OWN SOUL? In his judgment, it seems, the soul's *life* is depending. The account of gain and loss will soon be made up. And where *then* is he who has not minded religion as his first and great concern? And with all he can have acquired, what has he to give in exchange for his soul? O think of this now (p. 22).

84   Implying that every quarter of the town was engaged in the Concert: political, ecclesiastical, and lay.

85   Rev. David T. Kimball, "Centennial Discourse Delivered Before the First Church and Religious Society in Ipswich, August 10, 1834" (Published by request of the Church. Printed by Leonard W. Kimball, Pollock Press, 1834), pp. 17-18.

86   Kimball, *Ecclesiastical History of Ipswich*, p. 35.

87   The reputation of John Rogers's preaching was so great that young men would *walk* from Boston to Ipswich just to hear his Thursday lectures, a trip of about forty miles. In Kimball's day, however, few would even *ride* to the next town for the Concert of Prayer, perhaps an hour's trip by horseback.

88   Kimball, *Ecclesiastical History of Ipswich*, p. 34.

89   Crowell, *History of Essex*, p. 337: "December 31, 1859, the centennial observance of the 'Quarterly Fast' . . . A large delegation from the South Church in Ipswich was present, strongly reminding many of the former years when *the fullest meetings of the year were the Quarterly Fast day*" (emphasis added). Compare the "Quarterly Fast" with the COPs and Edwards's "Quarterly Day for Prayer" in Dwight, *Life*, Vol. 1, p. 262, Letter to M'Culloch, October 1748.

90   They may have remained orthodox and evangelical, but they were not always warm and inviting to people unlike themselves. Though The COP was by no means "to be understood as restricted to any particular *Denomination* or *Party*, or to those who are of such or have such Opinions about any former Instances of remarkable religious Concern; but [is] to be extended to *All*" (see Appendix 1). In Ipswich the members of the COP weren't always so gracious and ecumenical to people who weren't Congregationalist or Presbyterian. During the last part of the eighteenth century came the tumultuous rise of Baptist churches. In one such account, Isaac Backus (*A History of New England*, Vol. 2, ed. David Weston [Newton, Mass: Backus Historical Society, 1871]) tells about one Rev. Hezekiah Smith, who as an itinerant preacher spoke in the pulpits of both Cleaveland and Parsons of Newbury in 1764. But when Smith returned to the area as the pastor of the First Baptist Church of Haverhill (the only Baptist church north of Boston) to attend a June 13, 1765, "fast" at Bradford, his apartment was pelted with rocks. When on July 10 he appeared with Cleaveland and Parsons for an ordination service in Newbury, Parsons and Cleaveland ignored him. "Yet this was Mr. Cleaveland who had given Mr. Smith such a cordial welcome at Chebacco, and for whom he preached with such tokens of divine favor; and this was Mr. Parson's meeting-house, in which Mr. Smith had preached to about four thousand people, as it was supposed, less than twelvemonth before" (Backus quoting from Rev. A. S. Train, D.D., *The Centennial Discourse of the First Baptist Church, Haverhill*, p. 20).

91 See a collection of uncategorized sermons in the librarian's office of the Ipswich Public Library.

92 From conversations I had with her in August 1992.

93 Heimert speaks of "the 1763-64 Revivals" that "spread throughout the colonies." He says of them: "the prayers of the faithful seemed answered in an outpouring of the Spirit" (see *Religion and the American Mind*, p. 81).

94 To Buell, these days of harvest were evidence of the greater work of the Lord soon to come. They "served for confirmation of the reality of the Lord's work in such days. No doubt the days are coming when immense plenty of the Lord's spiritual waters will be poured upon the dry ground: and it will seem as if the very heavens were rent asunder, and as if were dropt down from above, as at once. The coming of our Lord Christ in his Kingdom among men will be in a sudden, amazing and irresistible manner, and with clear manifestation, like lightning that cannot be hid. . . . I freely profess I am in daily expectation of approaching terrible things in righteousness; amazing changes hastening on the earth; marvelous outpourings of the Holy Spirit; and following glories . . . [a] long prayed for day" (Buell, *Narrative*, pp. 43-44).

95 Ibid., 64.

96 Ibid., 66.

97 Ibid., 70.

98 Ibid., 81. Isaiah 66:8 would become a theme for united praying for the next century at least. It is found repeatedly in revival reports in the nineteenth century.

99 Ibid., 83. Buell ends his *Narrative* with speculations and hopes for the immanent inauguration of the millennium.

100 See Andrew Gunton Fuller, *The Complete Works of the Rev. Andrew Fuller with a Memoir of His Life,* Vol. 1 (Boston: Gould, Kendall and Lincoln, 1836), p. 42. Fuller was more optimistic than Jonathan Edwards about how soon the millennium would arrive: "This glorious period is now" (ibid., Vol. 2, p. 16). See also Fawcett, *Cambuslang*, p. 229.

101 Thomas E. Fuller, *A Memoir of the Life and Writings of Andrew Fuller* (London: J. Wheaton & Sons, 1863), p. 42.

102 Andrew Gunton Fuller, *The Nature and Importance of WALKING by FAITH* (London: Vernor, 1791), p. 37.

103 Ibid. T. Fuller adds: "These services were the commencement of the well-known missionary prayer-meetings of modern days. They met, then, when the stillness of death rested upon the churches, and no voice was heard crying in the wilderness, 'Prepare ye the way of the Lord,' but now a thousand labourers in all parts of the earth are commending to the keeping of the 'King of kings.' These gatherings may very often be found profitless and formal, but let it be remembered that from that day their succession has been unbroken. The voice of prayer awakes the zeal it still feeds!" (*Memoir of Andrew Fuller*).

104 *Walking by Faith*, in A. G. Fuller, *Complete Works*, Vol. 2, pp. 180-81.

105 T. Fuller, *Memoir of Andrew Fuller*, p. 43.

106 Ibid.

107 Ibid.

108 Ibid. The influence of Jonathan Edwards can be clearly seen in Fuller's Discourse IX: *The Subdivision of the Seventh Seal into Seven Trumpets,* found in A. G. Fuller, *Complete Works*, Vol. 2, p. 32:

> . . . prior to the sounding of the trumpets [in Revelation 8], "another angel" comes forward, and stands at the altar, "having a golden censor," to whom much incense is given, that he should offer it with the prayer of all saints upon the golden altar before the throne. . . . The "prayers" here referred to appear to have a special relation to the events about to be predicted by the sounding of the trumpets. The events would occur in answer to these prayers; which might be so many intercessions for the success of Christ's cause.

109 A. G. Fuller, *PERSUASIVES,* in *Nature and Importance*, pp. 40-41. From Fuller's circular

letter, *Causes of Declension in Religion and Means of Revival*, we read: " . . . regard for our countrymen, connections and friends inspire us [to pray], and what is asked for is so small. . . . As to the *Times* that are proposed [for the Concert of Prayer], nothing can be less burdensome than *once a month*—but what did I say? *Burdensome*? God forbid that any employment of this sort should ever prove a burden! It is hoped it will be attended to as a *privilege* rather than merely as a duty. . . . Our petitions may prove like seed in our days . . . what if we should be the sowers and our posterity the reapers! Shall we think much at this?" (A. G. Fuller, *Complete Works*, Vol. 2, p. 566.)

110 Ibid., pp. 46-47.

111 Along with Mr. Ryland of Northampton, Sutcliff, we can guess, was one of the ministers with whom Fuller prayed in concert (see T. Fuller, *Memoir of Andrew Fuller*, p. 42). Five years later, Sutcliff's passion for Jonathan Edwards's call to prayer had not waned. In 1789 he had *Humble Attempt* republished: *An HUMBLE ATTEMPT To promote Explicit Agreement and Visible UNION among God's People, in Extraordinary Prayer for the REVIVAL of Religion, and the Advancement of Christ's Kingdom on Earth, pursuant to Scripture Promises, and Prophecies concerning the last Time* (Boston: Printed for D. Henchman in Cornhil, 1747, ed. John Sutcliff; Reprinted at Northampton: T. Dicey and Co., 1789).

112 Olney was also the parish of John Newton before 1780 (John Sutcliff became the Baptist pastor at Olney in 1775). It is uncertain whether Newton ever participated in the Concert of Prayer, but his ministry is suggestive of it (he may have influenced Sutcliff). We know Newton was familiar with Edwards's works (see Letter to the Rev. Thomas Bowman, January 21, 1766, in *Letters by the Rev. John Newton*, ed. Josiah Bull [London: The Religious Tract Society, 1869], p. 125). While at Olney, Newton's diaries speak of the regular prayer meeting at the "Great House," an unoccupied mansion in town he used for prayer meetings. The meetings grew so large he first moved them to a larger room (seating 130); then they outgrew this, and he moved them into the sanctuary of the church. Other ministers and notables such as William Bull and William Cowper participated. It was for this prayer meeting that Newton wrote the hymn: "O Lord, Our Languid Frame Inspire," and his friend William Cowper wrote "Jesus, Where'er Thy People Meet" (Letter to Captain Clunie, April 1, 1769, ibid., p. 65, see note).

It is also noteworthy that the Olney church experienced numerous revivals throughout Newton's stay. To Captain Clunie, Newton wrote, "Pray for us that the Lord may be in the midst of us . . . and that as He has now given us a Rehoboth, and has made room for us [in the Great House], so that He may be pleased to add to our numbers, and make us fruitful in the land. Surely there is a need of prayer to disperse the clouds which seem to be gathering around us. Every newspaper brings us sad tidings from [London], but I hope there will be mercy afforded for the sake of the remnant. Oh, that all who know his name may be found crying out day and night before him, that iniquity may not be our ruin!" (ibid., p. 66).

To Mrs. Place, Newton wrote, "I hope the good people at Bristol, and everywhere else, are praying for our sinful, distracted land, in this dark day. The Lord is angry, the sword is drawn, and I am afraid nothing but the spirit of wrestling prayer can prevail for the returning it into the scabbard. . . . It is a time of prayer. . . . Since we received the news of the first hostilities in America, we have had an additional prayer meeting. Could I hear that [Christians] in general, instead of wasting their breath in censuring men and measures, were plying the throne of grace, I should still hope for a respite. . . ." (Letter to Mrs. Place, August 1775, ibid., pp. 234-35).

Elsewhere he wrote: "In the prayers of true believers is our best visible resource. . . . United prayer, humiliation of heart, a mourning for sin in secret, and a faithful testimony against it in public will more essentially contribute to the safety and welfare of the nation, than all our military preparations without them." (Richard Cecil, ed., *Works of John Newton, with Memoirs of the Author*, Vol. 5 [London: Hamilton, Adams and Co., 1816], p. 159.)

It was, by the way, the combination of Francke's work among the orphans and Newton's life of prayer that galvanized the call of God in George Muller's life in Bristol

(Arthur T. Pierson, *George Muller of Bristol and His Witness to a Prayer-Hearing God* [Old Tappan, N.J.: Fleming H. Revell, 1899], pp. 120, 137.)

113 Internet site: www.rpc.ox.ac.uk/rpc/bq/elwyn_n.htm#49 Particular Baptists of the Northamptonshire Baptist Association as Reflected in the Circular Letters, 1765-1820, Thornton Elwyn, Treasurer, Baptist Historical Society, Northamtonshire, England. "The Association Circular Letters and other records are now deposited in the Northamptonshire County Record Office, Wootton Park, Northampton. There is also a bound set of Circular Letters in the Archive Room at the Fuller Baptist Church, Kettering, under the keeping of Mr. J. Pemble."

114 The spirit of unity in prayer in Christ was carried over into their missionary endeavors:

> When William Carey and his friends established the missionary society in 1792 and went to Serampore, Americans were thrilled and stimulated by his reports. American Congregationalists and Presbyterians contributed more to the Serampore work than did the Baptists. The London Missionary Society, founded in 1795, was a united effort of British evangelicals in four or more communions. . . . It resolved "not to send Presbyterianism, Independency, Episcopacy, or any other form of Church Order and Government . . . but the glorious Gospel of the Blessed God to the Heathen." (R. Pierce Beaver, *Ecumenical Beginnings in Protestant World Mission: A History of Comity* [New York: Thomas Nelson, 1962], p. 21.)

115 The Baptists republished *Humble Attempt* at the turn of our century: *A Call To Prayer: An HUMBLE ATTEMPT To promote Explicit Agreement and Visible UNION among God's People, in Extraordinary Prayer for the REVIVAL of Religion, and the Advancement of Christ's Kingdom on Earth, pursuant to Scripture Promises, and Prophecies concerning the last Time* (Boston: Printed for D. Henchman in Cornhil, 1747; Reprinted London: Unwin Brothers, Limited, 1902).

> [All throughout the first half of the nineteenth century] [e]very missionary society published news about the activities of the others in its magazine. These accounts were read in the Monthly Concert of Prayer for Missions. Thus the early participants in the Protestant missionary enterprise were drawn together, influenced each other, supported each other, and felt a sense of unity and brotherhood not known to the other clergy and laity in the churches in a time of denominational isolation. The very battle against indifference, inertia, and official opposition which they had to wage for recognition of the missionary privilege and obligation sharpened their sense of unity and common purpose (Beaver, *Ecumenical Beginnings,* p. 22).

116 The Scots who supported [The Society in Scotland for the Propagation of Christian Knowledge] were responsible for the Quarterly Concert of Prayer. Jonathan Edwards, the greatest American theologian of the time and missionary to Stockbridge Indians, wrote his book, *An Humble Attempt,* &c, and gave power to the movement as well as relating it to the missionary vision. The English Baptists made the prayer movement a Monthly Concert, and the ideas connected with it influenced William Carey and his brethren. The London Missionary Society (L.M.S.) made it the Monthly Concert of Prayer for Missions, and it became on both sides of the Atlantic the most potent means of missionary education and support (Beaver, *Ecumenical Beginnings,* pp. 19, 22).

> "For the young people's missionary meetings especially, the United Society of Christian Endeavor, Boston, and some of the denominational missionary boards *publish missionary concert exercises* for all the prominent mission fields." (John F. Cowan, *New Life in the Old Prayer-Meeting* [New York: Fleming H. Revell, 1906], p. 164.)

117 "Dr. F. A. Cox, seeking for 'the primary cause of the missionary excitement in Carey's mind' and its influence among Carey's ministerial brethren, found it in" Fuller's 1784 call to prayer. (E. A. Payne, *The Prayer Call of 1784* [London, 1941], pp. 6-7.)

118 Carey's famous sermon from Isaiah 54:2, "Expect great things from God, and attempt great things for God," was a prime example of the positive and hopeful expectations arising from the millennial expectations of his day.

119 William Carey, *An ENQUIRY Into the OBLIGATIONS OF CHRISTIANS, to use Means for the CONVERSION of the HEATHENS. In Which the Religious State of the Different Nations of the*

World, the Success of Former Undertakings, and the Practicability of Further Undertakings, Are Considered (Leicester: Ann Ireland, 1792. Introduction by Earnest Payne. London: New Facsimile Edition, 1961).

120 Carey bore testimony to the effect the special monthly prayer meetings had had on his life, though he expressed in parenthesis his doubt about certain aspects of Edwards's interpretation of prophecy (see ibid., p. xii):

> On the first, and most important of those duties which are incumbent upon us, is *fervent and united prayer*. However the influence of the Holy Spirit may be set at naught, and run down by many, it will be found upon trial, that all means which we can use, without it, will be ineffectual. If a temple is raised for God in the heathen world, it will not be *by might, nor by power*, nor by the authority of the magistrate, or the eloquence of the orator; *but by my Spirit, saith the Lord of Hosts*. We must therefore be in real earnest in supplicating his blessing upon our labours.
>
> . . . It is represented in the prophets, that when there shall be *a great mourning in the land, as the mourning of Hadadrimmon in the valley of Megiddon, and every family shall mourn apart, and their wives apart*, it shall all follow upon a *Spirit of grace and supplication*. And when these things shall take place, it is promised that *there shall be a fountain opened for the house of David, and for the inhabitants of Jerusalem, for sin, and for uncleanness*—and that *the idols shall be destroyed*, and *the false prophets ashamed* of their profession (Zech. 12:10, 14—13:1, 6). This prophecy seems to teach that when there shall be an universal conjunction in fervent prayer, and all shall esteem Zion's welfare as their own, then copious influences of the Spirit shall be shed upon the churches, which like a purifying *fountain* shall cleanse the servant of the Lord. Nor shall this cleansing influence stop here; all old idolatrous prejudices shall be rooted out, and truth prevail so gloriously that false teachers shall be so ashamed as rather to wish to be classed with obscure herdsmen, or the meanest peasants, than bear the ignominy attendant on their detection.
>
> The most glorious works of grace that have ever taken place have been in answer to prayer; and it is in this way, we have the greatest reason to suppose that the glorious out-pouring of the Spirit, which we expect at last, will be bestowed.
>
> With respect to our own immediate connections, we have within these few years been favoured with some tokens for good, granted in answer to prayer, which should encourage us to persist, and increase in that important duty. I trust our *monthly prayer-meetings* for the success of the gospel have not been in vain. It is true a want of importunity too generally attends our prayers; yet unimportunate, and feeble as they have been, it is to be believed that God has heard, and in a measure answered them. The churches that have engaged in the practice have in general since that time been evidently on the increase; some controversies which have long perplexed and divided the church, are more clearly stated than ever; there are calls to preach the gospel in many places where it has not been usually published; yea, a glorious door is opened, and is likely to be opened wider and wider, by the spread of civil and religious liberty, accompanied also by a diminution of the spirit of popery. . . .
>
> If an holy solicitude had prevailed in all the assemblies of Christians in behalf of their Redeemer's kingdom, we might probably have seen before now, not only an *open door* for the gospel, but *many running to and fro, and knowledge increases*; or a diligent use of those means which providence has put in our power, accompanied with a greater blessing than ordinary from heaven.
>
> . . . We must not be contented however with praying, without *exerting ourselves in the use of the means* for obtaining of those things we pray for. We're *the children of the light*, but *as wise in their generation as the children of this world*, they would stretch every nerve to gain so glorious a prize, nor ever imagine that it was to be obtained in any other way.

121 Ibid., *Introduction*; see also pp. 14, 15.

122 Ibid., p. 77. See Appendix 2 for more lengthy excerpts.

123 See *Letters by the Rev. John Newton*, ed. Josiah Bull (London: The Religious Tract Society, 1869).

124 Fawcett, *Cambuslang*, pp. 234-35.

125 *Thoughts on the PLAN FOR SOCIAL PRAYER proposed by the DIRECTORS of the NEW-YORK MISSIONARY SOCIETY* (New York: T. & J. Swords, 1797).

126 Ibid., p. 4.

127 Ibid., p. 5.

128 Ibid., p. 8.

129 Ibid., p. 9.

130 Ibid., p. 10.

131 The Sunday-School concert . . . gained a national prominence through its recommendation by the Board of Managers of the American Sunday-School Union, in September, 1824, and its growth was thenceforward correspondent with the extension of the Sunday-School system. Both the missionary and Sunday-School concerts were, after a time, changed from Monday to Sunday evenings. (Clay Trumbull, *Children in the Temple: A Handbook for the Sunday-School Concert and a Guide for the Children's Preacher* [Springfield, Mass: Holland & Company, 1869], pp. 15-16.)

132 *Union Hymns* (Philadelphia: American Sunday-School Union, 1845). "More than 300,000 copies sold."

133 Ibid., Hymn no. 424.

134 Ibid., Hymn no. 430.

135 *A Concert of Prayer propounded to the citizens of the United States of America. By an association of Christian ministers* (Exeter, N. H.: Lamson and Ranlet, 1787).

136 Joseph Bellamy, *The MILLENNIUM, or the THOUSAND YEARS OF PROSPERITY promised to the CHURCH OF GOD, in the OLD TESTAMENT and in the NEW, shortly to COMMENCE and to be carried on to PERFECTION under the auspices of HIM; WHO, IN THE VISION, was presented to St. JOHN*, ed. David Austin (Boston, 1758; Elizabethtown: Shepard Kollock, 1794). In 1793 Austin also had Jonathan Edwards's *History of Redemption* republished: (New York: T. & T. Swords, 1793). Writing in its foreword, Austin hails the glory and "the approach of the millennial Day!"

137 Inside the front cover is a picture of Jonathan Edwards.

138 Ibid., p. iii.

139 Ibid., p. v.

140 Ibid., pp. vii-viii.

141 See Appendix 3.

142 Ibid.

143 Ibid.

144 *THE DAWN OF DAY, Introductory to the RISING SUN, whose Rays Shall Gild the Clouds . . . in Nine Letters* (New Haven: Read and Morse, 1800). Included were open letters to King George III, Pius VII, Napoleon Bonaparte, the French nation, etc., warning them all of the impending judgment of God upon them. Austin got a bit carried away, we may suppose. He envisioned "Joshua arising out of the ashes of [George] Washington" (p. 10), and sees Christ's new temple rising "from the Washington base" (p. 16). In his letter "To the Christian Church Throughout the World," he wrote urgently: "Prepare yourselves for an acknowledgment of one common supreme . . . favour—of one common Jerusalem—of one common altar—of one common Melchisedeck, king of Salem, and Priest of the Most High God" (p 18).

Heimert reports on a remarkable campaign engineered by Austin: "*Humble Attempt* inspired David Austin in the series of speculations and ventures by which he persuaded himself, and a large part of the dissenter population of New England and the Middle Colonies, to exert themselves on behalf of the election of Jefferson so the millennium might be inaugurated before the beginning of the nineteenth century" (Heimert, *Religion and the American Mind*, p. 81).

Austin believed that Jefferson embodied the very essence of the Antichrist. Jefferson's election, Austin thought, would hasten the day of Satan's prominence foretold in the Scriptures, thus the day of Satan's utter defeat, and thus hasten the inauguration of the millennial kingdom! (Heimert, citing David Austin, *The Millennium* [Elizabethtown, N. J., 1794], pp. v-vi.)

145 Letter to Fifteen Divines, New Haven, October 20, 1800, from Heimert, ibid., p. 32.

146 *The Diary of Isaac Backus,* ed. William G. McLoughlin, Vol. 3 (Providence: Brown University Press, 1979), p. 1283.

147 Ibid., p. 1342. See The Sedition Act, July 14, 1797, *The Laws of the United States of America* (Philadelphia: Richard Folwell, 1796-1798).

148 McLoughlin, ibid.

149 Ibid., p. 1447, quoting from the "Warren Commission" of 1799.

150 Alvah Hovey, *The Life and Times of Isaac Backus* (Boston: Gould and Lincoln, 1859), pp. 304-5.

151 Paul Keith Conkin, *Cane Ridge: America's Pentecost* (Madison, Wis.: The University of Wisconsin Press, 1990). See his Introduction.

152 See discussion in Winthrop S. Hudson, *Religion in America* (New York: Charles Scribners Sons, 1965), pp. 118-19. John Blair Smith was a chief supporter of this union measure, especially for the settling of the frontier.

153 One of the principal influences in the South, was Virginian Samuel Davies, another Jonathan Edwards disciple and trustee at Princeton. He was a powerful voice in Presbyterianism and one of America's great preachers. In 1751 Davies led an attempt to move Jonathan Edwards, recently deposed from his pulpit in Northampton, Massachusetts, to Virginia. Later, in 1758, he would succeed Jonathan Edwards as president of the College of New Jersey (Princeton). (See Conkin, *Pentecost,* p. 35.)

154 See chapter 2, "The Feeling of Crisis," in John Boles, *The Great Revival 1787-1805* (Lexington, Ky.: University of Kentucky Press, 1972), pp. 12ff.

155 Benjamin Rice Lacy, *Revivals in the Midst of the Years* (Hopewell, Va.: Royal Publishers, Inc., 1968), p. 68.

156 Ibid.

157 Ibid., quoting Dr. William Hill, the next student saved.

158 Boles, *Great Revival,* p. 39.

159 Ibid., p. 47.

160 See Lacy, *Revivals in the Midst,* p. 74. The Saturday evening and Sabbath morning Concert come right out of the Cambuslang memorial. McCready, like the English Baptists under Fuller, increased the frequency of the large-group meeting to once a month.

In Richard M'Nemar, *The Kentucky Revival; or A Short History of the Late Extraordinary Outpouring of the Spirit of God in the Western States of America* (New York: Edward O. Jenkins, 1846), we find recorded the formation of "praying societies" prior to the Kentucky revival, the members of which cried out to God "for the accomplishment of those blessed promises which respected the coming of Christ and the glory of the latter days" (p. 12).

M'Nemar also wrote:
[Before the revival, the churches] instead of uniting . . . in righteousness and peace, had kindled up endless controversies and angry disputes. . . . [They] were full of envy and strife, railing and backbiting, hateful and hating one another. . . . [Eventually, the Christians understood that there] would be glorious times upon the earth, and Christ would appear again, and set up his kingdom, and gather the nations into it. . . . [So] many began to apprehend that this period was not far off; and concluded it was time to leave off their vain disputes, and unite in prayer, for Christ to come and pour out his spirit, gather his people into one, make an end of sin, and fill the earth with his glory. . . . When any one prays for a thing, it is a sure and certain evidence that he has not got that thing in possession; and hence the united prayers of hundreds of

the warmest professors, entreating Christ to come and visit the churches, loudly proclaimed that he was not already there (pp. 11-13).

Boles cites Burkitt and Read, *History of the Kekhukee Baptist Association* (Halifax, N. C., 1803), who record that the Kehukee Association was busy setting up prayer societies.

161 Catherine Cleaveland, *The Great Revival in the West* (Gloucester, Mass: Peter Smith, 1959), p. 40, footnote.

162 Boles, *Revival*, p. 48.

163 *Western Missionary Magazine and REPOSITORY of Religious Intelligence*, Vol. 1 (Washington, Penn: John Collerick, 1803-4), February, p. 27.

164 For a full-blown account of this remarkable series of events, see James McCready, "Short Narrative of the Revival of Religion in Logan County, in the State of Kentucky, and the adjacent settlements in the State of Tennessee, from May 1797-1800," in ibid. (February 1803), pp. 27-28; (March 1803), pp. 45-54; (April 1803), pp. 99-103. McCready's complete "Narrative" can be found in *New York Missionary Magazine*, 1800-1803 (New York), see 1802, p. 160.

Conkin argues that the Presbyterian Sacrament meeting (the serving of Communion to large outdoor assemblies) was critical for the revival of 1800. It created an environment perfectly suited for what followed and set the precedent for the camp meetings: "[McCready] timed the communions so that members of each small congregation could travel to each one by horseback or wagon, thus creating the critical mass of people needed for a fervent revival. The travel, the home hospitality, the break from normal routines, the all-day and, often, almost all-night services also created a special atmosphere" (*Pentecost*, p. 57). Conkin argues, too, that the Cane Ridge revival "was the next Cambuslang" (p. 25) since it was "eerily similar" to that revival centered on Whitefield's preaching at the Sacrament, where the crowds reached 30,000. At Cane Ridge attendance approached 25,000. Conkin points out, too, that the Communion services created so much interest in Cambuslang that *Western Missionary Magazine* reprinted M'Culloch's "Attestations" in the August 1804 issue.

165 Boles, *Revival*, p. 49.

166 See Lacy, *Revivals in the Midst*, pp. 74-75.

167 Ibid., p. 50.

168 Ibid., p. 51.

169 Conkin, *Pentecost*, p. 59.

170 Levi Purviance, *The Biography of Elder David Purviance* (Dayton: B. F. & G. W. Ells, 1848), pp. 242-43.

171 Ibid.

172 Lacy, *Revivals in the Midst*, p. 75. Purviance, *Biography*, p. 244.

173 Baptist H. Tolar, writing from Virginia to Isaac Backus, August 8, 1801: "May the many revivals begun in different states of this union, spread, till the earth shall be full of the knowledge of the Lord." (Hovey, *Life and Times*, pp. 296-97.)

174 Purviance, *Biography*, p. 245: "Bigotry, selfishness and sectarianism gave way before the spirit that accompanied this work. A great regard was manifested for the salvation of souls and a very extraordinary spirit of prayer was felt among Christians. So much love, peace and unanimity, forbearance, brotherly kindness and charity, must be from the source and fountain of all GOODNESS."

175 *Western Missionary Magazine*, Vol. 1, October 1803, p. 312.

176 M'Nemar, *Kentucky Revival*, p. 78.

177 With regard to the lasting influence of Jonathan Edwards, *Western Missionary Magazine*'s first nine installments (February-October) ran Jonathan Edwards's *Distinguishing Marks* and in April printed his sermon "On Fulfilling Engagements and Praying Debts."

178 Ibid., "*REVIVAL OF RELIGION In the Western Country*," October, p. 328.

179 Ibid.

180 Ibid., September, pp. 292ff.

181 Ibid.

182 M'Nemar, *Kentucky Revival*, p. 87.

183 Ibid., July, pp. 216ff.

184 By "the wretch," Voltaire meant the Christian church.

185 Ibid., pp. 222-23.

186 Its "end" or "point of consummation to which all things are flowing."

187 Boles, *Revival*, p. 103: "Post-millennialism dominated by far," Boles noted. He cited Levi Purviance as an example of the commonly held convictions: "Levi Purviance recalled that in Kentucky, 'The good work of reformation went on with irresistible force, and appeared like carrying everything before it. May we be fully persuaded that the glorious Millennial Day had commenced' " (quoting from Levi Purviance, *Biography*).

188 Alexander Pringle, *Prayer for the Revival of Religion in all the Protestant Churches and for the Spread of the Gospel among Heathen Nations, Recommended. Also Outlines of a Plan for the Erection of Monthly Societies for Prayer, Among Friends of Real Religion of all Denominations, in Scotland. With Extracts Concerning the Begun Revival of Religion in Some Churches* (Edinburgh: Printed by Shaw and Pillane and sold by J. Guthrie, J. Ogle, and J. Galbraith, 1796), pp. 2-4.

189 James H. Stewart, *THOUGHTS on the IMPORTANCE OF SPECIAL PRAYER for the GENERAL OUTPOURING of THE HOLY SPIRIT* (London: Printed for The Religious Tract Society, c. 1825), p. 42. (This tract, ed. Samuel Davies, is bound with Jonathan Edwards's *A Faithful Narrative*.) Stewart's involvement means that the COP was not the exclusive domain of the low churches.

190 Ibid., p. 30.

191 Ibid., p. 4.

192 Ibid., p. 16. To proof-text this assertion, Stewart points to some of Jonathan Edwards's favorite texts, including Zechariah 8:21, 12:10, Jeremiah 31:6, and Isaiah 62:6-7.

193 Ibid., p. 4.

194 Ibid., p. 31.

195 Ibid. As in the Cambuslang memorial, on page 5 Stewart suggests "Sabbath mornings" for this concert. He adds to this, however, "Monday evenings for the family" prayers.

196 Ibid., p. 32.

197 Ibid.

198 *Calcutta Christian Observer* 2 (December 1833), p. 599.

199 Ibid., pp. 21-22.

200 David Slie, *The Holy of Holies, or, World's Tri-Daily Concert of Prayer* (Rochester, N.Y.: A. Strong & Company, Democrat and American Office, 1861).

201 Ibid., p. vi.

202 Ibid., p. 11.

203 Ibid., pp. 11-12.

204 Ibid., p. 27.

205 Ibid., p. 94.

206 See "My Conversion to Christ," chapter 2 of *The Memoirs of Charles G. Finney*, ed. Garth Rosell and Richard A. G. Dupuis (Grand Rapids: Zondervan, 1989), pp. 16ff.

207 Ibid., p. 33.

208 Ibid.

209 Ibid., pp. 33-35. Compare the Finney account of the Adams, New York, revival with an account of a revival in Northern Scotland ("Revival of Religion in the North of Scotland," June 10, 1802, in *Western Missionary Magazine*, Vol. 1, March 1803, pp. 54-55):

The manner in which many of [the revived people] were impressed was to me at first surprising: they were suddenly struck during the time of prayer, they fell to the ground, and many of them, both old and young, continued speechless for twenty minutes, or half an hour, and the first language they uttered was, "Praise the Lord!— O praise and magnify his ever-blessed name, for his great love wherewith he loved us, and gave himself for the unjust, that he might bring us unto God." &c. . . . It began in the prayer meetings which I mentioned in the journal. . . . They all flocked together in each of these places, and continued to go from house to house, praying and praising God for eight to ten days and nights, with only about two hours sleep each morning, and many several nights without any sleep.

210 Charles G. Finney, *Lectures on Revivals of Religion* (New York, Chicago, Toronto, London and Edinburgh: Fleming H. Revell, 1868).

211 For further discussion, see "Charles Finney," in *Christian History* , Vol. 7, No. 4, Issue 20, 1988, p. 2. For a discussion of how Finney's theology of revival is a logical extension of Jonathan Edwards's theology, see "Background to Awakenings," in *Christian History*, Vol. 8, No. 3, Issue 23, p. 6.

212 Stewart, *THOUGHTS on the IMPORTANCE*, p. 4. One incident in particular demonstrated Finney's commitment to united prayer. In April 1824, he came to the town of Evans Mills for meetings. Gorham Cross, a young boy at the time,

> was at the house of the deacon of the church upon Finney's arrival. As soon as he had taken off his overcoat, [Finney] asked what praying persons there were in the neighborhood. He was informed that there were a very few. Two or three women in humble circumstances were mentioned, however, who were of recognized piety. His instant reply was, "I must see them," and he immediately put on his overcoat and set out to look them up. This will illustrate what was his universal practice in subsequent years. (*Lectures on Revivals*, p. 98, footnote, quoting *Charles Grandison Finney* [Boston and New York: Houghton Mifflin, 1891], pp. 29-30.)

213 Ibid.

214 Ibid., from "Necessity and Effect of Union," p. 294.

215 Professor of Ecclesiastical History and Church Government until his death in 1850.

216 Samuel Miller, *Letters on the Observance of the Monthly Concert of Prayer* (Philadelphia: Presbyterian Board of Publication, 1845).

217 Ibid., p. 16.

218 Ibid., p. 17.

219 Cairns, among others, entitles this work of God "The Lay Prayer Revival." Earl E. Cairns, *An Endless Line of Splendor* (Wheaton, Ill.: Tyndale, 1986), p. 147.

220 See, for example, Talbot Chambers, *The Noon Prayer Meeting of the North Dutch Church* (New York: Board of Publication of the Reformed Protestant Dutch Church, 1858); Cairns begins his discussion of the revival in the United States with: "The officials of the old North Dutch Reformed Church at Fulton Street and Williams Streets in New York became concerned . . ." (Cairns, ibid., pp. 148ff.

221 *Old South Chapel Prayer Meeting: Its Origins and History* (Boston: J. E. Tilton & Company, 1859), pp. 17ff.

222 Ibid., p. 20.

223 Ibid.

224 Ibid., p. 22.

225 Ibid. Each year's statistics are listed in the minutes.

226 Ibid., p. 27.

227 Ibid., p. 30 (emphasis added).

228 Ibid., p. 31. The Brooklyn, New York, meeting was called the Union Prayer Meeting.

229 Ibid.

230 Ibid.

231 Ibid., p. 37.

232 Ibid., pp. 9ff:

The meeting is held every morning, Sunday excepted, in the Old South Chapel . . . commencing in the warm season at eight o'clock, and in the cold season at half-past eight. It continues one hour only. . . . The time allotted to each speaker is three minutes, and those who conduct the meeting are expected to enforce this rule except in special cases. The leader of the meeting is allowed ten minutes to open it, including prayer, reading of Scriptures, singing, and remarks. [A] committee secures someone to be responsible for the meeting each day in the week for a number of months at a time, and he must either take charge of it himself or see that someone is provided. . . . The rules are placed upon the table so that the leader may see them. A little bell is also provided, which he is expected to use when necessary in enforcing the three-minute rule.

233 Ibid., p. 11:

There is a general understanding that on Monday morning special opportunity will be given for the communication of religious intelligence; consequently, there is more religious news presented on that morning than on any other. Clergymen from abroad are often present, and they are called upon, if they do not rise voluntarily, to take part in the meeting.

On Saturday, the Jews are especially remembered in the prayers, and interesting intelligence is often presented respecting the work of the Lord among them. Occasionally, converted Jews have been present, which has added very much to the interest of the meeting. Rev. Dr. [William] Jenks, who has always felt a deep interest in their welfare, has often given very valuable information respecting them, which has quickened the faith of God's people, and incited them to earnest prayer in their behalf.

234 Ibid., p. 65.

235 Ibid., p. 88.

236 Ibid.

237 Ibid. In *The Autobiography of Lyman Beecher*, ed. Barbara M. Cross, Vol. 2 (Cambridge, Mass: The Belknap Press of Harvard University Press, 1961), p. 412, we read: "[In his waning years] the Old South morning prayer-meeting became, while he continued to reside in Boston, his main dependence—a kind of citadel on which he fell back to fight against decay to the last, and many were the brilliant flashes and bold sallies which reminded his brethren of what he had been."

238 For well over a year *The Congregationalist* had been reporting revival-like activities from around the nation. It is of great interest, too, that in the issue dated April 24, 1857, Jonathan Edwards made his mark once again. An article speaks about the Chauncy/Edwards debates over the authenticity of the revival and concludes:

[The Awakening in the 1730s and 1740s] was pre-eminently a work of God's grace, carried on with great power, and productive of vast results . . . [including binding] the growth of Arminianism, Pelagianism, and Socinianism . . . and the prominence which the doctrines of grace have ever since held in the system of New England theology. . . . Princeton and Dartmouth Colleges both grew indirectly out of it; as also the mission of David Brainerd to the heathen, and *the monthly concert of prayer* for the world (emphasis added).

239 *Old South Chapel Prayer*, p. 50. See Fuller's *Persuasives*, pp. 40-41.

240 Ibid., p. 119.

241 Rosell and Dupuis, *Memoirs*, pp. 559ff.

242 Ibid., p. 562, footnote.

243 Ibid. In *The Congregationalist*, April 24, 1857, under the heading "Morning Prayer Meeting," we read of Tennent's visit to one of the large meetings:

The prayer meeting which has been held on every weekday morning, in the Old South Chapel in this city for several years past, was appointed in Tremont Temple for Fast Day, where a large audience assembled, nearly filling the room [Tremont Temple seats several thousand people]. . . . The meeting in the Chapel on Monday morning last, was prolonged nearly half an hour beyond its ordinary length, which is three-fourths of an hour. . . . Lewis Tappan of New York, was present, and in brief remarks referred to the experience of by-gone days when he was a resident of Boston and a disciple of Unitarianism.

Tappan used *American Missionary Magazine* to promote the New York prayer meeting. It was reprinted in *The Congregationalist*, Boston, October 2, 1857.

244 Ibid.

245 See Chambers, *Noon Prayer Meeting*, pp. 47ff. What made the Lanphier meetings so important? Two things: 1) his proximity to the financial district of New York (his meetings swelled in October of 1857 after the Bank of Philadelphia went under, and then they exploded in November, December, and January after the stock market crashed), and 2) his proximity to the New York press (they made his meetings a national byword).

CHAPTER 4: BACK TO THE FUTURE?

1   More than any single person, Steve has promoted and popularized Prayer Walking.

2   Acts 6:2.

3   Luke 24:49.

4   The word *together* is vital to understanding the type of prayer Luke is describing and goes to the heart of praying "in concert." The word is *homothymadon*, otherwise translated "one mind," "one heart," or "one accord." "[*Homothymadon*] is first found in the fifth and fourth centuries B.C. (Aristophanes, Plato, Demosthenes) and in the political sphere is used especially for the visible, inner unity of a group faced by a common duty or danger. The unanimity is not based on common personal feelings but on a cause greater than the individual." (Colin Brown, ed., *Dictionary of New Testament Theology*, Vol. 3. [Grand Rapids: Zondervan, 1980], p. 908.) See Acts 1:14; 2:46; 4:24; 5:12; Rom. 15:5-6. On Romans 15, Kittel writes: "[*Homothymadon* is] the goal of the church . . . unanimous praise of God *en heni stomati* ['with one mouth'], is also envisaged by Paul . . . when he prays to God for the unanimity in service that comes from Christ Jesus, and that *surmounts all differences in understanding and knowledge.*" (Gerhard Kittel and Gerhard Friedrich, eds., *Theological Dictionary of the New Testament*, abridged [Grand Rapids: Eerdmans and Paternoster Press, 1985], p. 684.)

5   Luke 4:1.

6   Matthew 4.

7   John 2:24.

8   Luke 6:12.

9   Mark 6:45ff.

10   Luke 23:46.

11   Luke 11:1.

12   G. I. Williamson, *The Westminster Confession of Faith for Study Classes* (Philadelphia: Presbyterian and Reformed Publishing Company, 1964), p. 88, Confession X: "Effectual Calling."

13   John 15:5.

14   Zechariah 4:6.

15   John Piper, *Desiring God* (Portland, Ore.: Multnomah, 1996).

16   Charles Haddon Spurgeon, *Three Sermons on Revival* (Pasadena, Tex.: Pilgrim Publications), pp. 31-32.

17   David Wayne Henderson, *The Ecclesiastical and Social Impact of the Clapham Sect: A Case Study for Renewal*, unpublished M.A. thesis, Gordon-Conwell Theological Seminary, April 1984, p. 4.

18   Ibid., p. 5.

19   David Fuller, ed., *Spurgeon's Lectures to His Students* (Grand Rapids: Zondervan, 1955), p. 43.

20   Nathaniel Appleton, *Faithful Ministers of Christ, the Salt of the Earth, and the Light of the World* (Boston: Printed by Rogers and Fowle for Samuel Elliot, 1743), p. 30.

21   Hebrews 11:1 (KJV). See Andrew Gunton Fuller, *The Nature and Importance of WALKING by FAITH* (London: Vernor, 1791).

22   Thomas E. Fuller, *A Memoir of the Life and Writings of Andrew Fuller* (London: J. Wheaton & Sons, 1863), p. 48.

23   Letter to William M'Culloch, October 7, 1748, in S. E. Dwight, *The Life of President Edwards,* Vol. 1 (New York: G.&C.&H. Carvill, 1830), p. 262.

24   Richard Lovelace, *Dynamics of Spiritual Life* (Downers Grove, Ill.: InterVarsity Press, 1979), p. 402, quoting Calvin Colton, *History and Character of American Revivals of Religion,* 2nd. ed. (London: Fredrick Westley and A. H. Davis, 1838), pp. 141-43. See also the lyrics of "Onward Christian Soldiers," #620, and "Stand Up, Stand Up for Jesus," #618, in Alfred Smith, ed., *Living Hymns* (Montrose, Penn: Encore Publications, 1972).

25   David Slie, *The Holy of Holies, or, World's Tri-Daily Concert of Prayer* (Rochester, N.Y.: A. Strong & Company, Democrat and American Office, 1861), p. 36.

26   Not even "intellectually respectable" (Stephen J. Stein, ed., *The Works of Jonathan Edwards,* Vol. 5, *Apocalyptic Writings* [New Haven, London: Yale University Press, 1977], p. 1.)

27   "There is a mood among . . . Christians of '*Aprés moi, le deluge*'" ("After me, the deluge," Lovelace, *Dynamics,* p. 404).

28   Jonathan Edwards, *The Works of Jonathan Edwards,* 10th ed., Vol. 1 (London: Henry G. Bohn, 1845), p. 369.

29   Issued by the Northfield Convention, August 14, 1885. From *Crisis in Missions,* by A. T. Pierson, appendix.

30   Northampton, Edwards's home, could have been reached in a day from Northfield by horseback.

APPENDIX 1

1   Jonathan Edwards, *An HUMBLE ATTEMPT To promote Explicit Agreement and Visible UNION among God's People, in Extraordinary Prayer for the REVIVAL of Religion, and the Advancement of Christ's Kingdom on Earth, pursuant to Scripture Promises, and Prophecies concerning the last Time* (Boston, New-England: Printed for D. Henchman in Cornhil, 1747), pp. 20ff.

2   Joseph Sewell (Old South Church), Thomas Prince, John Webb (New North Church), Thomas Foxcroft (First Church; one of the most prominent people to side with Edwards regarding the Communion controversy in Northampton), and Joshua Gee (North Church, pastored with and after Cotton Mather). Sewell and Prince were among the oldest and most highly esteemed pastors in Boston.

APPENDIX 2

1   From Section V of William Carey's *An ENQUIRY Into the OBLIGATIONS OF CHRISTIANS, to use Means for the CONVERSION of the HEATHENS. In Which The Religious State of the Different Nations of the World, the Success of Former Undertakings, and the Praticability of Further Undertakings, Are Considered,* Introduction by Earnest Payne (Leicester: Ann Ireland, 1792; New Facsimile Edition, London: 1961), pp. 77-81.

BIBLIOGRAPHY

Alleine, Richard. *A Companion for PRAYER In times of extraordinary Danger. To which is added, by way of Appendix, from Dr. Increase Mather's Discourse of the Prevalency of Prayer, &c.* Printed and sold by S. Kneeland, opposite the Prison, in Queen Street, 1750.

Appleton, Nathaniel. *(Mr.) Appleton's Discourse on the General Fast.* To the Session of the General Court, Cambridge, April 5, 1770.

_____. *Faithful Ministers of Christ, the Salt of the Earth, and the Light of the World.* Boston: Printed by Rogers and Fowle for Samuel Elliot, 1743.

Augustine, Bishop of Hippo. *Preaching and Teaching.* Oxford: A. R. Mowbray & Co., 1907.

Austin, David. *The DAWN OF DAY . . . in Nine Letters.* New Haven: Printed by Read and Morse, 1800.

Autrey, C. E. *Revivals of the Old Testament.* Grand Rapids: Zondervan, 1960.

Backus, Isaac. *Church History of New England from 1620-1804.* Philadelphia: American Baptist Publishing, 1853.

_____. *A History of New England.* 2 vols., ed. David Weston. Newton, Mass., 1871.

_____. *The Diary of Isaac Backus.* Ed. William G. McLoughlin, Vol. 3. Providence: Brown University Press, 1979.

Barth, Karl. *Preaching the Gospel.* Philadelphia: Westminster, 1963.

Baxter, Richard. *The Reformed Pastor.* Ed. William Brown. Edinburgh: Banner of Truth/ Puritan Paperbacks, 1974.

Beaver, R. Pierce. *Ecumenical Beginnings in Protestant World Mission. A History of Comity.* Nashville: Thomas Nelson, 1962.

Beecher, Lyman. *The Autobiography of Lyman Beecher.* Ed. Barbara M. Cross, Vol. 2. Cambridge, Mass.: The Belknap Press of Harvard University Press, 1961.

Bellamy, Joseph. *The MILLENNIUM, or the THOUSAND YEARS OF PROSPERITY promised to the CHURCH OF GOD, in the OLD TESTAMENT and in the NEW, shortly to COMMENCE and to be carried on to PERFECTION under the auspices of HIM; WHO, IN THE VISION, was presented to St. JOHN.* Ed. David Austin. Boston, 1758; Elizabethtown: Shepard Kollock, 1794.

Beveridge, W. *A Short History of the Westminster Assembly.* Edinburgh: T. & T. Clark, 1904.

Bloch, Ruth. *Visionary Republic: Millennial Themes in American Thought, 1756-1800.* Cambridge, Mass.: Harvard University Press, 1985.

Boles, John B. *The Great Revival 1787-1805.* Lexington, Ky.: University of Kentucky, 1972.

Bonhoeffer, Dietrich. *The Cost of Discipleship.* New York: Macmillan Publishing Co., 1963.

Bounds, E. M. *Power Through Prayer.* Springdale, Penn.: Whitaker House, 1982.

Brown, Colin, ed. *Dictionary of New Testament Theology.* 3 vols. [Translated, with additions and revisions, from the German: *Theologishes Begriffslexikon Zum Neuen Testament.* Eds. Lothar Coenen, Erich Beyreuther, and Hans Bietenhard] Grand Rapids: Zondervan, 1980.

Bruce, Alexander Balmine. *The Training of the Twelve, or Passages Out of the Gospels Exhibiting the Twelve Disciples of Jesus Under Discipline for the Apostleship.* 4th edn. A. C. Armstrong and Son, 1894; Grand Rapids: Kregel Publications, 1971.

Bryant, David. *With Concerts of Prayer Christians Join for Spiritual Awakening and World Evangelization.* Ventura, Ca.: Regal Books, 1985.

_____. "Special Report: The Most Hopeful Sign of Our Times: A Growing Prayer Movement Points America Toward Spiritual Revival," in *National & International Religion Report.* Stephen M. Wike, Publisher. Copyright 1992 by Media Management, P.O. Box 21433, Roanoke, VA 24018.

Buchanan, Claudius. *The Works of the Reverend Claudius Buchanan.* Comprising his *Eras of Light, Light of the World,* and *Star in the East,* to which is added *Christian Researches in Asia.* Boston: Samuel T. Armstrong, 1812.

Buell, Samuel. *A FAITHFUL NARRATIVE of the Remarkable Revival of Religion in the CONGREGATION of EASTHAMPTON on Long Island, In the year of our Lord, 1764.* Sag Harbor: Printed by Aiden Spooner, 1808.

Bull, Josiah, ed. *Letters by the Rev. John Newton.* London: The Religious Tract Society, 1869.

Burns, James. *Revivals: Their Laws and Leaders.* Grand Rapids: Baker Book House, 1960.

Cairns, Earle E. *An Endless Line of Splendor. Revivals and Their Leaders from the Great Awakening to the Present.* Wheaton, Ill.: Tyndale House Publishers Inc., 1986.

Calvin, John. *Institutes of the Christian Religion.* Trans. Henry Beveridge. Grand Rapids: Wm. B. Eerdmans, reprinted 1975.

Carey, William. *An ENQUIRY Into the OBLIGATIONS OF CHRISTIANS, to use Means for the CONVERSION of the HEATHENS. In Which the Religious State of the Different Nations of the World, the Success of Former Undertakings, and the Practicability of Further Undertakings, Are Considered.* Introduction by Earnest Payne. Leicester: Ann Ireland, 1792; New Facsimile edition, London, 1961.

Cecil, Richard, ed. *Works of John Newton. With Memoirs of the Author.* 6 vols, 2nd edn. London: Hamilton, Adams and Co., 1816.

Cedar, Paul, Kent Hughes, and Ben Paterson. *Mastering the Pastoral Role.* Portland, Ore.: Multnomah, 1991.

Clark, Calvin Montague. *History of the Congregational Churches in Maine.* Vol. 2. Portland, Maine: The Congregational Christian Conference of Maine, 1935.

Chambers, Talbot. *The Noon Prayer Meeting of the North Dutch Church.* New York: Board of Publication of the Reformed Protestant Dutch Church, 1858.

Christian History. Vol. 5, No. 2. Christian History Institute, 1986.

Christian History, The. Edinburgh, Scotland: Bound edition, 1943. Boston, N.E.: Kneeland and Green for Thomas Prince, 1743.

Cleveland, Catharine C. *The Great Revival in the West.* Gloucester, Mass.: Peter Smith, 1959.

Cleaveland, John. *A SHORT and PLAIN NARRATIVE of the late WORK of GOD's SPIRIT at CHEBACCO in IPSWICH, in the YEARS 1763 and 1764: Together with Some Accounts of the Conduct of the Fourth Church of Christ in IPSWICH, in admitting MEMBERS— and their Defense of said Conduct.* Boston: Z. Fowle, P. Freeman, 1767.

_____. MSS Collection. Four folders. Salem, Mass.: Essex Institute.

Congregationalist, The. Boston. April 3, 1857; April 24, 1857; May 1, 1857; October 2, 1857.

Congregational Quarterly, The. Whole No. 9. January 1861. Vol. 3, No. 1. Boston, 1861.

Cowan, John F. *New Life in the Old Prayer-Meeting.* New York: Fleming H. Revell, 1906.

Crowell, Robert. *History of the Town of Essex from 1634 to 1868.* Published by the town of Essex, Mass., 1868.

Curnock, N., ed. *The Letters of the Rev. John Wesley.* Standard edn. Vol. 2. London: Epworth Press, 1909.

Cutler, William P. and Julia P. Cutler. *Life Journals and Correspondence of Rev. Manasseh Cutler.* Vol. 2. Cincinnati: Robert Clarke & Co., 1888.

Dana, Joseph. *A Sermon Delivered at Ipswich, on a Day of Prayer, August 4, 1807.* Newburyport: Ephraim W. Allen, 1808.

Dallimore, Arnold A. *George Whitefield: The Life and Times of the Great Evangelist of the Eighteenth-Century Revival.* 2 vols. Westchester, Ill.: Cornerstone Books, 1979.

Demaray, Donald E. *The Innovation of John Newton.* Texts and Studies in Religion, Vol. 36. Lewiston/Queenston: The Edwin Mellen Press, 1988.

Edwards, Jonathan. *History of Redemption.* Ed. David Austin. New York: T. and J. Swords, 1793.

_____. *An HUMBLE ATTEMPT To promote Explicit Agreement and Visible UNION among God's People, in Extraordinary Prayer for the REVIVAL of Religion, and the Advancement of Christ's Kingdom on Earth, pursuant to Scripture Promises, and Prophecies concerning the last Time.* Boston: Printed for D. Henchman in Cornhil, 1747. Ed. John Sutcliff. Reprinted at Northampton, England: T. Dicey and Co., 1789.

_____, ed. *The Life of David Brainerd.* Grand Rapids: Baker Book House, American Tract Society Edition, 1983.

_____. *The Life of President Edwards.* Ed. Sereno E. Dwight. 10 vols. New York: G.&C.&H. Carvill, 1830.

_____. *Selected Works of Jonathan Edwards.* Vol. 1. London: Banner of Truth, 1965.

_____. *The Works of Jonathan Edwards.* 2 vols, 10th edn. London: Henry G. Bohn, 1845.

_____. *The Works of Jonathan Edwards.* Ed. Stephen J. Stein. *Apocalyptic Writings.* Vol. 5. New Haven, London: Yale University Press, 1977.

_____. *The Works of President Edwards.* Vol. 5. Worcester, Mass.: Isaiah Thomas, 1808.

_____. *The Works of President Edwards.* Vol. 2. New York: Burt Franklin, 1968.

_____. *The Works of President Edwards with a Memoir of His Life.* 10 vols. New York: S. Converse, 1829-30.

Elwell, Walter A., ed. *Evangelical Dictionary of Theology.* Grand Rapids: Baker Book House, 1984.

Fawcett, Arthur. *The Cambuslang Revival.* London: Banner of Truth, 1971.

Felt, Joseph. *History of Ipswich, Essex, and Hamilton.* Cambridge, Mass.: Charles Folsom, 1834.

Finney, Charles G. *The Memoirs of Charles G. Finney.* Ed. Garth Rosell and Richard A. G. Dupuis. Grand Rapids: Zondervan, 1989.

_____. *Lectures on Revivals of Religion.* New York, Chicago, Toronto, London, and Edinburgh: Fleming H. Revell, 1868.

Foxcroft, Thomas. *An Essay shewing the exact Accomplishment of the WORD of GOD, in his WORKS performed and to be performed. For confirming of Believers, and convincing Atheists of the present Time.* Boston: Printed by Rogers and Fowle for Walter McAlpine near Mill-Bridge, 1743.

Fuller, Andrew. *The Nature and Importance of WALKING by FAITH, to which is added PER-SUASIVES to a GENERAL UNION in Extraordinary PRAYER for the Revival of Real Religion.* London: Vernor, 1791.

Fuller, Andrew Gunton, ed. *Fuller, The Complete Works of the Rev. Andrew, with a Memoir of His Life.* 2 vols. Boston: Gould, Kendall, and Lincoln, 1836.

Fuller, Thomas E. *A Memoir of the Life and Writings of Andrew Fuller.* London: J. Heaton & Sons, 1863.

Gillies, John, ed. *Historical Collections of Accounts of Revival*. London: Banner of Truth, 1981.

_____. *Historical Collections Related to Remarkable Periods of the Success of the Gospel and Eminent Instruments Employed in Promoting It*. 2 vols. Glasgow, 1754.

_____. *Sermons and Essays by the Late Reverend Mr. John M'Laurin*. Glasgow: James Knox, 1755.

Heimert, Alan. *Religion and the American Mind: From the Great Awakening to the Revolution*. Cambridge, Mass.: Harvard University Press, 1966.

Henderson, David Wayne. *The Ecclesiastical and Social Impact of the Clapham Sect: A Case Study for Renewal*. Unpublished M.A. thesis. Gordon-Conwell Theological Seminary, April 1984.

History of York County Maine. Philadelphia: Everts & Peck, 1880.

Hollis, Daniel W. *Look to the Rock*. Richmond: John Knox, 1961.

Hovey, Alvah. *The Life and Times of Isaac Backus*. Boston: Gould and Lincoln, 1859.

Howard, David, ed. *Declare His Glory*. Downers Grove, Ill.: InterVarsity Press, 1977.

Hudson, Winthrop S. *Religion in America*. New York: Charles Scribner's Sons, 1965.

Hurd, D. Hamilton. *History of Essex County Massachusetts*. 2 vols. Philadelphia: J. W. Lewis & Co., 1888.

Hybels, Bill, Stuart Briscoe, and Haddon Robinson. *Mastering Contemporary Preaching*. Portland, Ore.: Multnomah, 1989.

Jedfrey, Christopher M. *The World of John Cleaveland*. London, New York: W. W. Norton and Co., 1979.

Kemper, Deane A. *Effective Preaching*. Philadelphia: Westminster, 1985.

Kepler, Thomas. *An Anthology of Devotional Literature*. Grand Rapids: Baker Book House, 1947.

Kimball, Rev. David T. *Centennial Discourse Delivered Before the First Church and Religious Society in Ipswich, August 10, 1834*. Printed by Leonard W. Kimball, Pollock Press, 1834.

_____. *A Sketch of the Ecclesiastical History of Ipswich. The Substance of a Discourse in Two Parts, Delivered in That Town, December 1820*. Haverhill, Mass: *Gazette* and *Patriot* Office, 1823.

Lacy, Benjamin Rice. *Revivals in the Midst of the Years*. Hopewell, Va.: Royal Publishers, Inc., 1968.

Ladd, George Eldon. *The Presence of the Future*. Grand Rapids: Wm. B. Eerdmans, 1974.

Latourette, Kenneth Scott. *A History of Christianity*. Vol. 2. New York, Evanston, San Francisco, London: Harper and Row, Publishers, 1975.

Lewis, A. J. *Zinzendorf: The Ecumenical Pioneer*. Philadelphia: The Westminster Press, 1962.

Lloyd-Jones, David Martyn. *Preachers and Preaching*. Grand Rapids: Zondervan, 1972.

Lovelace, Richard F. *Dynamics of Spiritual Life*. Downers Grove: InterVarsity Press, 1979.

Luther, Martin. *Three Treatises*. Philadelphia, 1943.

Marsden, George M. *Fundamentalism and American Culture*. New York, Oxford: Oxford University Press, 1980.

Marshman, John Clark. *The Life and Times of Carey, Marshman, and Ward*. 2 vols. London: Longman, Brown, Green, & Roberts, 1859.

Mather, Cotton. *Private Meetings Animated and Regulated*. Boston: T. Green, 1706.

_____. *Proposals Concerning Religious Societies. Humbly Offered unto GOOD MEN, in sev-*

eral Towns of the County: For the Revival of DYING RELIGION. Boston: Printed by S. Kneeland, for John Phillips, 1724.

McCollough, William. *Narrative of the Extraordinary Work at Cambuslang In a Letter to a Friend with proper Attestations By Ministers, Preachers, and others*. Boston: S. Kneeland and T. Green, 1742.

McDermott, Gerald R. *One Holy and Happy Society. The Public Theology of Jonathan Edwards*. University Park, Penn.: The Pennsylvania State University Press, 1992.

M'Nemar, Richard. *The Kentucky Revival; or A Short History of the Late Extraordinary Outpouring of the Spirit of God in the Western States of America*. New York: Edward O. Jenkins, 1846.

Miller, Perry. *Errand into the Wilderness*. Cambridge, Mass.: Harvard University Press, 1956.

Morgan, G. Campbell. *Preaching*. New York: Fleming H. Revell, 1937.

Morris, E. J. *Prayer-Meeting Theology*. New York, London: G. P. Putnam & Sons, Knickerbocker Press, 1892.

Old South Chapel Prayer Meeting: Its Origins and History. Boston: J. E. Tilton & Co., 1859.

Orr, J. Edwin. *The Fervent Prayer*. Chicago: Moody Press, 1974.

Ortiz, Juan Carlos. *Disciple*. Carol Stream, Ill.: Creation House, 1975.

Packer, J. I. *Jonathan Edwards and the Theology of Revival. From Increasing in the Knowledge of God*. Papers read at the Puritan and Reformed Studies Conference, 1960.

_____. *Knowing God*. Downers Grove, Ill.: InterVarsity Press, 1973.

_____. *Knowing Man*. Westchester, Ill.: Cornerstone Books, 1978.

Parsons, Usher. *The Life of Sir William Pepperell*. London: Sampson Low, Son, & Co.; Boston: Little, Brown, & Co., 1856.

Patten, John A. *These Remarkable Men. The Beginnings of a World Enterprise*. London, Redhill: Lutterworth Press, 1945.

Philip, Robert. *The Life and Times of the Reverend George Whitefield, M.A.* New York: D. Appleton & Company, 1838.

Pierson, Arthur T. *George Muller of Bristol and His Witness to a Prayer-Hearing God*. Old Tappan, N. J.: Fleming H. Revell, 1899.

Prince, Rev. Thomas. *The Great Revival in Middleborough, Mass.* Boston: T. R. Marvin, 1842.

_____. *Extraordinary Events the doings of GOD, and marvellous in pious Eyes, Illustrated in a Sermon at the South Church in Boston, N.E., On the General Thanksgiving, Thursday, July 18, 1745*. Occasioned by taking the city of Louisbourg on the Isle of Cape Breton. Printed for D. Henchman in Cornhil, 1745.

Roberts, Richard Owen. *Revival*. Wheaton, Ill.: Tyndale, 1983.

Robinson, Haddon W. *Biblical Preaching*. Grand Rapids: Baker Book House, 1980.

Rutman, Darrett B., ed. *The Great Awakening: Event and Exegesis*. New York, London, and Toronto: John Wiley and Sons, 1970.

Schaller, Lyle E. *The Senior Minister*. Nashville: Abingdon Press, 1988.

Slie, David. *The Holy of Holies, or, World's Tri-Daily Concert of Prayer*. Rochester, N.Y.: A. Strong & Co., *Democrat* and *American* Office, 1861.

Smith, Alfred, ed. *Living Hymns*. Montrose, Penn.: Encore Publications, 1972.

Smith, Timothy. *Revivalism and Social Reform*. Baltimore: The Johns Hopkins University Press, 1980.

Spurgeon, Charles Haddon. *Spurgeon's Lectures to His Students*. David Fuller, ed. Grand Rapids: Zondervan, 1955.

Stackpole, Everett S. *Old Kittery and Her Families.* Somersworth: New England History Press, 1981.

Stewart, James H. *THOUGHTS on the IMPORTANCE OF SPECIAL PRAYER for the GENERAL OUTPOURING of THE HOLY SPIRIT.* London: The Religious Tract Society, c. 1825.

Stott, John R. W. *Between Two Worlds.* Grand Rapids: Wm. B. Eerdmans, 1982.

Stout, Harry S. *The Divine Dramatist.* Grand Rapids: Wm. B. Eerdmans, 1991.

Tennent, Gilbert. *Sermon Preached at Philadelphia, January 7, 1747 . . . A Day of Fasting and Prayer.* Philadelphia, 1748.

Theological Dictionary of the New Testament. Gerhard Kittel and Gerhard Friedrich, eds. Abridged in one volume by Geoffrey W. Bromiley. Grand Rapids: Wm. B. Eerdmans & Paternoster Press, 1985.

Trumbull, Clay. *Children in the Temple. A Handbook for the Sunday-School Concert and a Guide for the Children's Preacher.* Springfield, Mass.: Holland & Co., 1869.

Waters, Thomas Franklin. *Ipswich in the Massachusetts Bay Colony.* Vol. 2. Ipswich, Mass.: The Ipswich Historical Society, 1917.

Walker, Winston. *A History of the Christian Church.* New York: Charles Scribner's Sons, 1970.

Webb, John. *A SERMON Preach'd June 18, 1734, Being a Day of Prayer with Fasting observed by the NEW NORTH CHURCH in BOSTON. (A SERMON on a Day of Prayer, for the Reviving of GOD's Work).* Boston: S. Kneeland and T. Green, 1734.

Weisberger, Bernard A. *They Gathered by the River.* Boston: Little, Brown, & Co., 1958.

Wells, David F. *God the Evangelist.* Grand Rapids: Wm. B. Eerdmans, 1987.

William and Mary Quarterly, 3rd ser., Vol. 38, No. 2, April 1980.

Woodward, J. *Account of the Rise of the Religious Societies.* 3rd edn. London, 1701.

Wodrow, Robert. *Analecta, or Materials for a History of Remarkable Providences &c.* Maitland Club edn. Glasgow, 1842.

Worthley, Harold Field. *An Inventory of the Records of the Particular (Congregational) Churches of Massachusetts Gathered 1620-1805.* Cambridge, Mass.: Harvard University Press, 1970.

Young, Robert. *The Importance of Prayer Meetings in Promoting the Revival of Religion.* New York: Lane & Tippet, for the Methodist Episcopal Church, James Collord, printer, 1846.

GENERAL INDEX